Research Series on the Chinese Dream and China's Development Path

Project Director
Xie Shouguang, President, Social Sciences Academic Press

Series editors
Li Yang, Vice president, Chinese Academy of Social Sciences, Beijing, China
Li Peilin, Vice president, Chinese Academy of Social Sciences, Beijing, China

Academic Advisors
Cai Fang, Gao Peiyong, Li Lin, Li Qiang, Ma Huaide, Pan Jiahua, Pei Changhong, Qi Ye, Wang Lei, Wang Ming, Zhang Yuyan, Zheng Yongnian, Zhou Hong

Drawing on a large body of empirical studies done over the last two decades, the *Research Series on the Chinese Dream and China's Development Path* seeks to provide its readers with in-depth analyses of the past and present, and forecasts for the future course of China's development. Thanks to the adoption of Socialism with Chinese characteristics, and the implementation of comprehensive reform and opening, China has made tremendous achievements in areas such as political reform, economic development, and social construction, and is making great strides towards the realization of the Chinese dream of national rejuvenation. In addition to presenting a detailed account of many of these achievements, the authors also discuss what lessons other countries can learn from China's experience. This series will be an invaluable companion to every researcher who is trying to gain a deeper understanding of the development model, path and experience unique to China.

More information about this series at http://www.springer.com/series/13571

Zhou Li

Reform and Development of Agriculture in China

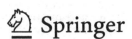

Zhou Li
CASS Rural Development Institute
Beijing
China

ISSN 2363-6866 ISSN 2363-6874 (electronic)
Research Series on the Chinese Dream and China's Development Path
ISBN 978-981-10-3460-2 ISBN 978-981-10-3462-6 (eBook)
DOI 10.1007/978-981-10-3462-6

Jointly published with Social Sciences Academic Press

Library of Congress Control Number: 2016963287

Printed on acid-free paper

This Springer imprint is published by Springer Nature
The registered company is Springer Nature Singapore Pte Ltd.
The registered company address is: 152 Beach Road, #22-06/08 Gateway East, Singapore 189721, Singapore

Series Preface

Since China's reform and opening began in 1978, the country has come a long way on the path of Socialism with Chinese Characteristics, under the leadership of the Communist Party of China. Over 30 years of reform efforts and sustained spectacular economic growth have turned China into the world's second largest economy, and wrought many profound changes in the Chinese society. These historically significant developments have been garnering increasing attention from scholars, governments and the public alike around the world since the 1990s, when the newest wave of China studies began to gather steam. Some of the hottest topics have included the so-called "China miracle", "Chinese phenomenon", "Chinese experience", "Chinese path" and the "Chinese model". Homegrown researchers have soon followed suit. Already hugely productive, this vibrant field is putting out a large number of books each year, with Social Sciences Academic Press alone having published hundreds of titles on a wide range of subjects.

Because most of these books have been written and published in Chinese, however, readership has been limited outside China—even among many who study China—for whom English is still the lingua franca. This language barrier has been an impediment to efforts by academia, business communities and policy-makers in other countries to form a thorough understanding of contemporary China, of what is distinct about China's past and present may mean not only for her future but also for the future of the world. The need to remove such an impediment is both real and urgent, and the *Research Series on the Chinese Dream and China's Development Path* is my answer to the call.

This series features some of the most notable achievements from the last 20 years by scholars in China in a variety of research topics related to reform and opening. They include both theoretical explorations and empirical studies, and cover economy, society, politics, law, culture and ecology, the six areas in which reform and opening policies have had the deepest impact and farthest-reaching consequences for the country. Authors for the series have also tried to articulate their visions of the "Chinese Dream" and how the country can realize it in these fields and beyond.

All of the editors and authors for the *Research Series on the Chinese Dream and China's Development Path* are both longtime students of reform and opening and recognized authorities in their respective academic fields. Their credentials and expertise lend credibility to these books, each of which having been subject to a rigorous peer-review process for inclusion in the series. As part of the Reform and Development Program under the State Administration of Press, Publication, Radio, Film and Television of the People's Republic of China, the series is published by Springer, a Germany-based academic publisher of international repute, and distributed overseas. I am confident that it will help fill a lacuna in studies of China in the era of reform and opening.

                                                                                     Xie Shouguang

Acknowledgements

After a relatively short gestation period, the *Research Series on the Chinese Dream and China's Development Path* has started to bear fruits. We have, first and foremost, the books' authors and editors to thank for making this possible. And it was the hard work by many people at Social Sciences Academic Press and Springer, the two collaborating publishers, that made it a reality. We are deeply grateful to all of them.

Mr. Xie Shouguang, president of Social Sciences Academic Press (SSAP), is the mastermind behind the project. In addition to defining the key missions to be accomplished by it and setting down the basic parameters for the project's execution, as the work has unfolded, Mr. Xie has provided critical input pertaining to its every aspect and at every step of the way. Thanks to the deft coordination by Ms. Li Yanling, all the constantly moving parts of the project, especially those on the SSAP side, are securely held together, and as well synchronized as is feasible for a project of this scale. Ms. Gao Jing, unfailingly diligent and meticulous, makes sure every aspect of each Chinese manuscript meets the highest standards for both publishers, something of critical importance to all subsequent steps in the publishing process. That high-quality if also at times stylistically as well as technically challenging scholarly writing in Chinese has turned into decent, readable English that readers see on these pages is largely thanks to Ms. Liang Fan, who oversees translator recruitment and translation quality control.

Ten other members of the SSAP staff have been intimately involved, primarily in the capacity of in-house editor, in the preparation of the Chinese manuscripts. It is a time-consuming work that requires attention to details, and each of them has done this, and is continuing to do this with superb skills. They are, in alphabetical order: Mr. Cai Jihui, Ms. Liu Xiaojun, Mr. Ren Wenwu, Ms. Shi Xiaolin, Ms. Song Yuehua, Mr. Tong Genxing, Ms. Wu Dan, Ms. Yao Dongmei, Ms. Yun Wei and Ms. Zhou Qiong. In addition, Xie Shouguang and Li Yanling have also taken part in this work.

Ms. Yun Wei is the SSAP in-house editor for the current volume.

Our appreciation is also owed to Ms. Li Yan, Mr. Chai Ning, Ms. Wang Lei and Ms. Xu Yi from Springer's Beijing Representative Office. Their strong support for the SSAP team in various aspects of the project helped to make the latter's work much easier than it would have otherwise been.

We thank Mr. Evan Villarrubia for translating this book.

Last, but certainly not least, it must be mentioned that funding for this project comes from the Ministry of Finance of the People's Republic of China. Our profound gratitude, if we can be forgiven for a bit of apophasis, goes without saying.

Social Sciences Academic Press
Springer

Contents

1 History of Chinese Agriculture Before Reform and Opening   1
   1.1   Three Thousand Years of Agriculture in China   1
       1.1.1   The Origins of Agriculture   1
       1.1.2   The Development of Agriculture   3
       1.1.3   Agricultural Achievements   8
       1.1.4   Characteristics of Agriculture   12
   1.2   The Last 300 Years of Agriculture in China   13
       1.2.1   A Stage of Continued Slow Growth in Agriculture   14
       1.2.2   Why Agriculture Did Not Cause Economic Decline
              in China   18
       1.2.3   Reasons for China's Economic Decline   19
   1.3   Agriculture in China for the 30 Years Prior to Reform
      and Opening   23

2 Agricultural Reforms   27
   2.1   Reforms to Markets for Agricultural Products   31
       2.1.1   Gradually Shrinking the Scope of the Agricultural
              State Monopoly   31
       2.1.2   Gradually Reducing the Quantity of State Monopoly
              Purchases   32
       2.1.3   Gradually Developing a Market for Agricultural
              Products   32
       2.1.4   Expanding Channels for Circulation of Agricultural
              Products   33
   2.2   Agricultural Factor Market Reforms   35
       2.2.1   Reforms to Agricultural Input Markets   36
       2.2.2   Reforms to Agricultural Labor Markets   36
       2.2.3   Reforms to Rural Capital Markets   39

2.3   Reforms to the Agricultural Land System.   51
      2.3.1   Progress of Reforms to the Agricultural Land System   52
      2.3.2   Developing a Rural Land Market   53
      2.3.3   Scale and Pricing of the Land Market.   55
      2.3.4   Establishing Land Management and Farmland
              Protection Systems   56
2.4   Reforms to the System and Mechanisms for Agricultural
      Operations   57
      2.4.1   Reducing the Scope of Administrative Management,
              Establishing Norms for Administrative Management.   57
      2.4.2   Improving Laws and Regulations, Governing in Strict
              Accordance with the Law   59
      2.4.3   Expanding the Scope of Economic Administration,
              Improving Economic Management Methods   60
2.5   The Experience of China's Rural Reforms   62
      2.5.1   Enormous Potential for Rural Economic Growth   62
      2.5.2   Market Guidance: An Important Factor
              in Rural Growth   63
      2.5.3   Non-agricultural Enterprises to Become Mainstay
              of Rural Development.   63

3 China's Agricultural Basic Operating System.   65
3.1   Changes to China's Agricultural Basic Operating System   65
3.2   Environmental Changes Facing Construction of the Basic
      Operating System.   67
      3.2.1   Sustenance Fields Less Important   67
      3.2.2   Gradual Increases to Opportunity Costs of Agriculture   68
      3.2.3   Using Land to Provide for Old Age Less Important   68
      3.2.4   Differentiation in Production and Capital Functions
              of Agricultural Land   68
      3.2.5   Differentiation Between Rural Citizens   70
      3.2.6   Diversification of Organizational Market Entry
              Methods for Rural Citizens.   71
3.3   The Development of New Agricultural Operators in China   71
      3.3.1   Leading Farms   72
      3.3.2   Specialized Households.   73
      3.3.3   Specialized Farmer Cooperatives.   74
      3.3.4   Agricultural Companies.   74
3.4   The Thinking Behind Fostering Leading Rural Households   75
3.5   Summarizing Comments.   78

4   The Development of Agriculture in China.   81
   4.1   China's Natural Agricultural Resources   81
       4.1.1   Low Per Capita Quantities of Land.   81
       4.1.2   Big Regional Differences in Available Water   81
       4.1.3   Discoordination in Water and Land Resources   82
   4.2   Agricultural Inputs   82
       4.2.1   Labor   82
       4.2.2   Farmland.   84
       4.2.3   Water Resources   90
       4.2.4   Capital Inputs   93
       4.2.5   Adjustments to the Agricultural Structure   99
   4.3   Growth of Agriculture   100
       4.3.1   Material Productivity of Agriculture   100
       4.3.2   Value Productivity of Agriculture   102
       4.3.3   Technological Productivity of Agriculture.   103
   4.4   Development in Other Agricultural Sectors   106
       4.4.1   Forest Protection and Construction   108
       4.4.2   Grassland Protection and Construction   110
       4.4.3   Wetlands Protection and Construction.   113

5   Transformations to Agriculture and Agricultural Policies
in China.   115
   5.1   Changes to the Agricultural Operations Model.   115
       5.1.1   Transition from Collective to Household Operations.   115
       5.1.2   Transition from Scattered to Scale Operations.   117
       5.1.3   Transition from Coercive to Inductive Administration.   120
   5.2   Changes to the Agricultural Structure.   121
       5.2.1   Transition from Reliance on Rainwater to Irrigation   121
       5.2.2   Transition from Planting-Based to Husbandry-Based
               Agriculture   122
       5.2.3   Transition from Dispersed to Concentrated Husbandry   123
       5.2.4   Transition from Wild Catching to Farming in Fisheries . . .   124
       5.2.5   Transition from Net Exports to Net Imports
               of Agricultural Products   124
   5.3   Changes to Agricultural Policies.   127
       5.3.1   Transition from Concentrating Agricultural Surpluses
               to Supporting Agricultural Development.   127
       5.3.2   Transition from Comprehensive Support to Focus
               Support.   128
       5.3.3   Transition from Quantity Security to Quality Security   129
       5.3.4   Transition from Expanding Production to Protecting
               the Environment   129
       5.3.5   Transition from Economic Development to Social
               Development.   134

6   Grain Production and Food Security in China 141
   6.1   Grain Production 141
       6.1.1   Changes to Grain Yields and Per Capita Grain Shares 141
       6.1.2   Per Capita Grain Yields in China 150
   6.2   Analysis of Factors Affecting Grain Production 152
       6.2.1   Technological Advances 152
       6.2.2   Impact of Climate Change 154
       6.2.3   Agricultural Policies 154
       6.2.4   Reductions of Farmland 156
   6.3   Changes and Trends to Grain Production Distribution 156
       6.3.1   North Outstrips South in Grain Production 156
       6.3.2   Grain Production Concentrating in Central Region 157
       6.3.3   Expansion of Northeastern Superior Round-Grain Rice,
            Stable Advantages of Southern Rice 157
       6.3.4   Wheat Production Concentrating in Huang and Huai
            River Basins 157
       6.3.5   Corn Production Concentrating in Northeastern
            and Central Regions 158
       6.3.6   Overall Shrinking of Soybean Production 158
   6.4   China's Food Security Strategy 159
       6.4.1   Enactment of the Prime Farmland Protection Policy 159
       6.4.2   Strengthening Construction of Prime Farmland
            Infrastructure 159
       6.4.3   Optimizing the Distribution of Grain Production 159
       6.4.4   Promoting International Trade of Agricultural Products ... 160
   6.5   The Implications of Food Security 162
       6.5.1   Food Security at the Product Level 163
       6.5.2   Food Security at the Resource Level 164
       6.5.3   Food Security at the Environmental Level 166
       6.5.4   Food Security at the Consumption Level 166
   References 169

7   Challenges Facing Agricultural Development 171
   7.1   Challenges Facing Agricultural Production 171
       7.1.1   The Challenge of Non-agricultural Usage of Farmland 171
       7.1.2   The Challenge of Uses of Farmland Other Than
            Grain Production 175
       7.1.3   The Challenge of Low Efficiency Usage of Farmland 176
       7.1.4   The Challenge of Decreasing Cultivation Intensiveness ... 176
       7.1.5   The Challenge of Decreasing Agricultural
            Competitiveness 178
   7.2   Challenges in Other Areas 179
       7.2.1   The Challenge of Promoting Cooperation
            Among Rural Citizens 179

7.2.2 The Challenge of Rural Citizens Unwilling
to Abandon the Land 179
7.2.3 The Challenge of Rural Citizens Retaining
Land Rights 180
7.2.4 The Challenge of Agriculture Transitioning to Scale
Operations....................................... 181
7.2.5 The Challenge of Protecting Rural Citizen Land Rights ... 182
7.2.6 The Challenge of the Rural Community Administration
System 183
7.2.7 The Challenge of Rural Differentiation and Stability...... 183

8 Outlook and Vision for Agriculture in China 185
8.1 Objectives for Agricultural Development 185
8.1.1 Objectives of Agricultural Reforms.................. 185
8.1.2 Tasks of Rural Development....................... 187
8.1.3 The Course of Agricultural Development 189
8.1.4 Policies for Agricultural Development 196
8.2 Outlook for Agricultural Development in China.............. 201
8.2.1 Full Citizen Treatment for Rural Citizens 201
8.2.2 International Competitiveness in Agriculture........... 204
8.2.3 Comprehensive Development of Rural Society 209
References... 213

Chapter 1
History of Chinese Agriculture Before Reform and Opening

The objective of this book is to describe the development of agriculture in China over the 30-plus years of Reform and Opening. To give the reader a general understanding of the entire history of agricultural development in China, in this first chapter I give an overview of Chinese agriculture in the 30, 300, and 3000 years prior to Reform and Opening.

1.1 Three Thousand Years of Agriculture in China

1.1.1 The Origins of Agriculture

The ancestors of the present Chinese people spent the vast majority of the several million years of human history as gatherer-fisher-hunters.[1] Gradually over the long span of gathering-fishing-hunting, these peoples began to domesticate wild plants, large beasts, and birds, eventually giving rise to primitive agriculture. The rise of agriculture marked the first time that human beings used their own labor to produce requisite foodstuffs; it also marked the dawn of the era of civilization. Agriculture's origins spanned an extremely long period of time. Agriculture initially did not play a major role in our ancestors' lives, but rather was a supplement to the primary food-obtention activities of gathering, fishing, and hunting.

Primitive agriculture rose first in the easiest places to carry out land cultivation. The majority of the Yellow River Basin is composed of either primary or secondary loess[2]; the soil here is deep and loose with local flora highly spread out, making it

---

[1]Translator's note: essentially identical to "hunter-gatherers," a concept that also comprises fishing.

[2]Translator's note: known as "yellow earth" in Chinese, this is a yellow-tinted deposit of wind-blown sediment that is highly fertile. The word "loess" comes from the German *löss*, meaning "loose."

© Social Sciences Academic Press and Springer Nature Singapore Pte Ltd. 2017
Z. Li, *Reform and Development of Agriculture in China*,
Research Series on the Chinese Dream and China's Development Path,
DOI 10.1007/978-981-10-3462-6_1

extremely easy to farm. This is an important reason that this region was one of the first in China to play host to the origins of agriculture.

Our ancestors' first impression regarding water and agriculture was that water was a menace, not a boon, to agriculture, and so the first attempts at controlling water in areas under cultivation were intended to move it away from crops, not toward them. This is an important reason that drainage ditch systems, not irrigation systems, were first to appear in primitive agriculture. At first such ditches were built haphazardly without organization, but over time more rationally engineered systems of ditches began to appear.

Primitive peoples exerted great effort to build ditches for their fields, and as such were not willing to allow these fields to lie fallow. This led them to invent the "ridge agriculture method" (alternatively known as the ridge-and-furrow method) that allowed for consecutive plantings on a single plot. Under this method, rectangular fields six chi^3 wide were divided by three ridges and three furrows. Farmers planted seeds in the furrows, and after the seeds germinated, the earth from the ridges was hoed down to cover the seedlings until the field was entirely flat. The positions of the ridges and furrows alternated from year to year, effectively allowing for part of the field to remain fallow every other year, enabling early farmers to use all their fields every year while not exhausting them. This method of alternating ridges and furrows on the same fields every year was clearly more intensive than the two-field system employed in the West. To ensure the effectiveness of their consecutive plantings, our ancestors developed the crop rotation method. As not even these methods were sufficient to naturally restore sufficient soil fertility in land perennially planted, our ancestors employed fertilization. One major reason that farmland in China has remained fertile over the millennia is that our forebears systematized these methods of crop rotation and fertilization.

After the potential harms of water to agriculture had come under control, our ancestors began to consider bringing more of it into their fields to compensate for shortcomings in rainfall. Advances in iron-wrought tools laid a material foundation for the construction of irrigation works. In simple terms, the technological path taken in primitive agriculture was first to ensure any harvest at all and only then to seek greater yields. Although irrigation was developed in the Yellow River Basin, water scarcity in the region made dry farming the principal form of agriculture in the region. As our ancestors explored how to make ample use of water present in the soil, they gradually developed the dry agriculture technological system comprised of a synthesis of "plowing, harrowing, leveling, flattening, and hoeing," focused on preserving soil moisture but also including methods of fertilization, selection of outstanding cultivars, and crop rotation.

---

[3]Translator's note: *chi* is a traditional unit of length in China, comprised of 10 cun. Like the foot in the English system, the length this unit denoted changed over the centuries, from 23.09 cm in the Han Dynasty to 29.4 or 24.6 cm in the Sui and Tang Dynasties (either the a "big *chi*" or the "small *chi*"). In modern China, this unit denotes one third of a meter.

The origins of agriculture in other places were similar. The Yangtze River Basin, for example, is a subtropical region with a warm temperate climate, abundant rainfall, ample water resources, a dense system of rivers, alluvial flood plains on either side of major rivers and lakes in the region, and fertile soil; it is, therefore, extremely amenable to cultivation. That is why the Yangtze River Basin became another center for the origins of agriculture in China. Agriculture in lake regions began with the planting of rice along the banks of rivers in the dry season. "Plowing fire and hoeing water" (essentially "slash-and-burn") methods were employed for the earliest rice cultivation. That is, first the weeds and dead plants along lakeshores were burned, and then the areas were flooded. The "hoeing water" part referred to the continued flooding of rice seedlings as they grew. To further stabilize agriculture in lakeshore regions, our ancestors built embankments, converting lakeshore land into "lake-reclaimed fields." Embankments were also erected around the large area of lowland marshes to keep water out and preserve the integrity of the fields within. Sluices were installed on the embankments to allow drainage in case of floods or further flooding in case of drought. Fields within embankments were referred to as *weitian* or *yuantian*, either translated literally as "dike fields," or otherwise as "polders." Beaches or shoals made of sediment alongside or in the middle of rivers were drained via ditches and cultivated either as dry or wet fields; these were called *shatian*, "sand fields," or *zhutian*, "river bank fields." Most early agriculture in the mid to lower reaches of the Yangtze Basin was developed in lake fields or dike fields. Rivers were dredged at fixed intervals to facilitate the storage of floodwater or the drainage of flooded fields in this region; this is what gradually gave rise to the irrigation system built from the region's network of rivers.

As our ancestors in this region developed paddy agriculture, they eventually invented the *ba* and the *chao*, two early forms of harrows, in order to prepare paddies for the transplanting of rice seedlings. They also developed the *quyuanli*, curved-thill plow, and the *yundang*, or hand-drawn weeder. All these advances led to the paddy cultivation technological system of "plowing, raking, harrowing, weeding, and soil loosening"—consisting of such closely-related technologies as drying paddies in the sun, drainage and irrigation, and soil maturation—as well as alternating between dry and paddy farming and multi-cropping rice, wheat, and other cereal grains on the same fields. These advances marked the rise of intensive paddy cultivation technology.

1.1.2 The Development of Agriculture

Agriculture in ancient times developed through advances in four areas: farmland improvements, improvements in agricultural techniques, farming implement improvements, and compliance with farming seasons.

1.1.2.1   Farmland Improvements

Agriculture began with the cultivation of virgin land into arable fields, but focus areas of such cultivation differed across different time periods. The focus of development in the Qin-Han period was on the loess plains of the Yellow River basin. It shifted to the plains of the mid to lower reaches of the Yangtze basin in the Tang-Song-Yuan period, and then to the hill-and-mountain country of the central-west and the pasturelands and forests of the far frontiers in the Ming-Qing period. Table 1.1 demonstrates that arable land in China increased gradually over time, growing from 230 million μ in the Spring and Autumn/Warring States period to 572 million μ in the Qin-Han period, then to 1.07 billion μ in the Ming Dynasty and up to 1.6 billion μ by the late Qing Dynasty. The cultivation of virgin land took place in stages over a long time, but farmland improvements was a sustained, continuous effort; that is to say that agricultural production was more reliant upon fertilization by humans than on natural soil fertility. Farmland improvement technology developed considerably amid the sustained explorations in farmland improvements. Specific methods employed include the following:

One, changing the land. In the saline-alkali soil of China's North, many methods have been employed for increasing arability, including digging ditches to drain salt, flooding fields to wash the salt out, colmatage—allowing an inflow of silt-laden water—to bury saline soil, planting salt-resistant trees and deeply turning salt deposits under the soil. Other methods are employed on the low-yield fields soaked year-round by water from cold springs of China's south, including winter plowing of soaked fields to be dried in the sun, digging ditches to drain water and permit drying in the sun, the building of fires on such soil, and the application of lime, bone ash, or coal ash on such soil. The majority of arable lands in China were transformed into good farmland gradually over a long period of time.

Table 1.1   Changes to China's total area of land under cultivation

Dynasty	Area under cultivation (μ)	Rural (agricultural) population (mn)	Per capita rural land ownership (μ)
Spring and Autumn/Warring States	230 mn	22.40	10.27
Qin-Han	572 mn	42.00	13.62
Wei-Jin	385 mn	35.00	11.00
Sui-Tang	642 mn	63.00	10.20
Song-Liao-Jin-Yuan	720 mn	84.00	8.57
Ming, 1600	1.070 bn	140.00	7.64
Qing, 1800	1.050 bn	210.00	5.00
Qing, 1840	1.400 bn	280.00	5.00
Qing, 1911	1.600 bn	322.00	4.97

Data source Bu Fengxian, "Assessing Rural Food Security Levels in the Era of Traditional Agriculture", *Zhongguonongshi* [Agricultural History of China], 2007 (4)

Two, soil enrichment. As continuous planting would be impossible on the strength of the land's natural capacity to rejuvenate fertility, our ancestors adopted a series of measures to enrich soil. The first was to inundate fields with water or burn them to turn weeds and other unwanted plants into fertilizer. The second was to use stalks and chaff from crops as well as dry leaves and unused parts of animals as fertilizer. The third was to use human and animal manure as fertilizer. The fourth was to use mud from sodded areas, river mud, pond mud, and aquatic plants as fertilizer. The fifth was to plant alfalfa and other green manure crops. The sixth was to plant soybeans and other soil enriching crops. The seventh was to irrigate fields with nutrient-rich river water and floodwater, which achieved the dual effects of irrigation and fertilization simultaneously. The eighth was to use pressed cakes of oil-bearing crops and spent fermented grain from alcohol production as fertilizer. They also fermented or composted these materials to increase efficiency. This is an important reason that China's soil has remained continuously fertile for such a long period of time.

Third, soil preparation. As the weather is impossible to change and difficult to control, our ancestors expended efforts, suitable to the conditions of the agricultural environment, on preparing soil for agriculture. After turning the soil, they broke up the clumps with a rake and then used a *mo*—soil leveler—to pulverize and flatten surface soil. This was done to break up soil capillaries and prevent water loss through evaporation. Surface soil was made loose and lower soil left firm to create a good soil structure for preserving moisture and fertility. The soil was tamped down promptly after sowing to keep seeds in close contact with the soil and to open up soil capillaries and allow water from below to rise to the surface, to aid in germination.

Four, land usage. Here, "land usage" refers to optimizing the land use structure. In the Han Dynasty, farmers began using the method of pond water irrigation. In the ponds they raised fish and planted lotus, and on the banks they planted trees. In the Ming and Qing dynasties, this method evolved: farmers dug ponds in low-lying areas, filled them, and piled up embankments around them. In the ponds they raised fish, and on the banks they planted mulberry trees. Mulberry leaves were fed to silkworms, and silkworm feces was fed to the fish. There were many such land usage methods involving specific plants and ponds, including fish ponds and mulberry trees, fish ponds and fruit trees, fish ponds and sugarcane, and fish ponds and rice. Another method evolved in the late Qing and early Ming: raising fish outside embankments, mulberry trees on embankments, and rice within embankments, feeding mulberry leaves to sheep and using sheep feces to fertilize the mulberries. All these land usage methods benefitted from ingenious employment of syntrophy between various plants and animals. These methods brought about rational food chains and energy flows and increased the efficiency of land usage.

1.1.2.2 Improvements to Farming Techniques

One, plant cultivation. First was the alternating field method, in which rectangular fields six *chi* wide were divided into three ridges and three furrows. Farmers planted seeds in the furrows, and after the seeds germinated, the earth from the ridges was hoed down to cover the seedlings until the field was entirely flat. The positions of the ridges and furrows alternated from year to year, effectively allowing for part of the field to remain fallow every other year. This allowed for balance between land usage and allowing the land to rest, which enabled long-term usage of fields thus cultivated. Second was the "being close to the fields method," also known as the stage-by-stage method of soil improvement. Under this method, farmers chose a portion of their arable land to be intensely cultivated, fertilized, and irrigated; this was to be done to a different portion of land every year. Third was the intense cultivation method. This method eradicated the threats of spring drought and low temperatures, thereby encouraging crop growth, using the ingenious cultivation system of "plowing, harrowing, leveling, flattening, and hoeing." Farmers covered grain roots with soil using harrows and seed plows, which preserved moisture and warmth in the soil as well while also preventing wheat growth before winter.

Two, rational close planting. Farmers planted in concise, orderly rows, to enable ventilation and ample sunlight to each plant. This made weeding between the rows and irrigation more convenient and prevented alkalization of the soil from water-logging; this created a good microclimate for agriculture.

Three, crop rotation. First was rotation between beans or green manure crops and grain crops. These were rotated to increase soil fertility, decrease the risk of insect pests and plant diseases, and reduce the incidence of weed growth. Second was intercropping. This allowed for ample usage of land and mutual benefit to different crops planted together over different seasons. This method required rationally planting different varieties based on which required more or less sunlight, which were tall and which were short, which had deep or shallow roots, and soil fertility requirements, so that they would not impede but improve each other's growth. Third was multiple cropping. In the South, staple crops—primarily rice—were often planted twice or sometimes three times in a year, while in the North wheat and other staple grains were planted twice or three times. Multiple cropping was often practiced at the same time as crop rotation and intercropping. This allowed for a maximum area of land covered with green plants while also maximally extending the growing season. This, in turn, allowed for maximum benefit from soil fertility and the sun, thereby promoting higher yields per unit of area. Such a system of cultivation exerted rigorous requirements on water usage, fertilization, and land management.

Four, seed selection. China's traditional method is as follows: select seeds annually to accumulate good characteristics; change seeds often to prevent degeneration; and combine seed selection, seed reproduction, and retention of strain purity.

Five, breeding new strains. Farmers select individual plants with desired characteristics and breed them together over long periods of time until new cultivars are attained. The basic method involves planting these individuals with desired qualities separately and while taking measures to prevent cross-pollination, the collecting their seeds and storing them separately, and planting these seeds over a wide area in the following year. Seeds should be stored in a dry place to prevent damage through either rot or bug infestation. All other individuals of a certain species must be cleared from an area prior to planting. The seeds should be dried in the sun, and sometimes mixed with medicinal compounds to promote germination, and then planted.

Six, introduction of non-native varieties. Many plant varieties now common in China are not native to the country. Wheat, corn, sorghum, potatoes, and sweet potatoes among food crops, as well as cotton among fiber crops, and peanuts and sesame among oil crops are some of them. In ancient times Chinese excelled not only at creation but also at emulation; they experimented with nearly every kind of plant that they came across. Wheat is a perennial crop that originated in the Mediterranean climate of Western Asia, typified by rainy winters. Neither the Yellow River basin in the North, with its dry winter and spring, nor the waterlogged rice-growing regions of the South was suitable for growing wheat. In order to help this foreign crop adapt, ancient Chinese worked for a long time to develop a strain that could grow properly in local climates. During the Ming and Qing dynasties, the great expansion of arable land was closely linked to efforts to introduce and promote the growing of corn, potatoes, and sweet potatoes. These efforts facilitated the cultivation of lands with infertile soil, generally in mountainous regions. For example, corn can grow in a variety of different soil and climate conditions, is low-maintenance, high yield, provides feeling of satiety at small amounts, and can be harvested and eaten even when not fully ripe. This crop was first planted in mountainous regions as a substitute for millet and then later spread to the plains of Norther and Northeastern China, becoming a major grain crop. Sweet potatoes were introduced shortly after a typhoon-induced famine in Fujian; the crop was planted to relieve the crisis and played an important role in tiding locals through food shortages. This helped sweet potatoes spread rapidly across the basins of the Yellow and Yangtze Rivers. Potatoes grow quickly, are highly adaptable, and can be planted even in cold regions and highly infertile mountainous areas.

Seven, hybridization. One of the most common methods humans have employed to effect hereditary changes to animals is intra-species hybridization. In addition, hybridization has even been used to create entirely new species. A cross between a horse and a donkey, for example, yields a mule, which can survive on unrefined grains, is tolerant of heavy workloads, can carry a great deal of weight, and is highly disease-resistant. A cross between common cattle and a yak yields the dzo, which provides more meat, milk, and labor than either of its forebears.

1.1.2.3   Farming Implement Improvements

One, working tools. Wrought iron farm implements were more durable and sharper than the cast iron tools they replaced. The introduction of wrought iron also enabled the invention of more different kinds of tools and more highly specialized tools. For plowing paddy fields, there was the *geng* [till], the *ba*[harrow], the *chao* [harrow-like pulverizing implement], as well as the *pingban* for flattening rice-seedling beds, the *tiandang* for leveling large areas of rice-seedling beds, and the *yundang* for intertilling. After advances in tool-making science, many farming implements became more efficient, labor-saving, and ingenious. Examples include the *quyuanli* [curved-thill plow] used for plowing, the *louchu* [seed-plow hoe] used for intertilling, and the *tuilian* [push sickle] used for harvesting. The most noteworthy such improvement was the evolution of the *zhichangyuan* [straight, long shaft] plow into the *duanquyuan* [short, curved shaft] plow. There were three characteristics of the curved-shaft plow. First, it was highly maneuverable; it could be flexibly turned or adjusted in use to change the depth and breadth of plowing. Second, it was equipped with a curved moldboard, making it highly effective at turning and breaking up soil. Third, it could be pulled by a single ox and operated by a single person, making it extremely simple to operate.

Two, irrigation tools. During the Spring and Autumn period was invented the *jiegao* [well sweep], which allowed its user to raise water using leverage. At the end of the Eastern Han Dynasty, the *fanche* [water wheel] and *longguche* [square-pallet chain-pump] were invented, allowing users to draw water using gear wheels and chain pumps. The first human-powered water wheels were turned by hand, and then later by foot pedals. They first came to be powered by animals in the Tang Dynasty, and then finally by hydropower between the Song and Yuan dynasties. They first came to be wind-powered between the Yuan and Ming dynasties.

1.1.2.4 Compliance with Farming Seasons

Most crops are annual plants. In order to keep their germination, growth, flowering, and fruiting in pace with the rhythms of the local climate, one must master farming seasons per the information that different crops reveal to farmers in their reactions to climatic changes. One must then make skillful arrangements of all agricultural production activities on that basis. So ancient Chinese made concentrated observations of astronomical phenomena and arrived at the 24 solar terms. The 24 solar terms accurately reflect the relationship between the earth and the sun per the earth's revolutions around the sun as registered on a sundial. At the same time the solar terms came into use, ancients also arrived at the corresponding 72 pentads. Thus the Chinese agricultural principles of suiting measures to conditions of time, place, and species came to be.

1.1.3 Agricultural Achievements

The achievements of agricultural development can be expressed through changes to the average grain yield per unit of area under cultivation, total agricultural output, and per capita share of grain. Per capita grain yields per unit of area cultivated are, relatively speaking, amore reliable indicator. Historically, total agricultural output has been calculated by comparing total taxes paid to the area of cultivated land on which agricultural taxes are levied. The use of this indicator to measure the achievements of agricultural development is subject to influences from three areas: first, the influence of adjustments to things taxed and the amount they are taxed; second, the influence of the difference between the total area of cultivated land and the area of cultivated land upon which taxes are levied; and third, the vacillations of the frontiers of China over the various dynasties.

Academics have performed a great deal of analysis on China's grain yields per μ.[4] On the basis of available historical materials, some estimated grain yields per μ in specific dynasties or regions, while others estimated grain yields per μ over several dynasties. Per their findings, although different researchers arrived at different grain yields per μ, the majority agree that grain yields per μ have steadily increased over time. The differences in data lie in the fact that some researchers, such as Zhao Gang (2001) and Wu Cunjie (1996), have ironed out their data, while others, such as Wu Hui (1985) and Yu Yefei (1980), have not.

It is very normal for there to be fluctuations in data for grain yields per μ, whether such figures were derived from analysis of data in specific years or from randomly selected data over a number of years. However, if one is to use changes to grain yields per μ to estimate agricultural development in China over thousands of years, these fluctuations must be ironed out. There are three ways to iron out fluctuations. The first is to eliminate disparities between individual years when seeking to average grain yields per μ over several years. The second is to use mutually verified studies to eliminate extreme outliers that fall far from normal trends. The third is to link up near-term data and long-term data to resolve issues of long-term data being greater than near-term data. The basic assumption behind this adjustment is: grain yields per μ in specific years from long-term data may be greater than figures from specific years in near-term data, but the reverse is not possible.

The importance of emphasizing such fluctuations for academics is the influence of historical events such as disasters, wars, and the reclamation and cultivation of wasteland on grain yields per unit of area cultivated. The effects of such historical events on grain yields per μ in individual years or in a minority of years is indeed quite pronounced, but over periods of a hundred years or several hundreds of years, their overall impact on grain yields per μ is extremely limited. So when one is investigating agricultural development over the past 3000 years, it is essential that one iron out fluctuations and eliminate their influence on the data, and certainly not allow such influences to stand apart from the general trends.

---

[4]The *mu* is China's traditional unit for measuring area. At present, one *mu* is equivalent to 0.067 ha or 0.165 acres.

Natural disasters. Floods, droughts, and other natural disasters may result in reduced yields or complete crop failures, but at the same time, they also promote the growth and propagation of wild animals and plants that can adapt to such changes. For example, the relationship between plant cultivation and aquaculture in lake regions is: "On lakeshores where water rises quickly, crops fail but fish and shrimp thrive. If there is no flood or drought, annual grains [rice] grow well, but there are few fish." After great floods, farmers "collect caltrops, reeds, or lotus roots to make their living," "or collect fish, shrimp, or turtles for food provision."[5] In the 1930s, Ji Chaoding collected a great quantity of empirical evidence to prove the fertilizing effects of floodwaters on fields situated in alluvial flood plains, river valleys, and ancient riverbeds and lakebeds in both the North and South of China. This is what gave rise to the saying, "those crops lost in autumn will be compensated doubly in summer."[6]

Wars. The negative impact of wars on agriculture is enormous in the short term. In the long term, however, the impact of wars on agriculture is limited. It is not appropriate to exaggerate the negative impact of wars when researching the development of agriculture at the grand scale.

Reclamation and cultivation of wasteland. While the addition of land with infertile soil through reclamation or cultivation tends to drag down average grain yields per µ for the total cultivated area, the impact is often negligible since the size of the addition has always been puny. More importantly, soil fertility can be increased over time. In the long term, the impact of natural soil fertility on grain yields per µ tends to decrease.

Table 1.2 shows that some estimates of grain yields per µ from different studies are quite similar, while some differ somewhat. These data provide us with a very base for making inferences about fluctuations and disparities. Figure 1.1 shows that it took about 1500 years for average grain yields per µ to grow from 40[7] to 80 jin, and then about another 1500 years for that number to grow to 120 jin. It took about 600 years for the average to grow from 120 to 160 jin, and about 400 years to grow again to 200 jin. Over the past 4000 years, average grain yields per µ progressively decreased over the first 3000 years and then progressively increased over the latter 1000 years (see Fig. 1.1).

---

[5]Xia Mingfang, "Grain Production in Contemporary China and Climatic Fluctuations," *Shehui Kexue Zhanxian* (1998) 4.

[6]Ji Chaoding, *Basic Economic Regions and the Development of Irrigation Works in Chinese History*, (Zhongguo Shehui Kexue Chubanshe, 1992), 20–21.

[7]It has been estimated that the population carrying capacity in the era of gathering-fishing-hunting was 0.02–0.03 people/km², up to 0.5–2.7 people/km² in the era of primitive agriculture, an increase of between 25 and 90 times. This figure implies the assumption that about one percent of total land was devoted to primitive agriculture. From: *Reader on Strategies of Sustainable Development*, ed. Chen Yaobang, (Beijing: Zhongguo Tongji Chubanshe, 1996).

Table 1.2 Estimated grain yields per area in China over the dynasties, *unit jin/μ*

	Xia	Shang	Zhou	Warring States	Qin	Han	Wei	Jin	Sui	Tang	Song	Yuan	Ming	Qing
Yang Gui	40	61	83											
Wu Cunjie				91		110	120			124	142		155	155
Bu Fengxian				91	122	122			124	124	140	140	155	155
Zhao Gang						110				125	183			296
Min Zongdian						120				116				
Ge Jinfang											198			
Chen Xianchun												244		
Zhou Guolin						120								
Yu Yefei					88	97	94	94	91		84	116	156	
OnoueEtsuzō														214
Xu Daofu														
Cao Guanyi						88								
Jiang Shoupeng											165		245	
	40	61	83	91	105	110	107	94	108	122	152	167	178	212

In analysis of grain yields per μ in China, the research of Wu Hui has been used the most. If we use Wu's figures, then grain yields per μ fell by about 100 jin or by one third from the mid Qing to the late Qing Dynasty. I personally find this to be unlikely, and so I did not apply Wu's figures in this book

Data source Yang Gui, "Conjecture on Yields Per Mu in the Xia, Shang, and Zhou Dynasties", *Zhongguo Nongshi* (1988) 2; Wu Cunjie, *History of Agriculture in China*, (Beijing: Jingguan Jiaoyu Chubanshe, 1996), 63–84; Bu Fengxian, "Estimated Rural Food Security Levels in the Era of Traditional Agriculture," *Zhongguo Nongshi* (2007) 4; Zhao Gang, *Agricultural and Economic History Collection—Property Rights, Population, and Agricultural Production* (Beijing: Zhongguo Nongye Chubanshe, 2001), 20–32; Min Zongdian and Dong Kaichen, "On Several Historical Issues of China's Agricultural Technology," *Nongye Kaogu* (1982) 2; Ge Jinfang, *Economic Research and Analysis of the Song, Liao, Xia, and Jin Dynasties*, (Wuhan: Wuhan Chubanshe, 1991), 135. Chen Xianfeng, "Analysis of Grain Yields Per Mu in the Yuan Dynasty," *Lishi Yanjiu* (1995) 4; Zhou Guolin, "Estimates of Per Mu Grain Yields in the Han Dynasty," *Zhongguo Nongshi* (1887) 3; Yu Yefei, "Overview of Average Per Mu Grain Yields over the Dynasties in China," *Chongqing Normal University Journal (Philosophy and Social Sciences Edition)* (1980) 3; Wu Hui, *Research of Per Mu Grain Yields in China over the Dynasties*, (Beijing: Zhongguo Nongye Chubanshe, 1985), 198–199; Xu Daofu, *Statistical Materials of Chinese Agricultural Production and Trade in Recent Times*, (Shanghai: Shanghai Renmin Chubanshe, 1983), 338–339; Cao Guanyi, *Agricultural and Economic History of China*, (Beijing: Zhongguo Shehuikexue Chubanshe, 1989), 204; Jiang Shoupeng, *Research of Northern Markets in the Ming and Qing Dynasties, Volume Two*, (Beijing Normal University Press, 1996); Wang Baoqing, "Changes to Per Mu Grain Yields in China over the Dynasties and Analysis of their Causes," *Laiyang Agricultural University Journal (Social Sciences Edition)* (2005) 1

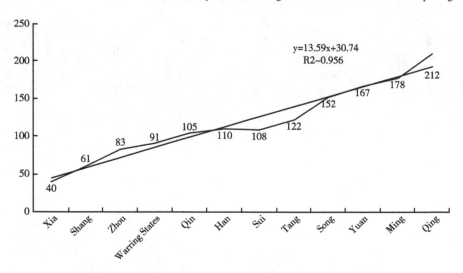

Fig. 1.1 Average grain production in China over the dynasties (jin/μ)

1.1.4 Characteristics of Agriculture

China, one of the three centers in the world for the origins of agriculture, was markedly different from the other two. First, China's major crops were millet and rice, as opposed to wheat and barley in Western Asia and potatoes, squash, and corn in Central and South America. Second, China's major domesticated animals were pigs, chickens, and water buffalo, as compared to sheep and goats in Western Asia and alpacas in Central and South America. Third, the origins of agriculture in China were diverse. Dry land agriculture based primarily on millet planting dominated the Yellow River Basin, while paddy agriculture and rice planting dominated the Yangtze River Basin. Agriculture in Northern China, by contrast, was dominated by the root tubers and stem tubers. Agriculture originating from each of these origins contributed it share to overall agricultural development and were of equal importance to this process.

Over the course of over 4000 years of recorded history, despite all manner of natural and man-made disasters, large and small, the development of agriculture never came to a complete halt. China's per area agricultural yields have reached considerable levels on the strength of China's compendium of intensive agricultural techniques. Remarkably, the country's arable lands continue to be fertile even after having been planted for thousands of years. The continuous flourishing of the Chinese culture has much to do with the formidable vitality of Chinese agriculture.

There are three primary reasons that agriculture developed better in the Yellow River Basin than in the Yangtze River Basin during the stage of primitive agriculture. First, conditions for gathering-fishing-hunting were not as good in the Yellow River Basin as in the Yangtze River Basin, and so there was a more urgent need there to find a substitute for gathering-fishing-hunting. That is to say that austere natural conditions stimulate human ingenuity, while munificent natural conditions encourage human reliance upon nature. So the key to agricultural development is not, then, bountiful natural conditions, but rather is the ability of ancient peoples to overcome difficulties. Second, the Yellow River Basin encompasses a large area of loess plateau, meaning that there was a larger area easily tilled in this basin than in its southern counterpart. Third, the larger the area of cultivation, the more people can participate, and thus the higher the probability and frequency of advances made to agricultural techniques, and ultimately the faster conditions for the development of agricultural systems come into place.

1.2 The Last 300 Years of Agriculture in China

China's economy grew quite well for a very long time. Economic declinein China, on the other hand, happened over a period of nearly 300 years (1644–1949); this is the primary reason that I have highlighted this period of history in specific for discussion and analysis. Bairoch's research indicates that before the Industrial Revolution (1750), economic levels indicated by real incomes were about the same for all nations. The difference between even the most developed and least developed nations at the time was only 1.8:1.[8] Maddison reached similar conclusions: prior to 1700, the level of development of every country in the world was approximately the same, with China's per capita GDP slightly higher than the global average. Over the years 1–1000 CE, China accounted for approximately 25% of the world economy, down to about 23% over the years 1000–1500. Despite that slight drop, China's share of the global economy remained larger than its share of global population. After 1700, economic growth in China fell behind the global average, and China's advantages gradually eroded. From 1840 to 1950, enormous, unprecedented strides were made in the global economy, which grew more than seven-fold. Per capita global GDP increased 3.8-fold over this period, but per capita GDP in China remained in a stage of sluggish growth, with the difference between China and the rest of the world growing steadily larger. In 1870, China accounted for only 17% of the global economy, down further to 8.9% in 1913 and finally to 4.5% in 1950. In 1820, China's per capita GDP was 90% of the global average, down to 61% in 1870, 37% in 1913, and finally 21% in 1950, making China the world's poorest country in that year.[9]

---

[8]Paul Bairoch, "The main trends in national economic disparities since the Industrial Revolution," *Disparities in Economic Development since the Industrial Revolution*, edit by Paul Bairochand Maurice Lévy-Leboyer, Londres, The Macmillan Press 1981.

[9]Angus Maddison, *The World Economy: A Millennial Perspective*, trans. Wu Xiaoying et al., (Beijing: Peking University Press, 2003); Angus Maddison, *Chinese Economic Performance in the Long Run: 960-2030*, trans. Wu Xiaoying and Ma Debin, (Shanghai: Shanghai Renmin Chubanshe, 2008).

In the long view of history, any country can fall into decline, and China is no exception. Nevertheless, it is still necessary to address the question of why China experienced its particular decline. In brief terms, the world entered the early stages of the Industrial Revolution over the years 1500–1800, but China, unfortunately, was not aware of this change. The global Industrial Revolution was in a period of acceleration from 1820 to 1949. Although some in China realized this, the country's leaders did not grasp the opportunity. This is the primary reason that China fell into a period of decline.

1.2.1   A Stage of Continued Slow Growth in Agriculture

Some academics hold that Chinese agriculture reached its apex in the Tang and Song dynasties,[10] and then fell into a period of stagnation in the Ming and Qing dynasties. If that were the case, analysis of China's economic decline could be begun from the country's agricultural decline. However, more academics hold that agriculture continued growing in the Ming and Qing dynasties. Continued rapid population growth over this period is proof to back up the latter position. Without continued growth in agriculture, continued population growth would have been impossible.

Table 1.3 indicates that over the 50 years from 1880 to 1930, net agricultural output grew from 9.987 to 16.641 billion yuan, an annual average growth of 1.05%. Area under cultivation grew from 63,047 to 93,886 kha, for an annual average growth of 0.80%. The employed population grew from 160,118,000 to 200,444,000, an annual average growth of 0.50%. Land productivity grew from 158.37 to 177.25 yuan/ha, an average annual growth of 0.23%, and labor productivity grew from 62.36 to 83.02 yuan/person, an average annual growth of 0.59%. These figures do not support the determination that China's economy fell into stagnation after the Ming and Qing dynasties, but do support the conclusion that agriculture entered a period of sluggish growth during this time.

Of all published materials on this topic, the figures outlining agricultural growth over this period given to us by Dwight Perkins and Angus Maddison are the most complete. It is a shame, however, that their figures assumed no changes to per capita grain shares. Perkins assumed a per capita grain share of 353 kg over the nearly 100-year period from 1840 to 1935, and Maddison assumed a per capita grain share of 285 kg over the over-300 year period from 1650 to 1952. They calculated total grain output based on population data assuming zero changes to per capita grain share. They then calculated area planted with grain per estimates of average grain yields per μ. Their use of this method would be understandable if the only data available were for population and grain yields per μ, but that simply

---

[10]Li Genpan, "On the Development of and Limitations on the Agricultural Economy in the Ming and Qing Periods," *Hebei Xuekan* (2003) 2.

Table 1.3 Development of agricultural production in China from the 1880s to the 1930s (all values in 1936 yuan)

	Net agricultural output (yuan)	Area under cultivation (kha)	Employed population	Land productivity (yuan/ha)	Labor productivity (yuan/person)
1880s	9.987 bn	63,047	160,118,000	158.37	62.36
1930s	16.641 bn	93,886	200,444,000	177.25	83.02
Annual growth rate (%)	1.05	0.80	0.50	0.23	0.59

Data source History of Chinese Economic Development in Recent Times, ed. Liu Foding, (Gaodeng jiaoyu chubanshe, 1999)

wasn't the case. Academics have made great efforts to ascertain the true area under cultivation over this period. A more appropriate method would be to calculate overall grain output in corresponding years using grain yields per μ and total area under cultivation, and then to calculate per capita grain share per population statistics.

As indicated in Table 1.4, the estimates of area under cultivation of He Bingdi, Wu Hui, and Shi Zhihong—all based on historical materials—are extremely similar, while the estimates of Zhou Rong are much higher than those of all other researchers, and thus I have excluded his figures from the composite. As can be seen in Fig. 1.2, although the estimates of the remaining four researchers vary widely, they all indicate a similar trend. I thus averaged their estimates in each year and analyzed the relationship between these figures. The results prove that these data are most effective when polynomial fitting is applied. The R2 value is 0.93, but its rate of change is excessive, and its effectiveness compared with extrapolation is weak. The results of applying exponential fitting come in second place, with the R2 value at 0.895, but the rate of change is relatively lower while effectiveness compared with extrapolation is better. Thus I chose an exponential form regression equation. All other methods resulted not only in poor goodness of fit but also in excessive rates of change, and so I chose to discard them (Fig. 1.3).

With that work completed, we can use fitting equations for area of land under cultivation (LuC) and average grain yields to make adjustments to said figures in corresponding years. We can make further adjustments to population figures in corresponding years using demographic statistics. Maddison's demographic data are of strong comparability, and so they are one of my major references for population data adjustments. I employ two principles when making adjustments. First, I eliminate all instances where fluctuations to per capita area of LuC are greater than fluctuations to yields per unit of area, and instances where fluctuations to yields per unit of area are greater than per capita grain share, and all other instances that do not conform to common sense. Second, I do my utmost to display changing trends and not merely fluctuations. In truth, most fluctuations in historical materials are attributable to attempts to reduce the amounts of taxes or tributes to be paid, and do not reflect reality at the time.

Table 1.4 Estimated changes to area under cultivation in China over the past 300 years, *unit* kilohectares

	Ge Quansheng et al.	He Bingdi	Zhou Rong	Wu Hui	Shi Zhihong	Zhang Youyi	Zheng Zheng et al.
1661	53,236	36,624	63,146	36,617	36,624		32,348
1685	59,288	40,523			40,523	42,575		37,346
1724	71,558	48,242	106,819	48,242	48,242		52,291
1753		49,014	118,661	49,015	49,018		45,172
1784	72,155				50,669		46,729
1812			149,331	52,595	52,810	70,017	48,472
1820	77,746	52,768		50,426	51,112		46,461
1851		50,426	140,282			71,790	46,467
1873	77,167	50,442		50,442			
1887	82,200	60,798		56,663		75,064	56,825
1893	79,076						56,519
1913	81,844					83,951	97,016
1933	82,684						
1949						96,293	

Data source Ge Quansheng et al., "Quantitative Changes in Resources of Area Under Cultivation in Some Chinese Provinces and Regions over the Past 300 Years and Analysis of Motivating Factors," *Zirankexuejinzhan* (2003) 8; He Bingdi, "Philological Studies and Assessments of Land Numbers from the Southern Song Dynasty to Present (Part Two)," *Zhongguoshehuikexue* (1985) 3; Zhou Rong, "A New Assessment of Overall Observations of Area Under Cultivation in the Early Qing Dynasty," *Zhongguoshehuijingjishiyanjiu* (2001) 3; Wu Hui, "Grain Yields Per Mu, Per Capita Grain Share, and Labor Productivity in the Early Qing Dynasty," *Zhongguojingjishiyanjiu* (1993) 1; Shi Zhihong, "A New Assessment of the Area Under Cultivation in China in the First Half of the Nineteenth Century," *Zhongguojingjishiyanjiu* (2011) 4; Zhang Youyi, "A New Assessment of China's Population and Area of Land Under Cultivation in the Recent Era," *Zhongguojingjishiyanjiu* (1991) 1; Zheng Zheng, Ma Li, and Wang Xingping, "The True Area of Land Under Cultivation in the Qing Dynasty," *Jianghaixuekan* (1998) 4

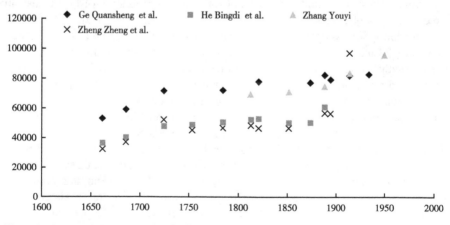

Fig. 1.2 Estimated changes to area under cultivation in China over the past 300 years

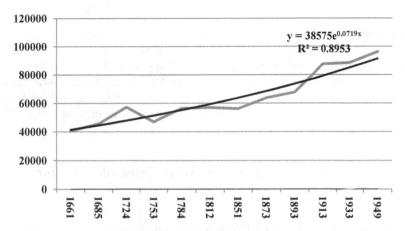

Fig. 1.3 Changes to area under cultivation in China over the past 300 years (Best Fit)

From Table 1.5 we can see that in the past 300 years, the population grew rapidly, from 141 million to 549 million, a 3.9-fold increase and an annual average growth of 0.47%. Next comes area of LuC, which grew from 41.41 to 90.43 million hectares, a 2.2-fold increase and average annual increase of 0.27%. Next comes average grain production per unit of area of LuC, which increased from 1350 to 1912 kg/ha, a 1.4-fold increase and an average annual increase of 0.12%. Driven by dual growth in both area of LuC and average yield per unit of area, total grain output grew from 55.91 million tonnes to 172.91 million tonnes, a 3.1-fold increase and an average annual growth of 0.39%. As the population grew even faster, the per

Table 1.5 Primary Grain Production Indicators in China over the Past 300 Years

Year	Area under cultivation (kha)	Per capita grain production (kg/ha)	Total output (tonnes)	Population	Per capita area under cultivation (ha)	Per capita grain share (kg)
1661	41,413	1350	55,908,084	140,831,000	0.29	397
1685	44,461	1402	62,333,823	170,950,000	0.26	365
1724	47,732	1455	69,450,224	224,380,000	0.21	310
1753	51,244	1504	77,071,428	264,110,000	0.19	292
1784	55,015	1553	85,438,169	286,460,000	0.19	298
1812	59,063	1606	94,855,152	327,686,000	0.18	289
1851	63,409	1658	105,131,974	368,913,000	0.17	285
1873	68,075	1711	116,475,668	381,027,000	0.18	306
1893	73,084	1763	128,846,439	393,500,000	0.19	327
1913	78,461	1812	142,171,718	432,000,000	0.18	329
1933	84,234	1860	156,676,142	473,530,000	0.18	331
1949	90,433	1912	172,907,058	548,770,000	0.16	315

capita share of land fell from 0.29 to 0.16 ha, a decrease of 44% and an average annual drop of 0.2%. Per capita grain share fell from 397 to 315 kg, a reduction of 21% and an average annual drop of 0.08%. This demonstrates that per capita grain shares were not fixed and unchanging. As 80% of China's LuC is used to produce grains, and at least 20% of all LuC is unreported,[11] in this book I have assumed that total area of LuC is equivalent to the area of land planted with grain. Henceforth I shall not make any adjustments upward or downward.

1.2.2   Why Agriculture Did Not Cause Economic Decline in China

1.2.2.1   China Still Possessed Comparative Advantages in Agriculture During This Period

Most assessments of agricultural productivity are made in light of natural conditions, land quality, laborer skills, technical levels, and so on. Actually, the simplest method is to assess agricultural productivity as a comparison between the amount of seeds sown and the size of the harvest. Such a comparison is not only easy to calculate, but also easy to observe. In China the ratio of seeds sown to harvest exceeds 1:20, while the same ratio is less than 1:15 in Europe and the Americas. This shows that agricultural productivity is relatively higher in China.

The research of Li Bozhong into the most densely populated regions of Jiangnan demonstrates the following figures for number of laborers per μ planted with rice: 12.1 at the end of the Ming Dynasty, 10.5 in the mid-Qing Dynasty, 13.75 in 1936, and 11.25 in 1941. There were no great changes across these centuries.[12] This further demonstrates that agriculture in China did not decline over this period.

1.2.2.2   Limited Disparities in Chinese Agricultural Technology During This Period

If China's economic decline were attributable to agriculture, then such decline would have been the result of a failure to keep up with advances in agricultural technology of the times. However, this is simply not the case. Although there were no major, earth-shattering innovations in agricultural technology made in China over the past 300 years, agricultural productivity in China has continued to increase. As ever greater attention has been paid to foreign affairs by China's

---

[11]Wu Chengming, "Observations of Agricultural Productivity in China in the Recent Era," *Zhongguojingjishiyanjiu* (1989) 2.

[12]Li Bozhong, "Increases to the Intensiveness of Rice Agriculture in Jiangnan In the Ming and Qing Dynasties," *Zhongguonongshi* (1984) 1.

agricultural sector, many foreign varieties have come to be widely applied in China; this has become one of the major channels through which agricultural development has been promoted. Thus Li Yuese thinks that from the third through the 13th centuries, the West couldn't hold a candle to China's technology and science, but beginning in the 15th century China gradually began falling behind Europe. The trend first cropped up in the fields of physics, astronomy, and mathematics, and only much later spread to chemistry, biology, medicine, and agronomy.[13]

1.2.2.3 Positive Impacts of the Industrial Revolution on Agriculture Still Highly Limited During This Period

Although the Industrial Revolution happened during this period, the achievements of the Industrial Revolution were not applied to agricultural sectors until much later. For example, although the tractor allowed for the emergence of commercialized production in the US in 1892, only 1000 tractors were produced in that country prior to 1914. The case was similar for chemical fertilizers and pesticides as well. That is to say that during this period, European and American countries were the same as China, in that agriculture remained stuck in the animal-powered era. Given similar conditions of productivity, development in agriculture would not have been markedly different.

1.2.3 Reasons for China's Economic Decline

1.2.3.1 Limitations on Division of Labor and Industries of Over-Small Scales of Operation

Different from many countries, China long ago replaced inheritance by only the elder son with equal inheritance among all the sons. That meant that a family's farmland was divided once about every 40 years. Very few families saw their land holdings grow by a factor of two or more over 30 years, but many families had to divide land between two or more brothers. As the expansion of arable land could not keep up with the growing number of adult males, the scale of land operations was forced to grow ever smaller. A survey conducted in 55 regions of 16 provinces revealed that the average family holding of farmland used for rice or other grain planting was 20.3 μ in 1890, 15.9 μ in 1910, and down to 13.8 μ in 1933.[14]

---

[13] Joseph Needham and Dorothy Needham, Science and Agriculture in China and the West Science Outpost, London: The Pibt Press LTD 253–258.

[14] Xu Daofu, *Agricultural and Trade Statistics for China in the Recent Era*, (Shanghai: Shanghai renmin chubanshe, 1983).

To resolve insufficient employment opportunities brought about by the excessively small scale of agricultural operations, most laborers participated in both agriculture and the family handicraft industry in order to better meet the various needs of their households. All laborers pursued methods of maximum skill diversity rather than maximum aptitude in a single skill. This limited the development of division of industries and division of labor to an extreme degree; it was thus difficult for industry to grow independently. And so even if the so-called "buds of capitalism" were sprouting, these buds were hard pressed to foment fundamental changes in rural industry structures.

With the scale of agricultural operations so small, it was difficult for home handicrafts industries to bring about specialized, scale development. All production activities relied upon human power, animal power, and natural power (such as hydro and wind power), which was sufficient for the needs of the time but could not drive innovations in machinery or other areas. So all non-agricultural activities focused on the continual improvement of luxury ornamental items, and all innovation and application in machinery likewise focused on the production of said luxury items.

All technical innovations in agriculture as well as livelihood strategies at the level of individual farming households were made under the limitations of extremely small scales of operation. On the one hand, intensive farming made such micro operation scales more highly adaptable, and on the other hand, adjustments to meal structures mitigated the impact of fluctuations to grain yields. That is to say that farmers either ate slightly better or slightly worse according to grain yield fluctuations in a given year, but they did not mitigate the impact of fluctuations through grain reserves. In 1931, the agricultural economics department of the Agriculture Institute of the University of Nanking (now merged with Nanjing University) conducted a survey into 131 counties of Hunan, Hubei, Jiangxi, Anhui, and Jiangsu that had been hit by floods. Surveyors found that flood victims ended up eating "one third less than usual." Some people summed up adjustments made to meal structures of flood victims as "husks and vegetables serve as grains for half the year."

1.2.3.2   Limitations on Industry Upgrading of Expansion of Arable Land

Many hilly and mountainous regions of China were long left wild as they were unsuited to planting millet or other crops. The great influx of corn, sweet potatoes, and potatoes, all of which give high yields and are tolerant of poor soil fertility, drove a movement of virgin cultivation of previously wild lands in China's hilly and mountainous areas. This movement also caused a major increase in the area of arable land in China during the Qing Dynasty. China's total arable land was a little over 500 million μ in 1661, up to 1.156 billion μ in 1911. Newly added LuC over this 250-year period exceeded the total of LuC accumulated over the several thousand years of China's agricultural history up to that point.

The development of hilly and mountainous areas went hand in hand with the movement of populations. The farmers who moved into such regions brought with them agricultural techniques of deep plowing, seed selection, fertilization, multiple cropping, and so on, all of which led to great increases in grain yields per μ in these areas. Over the same period, areas with highly developed agriculture also experienced ubiquitous increases in yields, only to a somewhat smaller extent.[15] The marked expansion in LuC and rapid increases to overall grain output strengthened the vitality of China's economic system, then centered on agriculture, and brought about a rapid surge in population growth. Grain prices slowly increased in the early Qing Dynasty, but then somewhere in the middle of the dynasty began a long, slow fall. This demonstrates that overall supply and demand for grain were on the whole balanced.

1.2.3.3   Limitations of "Celestial Empire Thinking" on Changing the Status Quo

By "Celestial Empire thinking," I mean a country's viewing itself as the center of the world. This was a problem shared by many countries, but it was most severe in China. The greatest pleasure of local officials in every part of China was to send reports of prosperity and the good life in their jurisdictions to the imperial court. Those in power were satisfied to see the achievements before their eyes, and in fact got drunk on this idea of prosperity. Even long after the country had succumbed to economic decline, they remained entranced by their pipe dream of China's being "the supreme nation of the Celestial Empire" and were unwilling to engage in equal relations with other countries. For example, on August 13, 1793, when receiving the English ambassador Earl George Macartney at his summer villa, the Qianlong Emperor haughtily declared:

> Our Celestial Empire possesses all things in prolific abundance and lacks no product within its own borders. There was therefore no need to import the manufactures of outside barbarians in exchange for our own produce. But as the tea, silk, and porcelain, which the Celestial Empire produces, are absolute necessities to European nations and to yourselves, we have permitted, as a signal mark of favor, that foreign hongs [groups of merchants] should be established at Canton, so that your wants might be supplied and your country thus participate in our beneficence.

Under the influence of such reasoning, officials at the time considered the only normal form of foreign relations to be for foreign countries to offer tribute at

---

[15]Fang Xing, introduction to *General History of Chinese Economy, Qing Dynasty Edition*, (Beijing: Jingji Ribao Chubanshe, 2000).

Table 1.6 Growth in agricultural labor productivity in various nations from 1913 to 1950

Region or nation	Labor pool		Change rate (%)	Per capita GDP (US$)		Change rate (%)
	1913 (mn)	1950 (mn)		1913	1950	
China	135.00	175.00	29.6	340	405	19.1
US	11.50	8.80	−23.5	6100	19,650	222.1
Japan	14.50	15.30	5.5	1300	2125	63.5
Western Europe	38.50	32.50	−15.6	3625	5550	53.1
Soviet Union	35.00	32.10	−8.3	1000	1560	56.0
Developed nations	124.00	112.50	−9.3	2475	6536	164.1
Developing nations	346.00	542.50	56.8	440	535	21.6

China's imperial court. They turned deaf ears to any news of the rapid development or astonishing feats of Western powers at the time. Even though it became necessary at this time to hire foreigners to make corrections to China's calendar system and to repair all clocks and other delicate machinery, Chinese officials still viewed all foreigners as barbarians.[16]

As demonstrated in Table 1.6, China's agricultural labor force grew from 135 million to 175 million between 1913 and 1950, an increase of 29.6%. Over the same period, Japan's labor force grew by only 5.5%, while that of the US grew by 23.5%, Western Europe by 15.6%, and the Soviet Union by 8.3%. A diversion of agricultural labor in those last three led to increases in agricultural productivity of 222.1, 53.1, and 57%, respectively. China's per capita gross domestic product (GDP) growth rate was only 19.1%, lower than the developing nation average of 21.6%.

China's economy did not decline because agriculture declined, but rather because the country's leaders continued to view agriculture as the foundation upon which the nation could grow. They continued to view agriculture as the nation's economic core, and so China remained stuck as an agricultural society, unable to keep up with the pace of economic transformations taking place in other countries, which were actively transforming their industry and employment structures. So any efforts to reverse China's economic decline would have had to be made by accelerating the pace of industrialization.

---

[16]John Barrow, *My View of the Flourishing Age of Qianlong*, (Beijing: Beijing Tushuguan Chubanshe, 2007), 260.

1.3 Agriculture in China for the 30 Years Prior to Reform and Opening

In 1949, when New China was founded, the country faced an economic system constituted primarily of peasant agriculture and with little accumulation. In order to accelerate the development of industry, particularly heavy industry, and achieve the goals of catching up to and exceeding developed economies as quickly as possible, it was necessary to concentrate agricultural surpluses to the greatest extent possible, achieve accumulation rates of 12% or higher, and reduce labor and material costs for industrial development to the greatest extent possible.

There were two methods available for concentrating agricultural surpluses: the financial and the fiscal. The financial method required precise, flexible financial policies, a rational distribution of financial organs, and intelligent, diversified financial tools. China had none of these things at the time, and so only the fiscal method was available. The fiscal method required either increasing taxation levels or distorting trade conditions. As the previous administration had already incurred the wrath of the people with high tax burdens, it was not an option for the new government to continue heavy taxation. So leaders opted to distort conditions for the trade of industrial and agricultural products. In China, this method is called price scissors for industrial and agricultural products. Another benefit of distorting trade conditions for industrial and agricultural products was that this allowed reducing the costs of labor and raw materials for industrial development to the greatest extent possible.

At the time, China's non-agricultural industries were controlled by private operators. Private operators were not satisfied with the benefits of distorted trade conditions going only to purchasers of agricultural and industrial products, and so they threw markets into disorder through speculation, hoarding, and other means. This drove the costs of urban livelihoods even higher. As the method of distorting trade conditions for industrial and agricultural products did not meet anticipated goals, the new government enacted the unified purchases and unified sales policy, better known as the state monopoly, for agricultural products.

The state monopoly on primary agricultural products effectively resolved the dilemma of how to concentrate agricultural surpluses while reducing the costs of urban livelihoods, but it was not possible for the government to include all agricultural products within the scope of the monopoly. The objective of most Chinese farmers at the time was self-sufficiency, and so agricultural products were not highly commercialized. To increase their incomes, rural citizens opted to produce less of the products included in the monopoly and more of the products not included. As the government could not make adjustments to the state monopoly on agricultural products at the level of individual households, there was an objective need for an organization system that would make managing peasants [*nongmin*, also referred to as rural citizens] more convenient. The people's commune was hailed as the best possible solution to this problem. Vice Premier Chen Yun, then in charge of economic work in China, used this vivid analogy: "Peasant households are like the hairs on a woman's head. They are many, and they're scattered, and it's not easy to grab them. The role of the people's commune is to tie the many, scattered hairs into a single braid, which is easy to grab." The people's commune system effectively resolved the problem of the state monopoly system's being unable to manage individual households by unifying the organization of production. The system met the goal of organizing agricultural production per the tasks set by the state monopoly.

This demonstrates that the tripartite system of distorted trade conditions, the state monopoly, and people's communes were born from a state strategy of concentrating agricultural surpluses, reducing the costs of urban livelihoods, and promoting industrial development. China's per capita gross national product (GNP), previously in a state of excessively low growth, reached an accumulation rate of over 12% on the strength of these policies. The goal of reducing wage rates and raw material costs for industry to the greatest extent possible was also met. In a relatively short time, China succeeded in building a relatively complete industrial system, and in developing atomic bombs, hydrogen bombs, and satellites.

Although trade conditions for industrial and agricultural products were distorted, officials effectively rejected rent-seeking on the strength of a rigorous set of fiscal accounting institutions. So the greatest problem with the planned economy wasn't corruption, but rather the inability of agricultural productivity to reach its full potential, as the majority of peasants remained in a state of poverty. Tables 1.7, 1.8 and 1.9 demonstrate that over the 20 years from 1958, the year that the people's

Table 1.7 Nationwide per capita shares of major agricultural products, 1957–1978, *unit* Kilograms

	1957	1962	1965	1970	1975	1978
Per capita grain share	306	240.5	272	293	310.5	318.5
Per capita cotton share	2.6	1.15	4.95	2.8	2.6	2.25
Per capita oil crop share	6.1	3.6	5.05	4.6	4.95	5.45
Per capita share of meat products	6.25	2.9	7.7	7.3	8.7	8.95
Per capita share of fisheries products	4.9	3.4	4.25	3.9	4.8	4.85

Data source Forty Years of Rural China, (Zhongyuan nongmin chubanshe, 1989), 132

Table 1.8 Average quantities of commercial agricultural products supplied per agriculturally-registered person, 1957–1978, *unit* Kilograms or head

	1957	1962	1965	1970	1975	1978
Grain	85.05	57.85	64.90	66.10	67.35	62.60
Cotton	2.65	1.15	3.25	2.90	2.85	2.60
Edible oil	1.95	0.65	1.40	1.45	1.00	1.10
Live pigs	0.075	0.034	0.130	0.108	0.132	0.135
Fisheries products	3.20	2.65	3.05	2.85	3.25	3.30

Data source Forty Years of Rural China, (Zhongyuan nongmin chubanshe, 1989), 133

Table 1.9 Rural per capita incomes, 1957–1978

	1957	1962	1965	1970	1975	1978
Per capita income (yuan)	87.57	111.53	117.27	129.25	133.45	133.59
Percentage of income from collective (%)	49.6	47.4	53.9	60.6	57.0	58.3
Percentage of income from sideline industries (%)	41.2	45.4	37.0	32.8	36.8	35.6
Percentage from other sources (%)	9.2	7.2	9.2	6.6	6.2	6.1

Data source Forty Years of Rural China, (Zhongyuan nongmin chubanshe, 1989), 130

commune system was established, through 1978, the first year of Reform and Opening, there was no marked growth to either the per capita share of agricultural products or the per capita supply of commercial agricultural products in China. Annual rural income growth was less than three yuan on average. Over the same period, focus development industries had to operate in a closed environment, as they possessed no comparative advantages in their industry sectors, enterprises in these sectors were not viable, and their products not competitive. This is the primary reason that the profits from agricultural surpluses were invested in heavy industry during this stage. Other reasons were: heavy industry was in a closed feedback loop; supply of light industrial products was severely lacking; and most of China's international trade at the time was done with agricultural products. To prevent this section growing too long and going off topic, I will leave discussion of these matters here.

Although total output of agricultural products never stopped growing in the 30 years prior to Reform and Opening, there were continuous, severe shortages of said products over that same period. Through the end of the 1970s, hundreds of millions of Chinese peasants were still struggling to feed and clothe themselves. In 1978, the rural annual per capita income in China was only a touch more than 70 yuan; in nearly a quarter of all production teams, per capita annual incomes from collective allocations were less than 50 yuan. Insufficient supply of agricultural products was a bottleneck restricting balanced growth of the economy from beginning to end. During the "Fifth Five-year Plan" period, imports of grain, cotton, and oil crops cost China USD $1.463 billion, accounting for 64% of total imported consumer goods and 12% of overall imports.

Although the share of domestic incomes from agriculture fell from 57.7% in 1952 to 28.4% in 1978, employment structures changed slowly. The proportion of agricultural labor to total labor fell from 83.5% in 1952 to 70.5% in 1978. Although nearly all capital was concentrated in cities during this period, the country's degree of urbanization, as measured by the urban share of total population, grew from 12.5% in 1952 to only 17.9% in 1978. Resultantly, average production per laborer in agriculture was only 16% of that for industry and 24% that of the service industry. The proportion of agricultural population to total population reached 83%

at its peak. Rural savings rates were less than 25% of urban savings rates, and rural consumption was only slightly above 40% of urban consumption.

Before Reform and Opening, extracting too much from agriculture was certainly a major reason that basic living requirements for many peasants were not met, but a more important reason was the lack of efficiency in rural economic organization. The results of investigations into total factor productivity of Chinese agriculture demonstrates that over the span of over 20 years during which the people's commune system was in place, total agricultural factor productivity was negative. There was certainly no retrogression of agricultural technology during this period, and so this could not have been the reason for total factor productivity going negative. So this negative value was entirely the product of a lack of efficiency in organization and institutional arrangements. Once the Household Responsibility System was implemented at a wide scale, agricultural factor productivity in China immediately became positive, proving the previous point.

Chapter 2
Agricultural Reforms

Reforms in China were first launched in poor rural areas. The earliest reform methods targeted individuals, were highly scattered, and affected only small areas at a time. The primary method of reforms was the implementation of the Household Responsibility System, which shifted the responsibility for both production and labor onto households. After agricultural collectivization in the 1950s, shifting responsibility onto households was one of the primary methods employed for peasants to respond to economic hardships around the country; that is to say that this was by no means a new tactic. What was new was the Chinese government allowing these methods to exist and offering support to the Household Responsibility System as it made possible marked gains in production. In order to bring about a consensus of the entire party and all of society, 1982s "Document Number One" demonstrated through argumentation the socialist nature of the Household Responsibility System and also advocated that no changes be made for a long time to either the public ownership system of land and other basic means of production or the Household Responsibility System. The centrally-issued "Document Number One" of 1983 made deep explanations to support the two conclusions that the Household Responsibility System was "a new development in the practical implementation of Marxist agricultural cooperative concepts in China" and "a great innovation of the Chinese peasantry." Yet another "Document Number One" issued in 1984 extended the term for land contracting from three to 15 years. With the three "Documents Number One" in place, the Household Responsibility System was universally established across rural China. Once granted operational autonomy, rural citizens became incentivized toward production in an unprecedented way. The gross agricultural product rose by an annual average of 7.6% from 1979 to 1984, as calculated based on constant prices. With increases to the prices of agricultural products over the same period, per capita incomes of rural citizens increased by an annual average of 15%, and thus basic life needs were met for the majority of Chinese dwelling in the countryside.

The major method employed in the early period of agricultural reforms was the Household Responsibility System, meaning the contracting of collective land to a

© Social Sciences Academic Press and Springer Nature Singapore Pte Ltd. 2017
Z. Li, *Reform and Development of Agriculture in China*,
Research Series on the Chinese Dream and China's Development Path,
DOI 10.1007/978-981-10-3462-6_2

household, which was to be responsible for production and management. All accounting and allocations of profits were still the responsibility of the village collective economic organization. Very quickly, however, the responsibility system came to encompass everything, with households now responsible for paying state taxes and fulfilling state agricultural product purchasing quotas, as well as paying contracting fees for the land to the collective; at this point village collective economic organizations no longer fulfilled obligations for unified accounting and allocations. Rural households were now the basic unit for production operations and economic accounting, and this set the scene for friction with the system of "three-tiered ownership with the production team as the foundation." To remedy this situation, reforms were enacted upon the people's commune system. These concrete measures were taken: production teams were reorganized into cooperatives; production brigades were abolished and replaced with administrative villages; and people's commune management committees were abolished, with township governments established in their stead. By May 1985, this reform was carried out completely. Around the country 91,138 town and township governments and 940,617 village people's committees were established, with villagers' small groups established under village people's committees.

Agricultural reforms in China were launched in line with two major themes. The first was the Household Responsibility System, aimed at tackling the challenge of rural poverty, and the second was opening to the outside, intended to tackle the challenge of development proceeding more rapidly in China's periphery. This is the basis for that assessment: On November 18, 1978, the processing plant of the Shangwu Brigade of the Shiyan Commune of Bao'an County signed an agreement with the Hong Kong Yigao Real Estate Company, a subsidiary of the Hong Kong Electrical Co., Ltd., creating the country's first "three imports and one compensation" enterprise, the Shangwu Electric (Shenzhen) Co., Ltd. This did not happen later than the Household Responsibility System of Xiaolan Village in Anhui. Shortly after reforms began, village collective economic organizations of Shenzhen not only adopted such reform measures as contracting responsibility to organizations, contracting production to households, contracting all responsibility to households, and allocating fields to households (Commune members were responsible only for turning over public grain and excess grain to higher authorities. Except that land still belonged to the collective, commune members had no economic relationship with their production teams.) and on the strength of their proximity to Hong Kong, they adopted measures for opening to the outside.

First, officials set their sights on the Hong Kong market and adjusted the agricultural production structure. From 1979 to 1980, Shenzhen converted 65,000 μ of rice paddies into 27,000 μ of fish ponds, 9250 μ of fish farms that included rice planting, 8621 μ of vegetable fields, 7910 μ of fruit orchards, and 12,000 μ of flower and medicinal herb gardens. These measures increased added value of agricultural products and rural incomes in the extreme. For example, the Fanshen Brigade of Nantou Commune raised fish and shrimp in 1350 μ of paddy fields suitable for aquaculture and developed an aquaculture industry geared toward export, earning over 126,000 yuan from the industry in 1980. The Xinzhou Brigade of Futian Commune developed over 50 μ of fish ponds and 250 μ of reclaimed ocean beach to raise fish and shrimp.

Second, officials developed cross-border cultivation. Production teams located along the border with Hong Kong's New Territories planted vegetables, flowers, and other cash crops to be sold in the New Territories for Hong Kong dollars (HKD), which were then used to purchase means of production. In 1980, the Liantang Brigade of Fucheng Commune, located on the border, opened a factory and a farm on the border to grow vegetables and raise fish, earning more than HKD $670,000 and earning income of 600,000 yuan for picking up waste. These two projects accounted for 44% of the brigade's total income in that year.

Third, officials developed horizontal alliances. The Futian Commune developed all manner of joint venture enterprises through such means as share-holding, dividend-sharing, and renting land. In 1980, these enterprises earned income of 2.7 million yuan, accounting for 24% of the commune's income in that year. The Xiamei Brigade, located in a rocky, mountainous area, cooperated with outsiders to develop quarries, tea fields, and other ventures, adding 126,000 yuan to income. The 15th Production Team of the Fenghuang Brigade of Fuyong Commune jointly operated a vegetable growing business with foreign merchants; revenues for the production team in 1980 were 43.1% greater than in 1979.

Fourth, officials developed a large-scale animal husbandry industry via compensation trade, establishing small processing companies for imported materials, assembly companies, and so on. There were a total of 426 compensation trade projects in Shenzhen by the end of 1979, which in 1980 generated over HKD $27 million in processing fees and profit sharing. The Buji Commune developed processing of imported materials and construction materials manufacturing, and the commune's income grew from over 1.69 million yuan in 1979 to over 5.2 million in 1980, more than a three-fold increase.

Fifth, officials developed petty trading in frontier areas. Rural communes and brigades along borders were allowed to autonomously export petty amounts of agricultural products and by-products to the New Territories after fulfilling state purchasing obligations. Per incomplete data, total petty cross-border trading in Shenzhen in 1980 came to 18.74 million yuan, accounting for a quarter of total income. The Luohu District of Shenzhen abuts the New Territories of Hong Kong. In 1980, after the allowance of petty cross-border trading, the district earned revenue of over 18 million yuan, a 2.5-fold increase over 1978. The Yumin Village Brigade of Fucheng Commune benefited from its proximity to Hong Kong to develop a commercial enterprise combining fisheries, industry, commerce, and agricultural by-products. The brigade paid per capita allocations of 2000 yuan and per capita labor compensations of over 3800 yuan in 1980.[1]

---

[1]Li et al., "A Look at the Superiority of Socialist Institutions from the Perspective of Changes in Rural Shenzhen," *Jinan University Journal (Philosophy and Social Sciences Edition)*, (1980) 4.

One perspective holds that the primary reason for the failures of collective operations in agriculture were the result of corporatization and communication causing work to be performed too hastily, too fast, and too crudely. Upon closer examination, however, one finds that this explanation isn't entirely tenable, as all problems caused by work being too hasty, too fast, or too crude will gradually be resolved over time, but these problems were never solved over a period of over 20 years. That proves that there were other reasons of inappropriate methods to blame in addition to work being too hasty, too fast, and too crude.

Agriculture's suitability to the Household Responsibility System is determined by some specific characteristics, such as the difficulty in effectively overseeing agricultural production, the difficulty of accurately measuring labor quality, and so on. Household operations bring about integration of production units and living units, as well as integration of production operations and family livelihood planning. Harmonious relationships founded upon blood ties can also maximally reduce costs of oversight, and so for all these reasons, household operations meet the demands of agricultural production rather well. It is difficult for collective operations to bring about effective oversight over agricultural laborers and to accurately measure the quality of their labor. It is also difficult for it to prevent some people from taking a free ride, and as time goes on more and more rural citizens feel less and less incentivized to engage in production. This is an important reason that we must persist in the Household Responsibility System for agriculture.

In addition to the Household Responsibility System, spurring incentives to produce of rural citizens by increasing the prices of agricultural products is another major reason that agricultural productivity grew during this stage. Per records, state grain purchase prices increased 20% at the time 1979s summer grains hit markets; prices for grain sold in excess of quota requirements rose 50%. There were also corresponding increases to prices of other agricultural products and by-products. In addition, prices for industrial products intended for agriculture, such as farm equipment, chemical fertilizers, pesticides, and agricultural plastic sheeting, all fell between 10 and 15% in 1979 and 1980.

The implementation of the Household Responsibility System triggered unconventional growth in agriculture from the beginning of Reform and Opening through 1984. The growth in agriculture it set off, however, was a one-time-only event. After the mid-1980s, growth in agriculture was primarily attributable to reforms to the circulation system for agricultural products, the fostering of a rural market system, and the effects of market mechanisms. In order to develop markets for agricultural products, China employed a method of gradual reforms, meaning a gradual transition from the planned economy into the market economy through price formation and the "dual-track system" of resource allocations.

The "dual-track" system of markets for agricultural products meant a synthesis of "adjustments" and "deregulation" to prices for agricultural products. In the early period of Reform and Opening, the central government greatly increased the purchase prices of agricultural products such as grains and also greatly increased the purchase prices for all grains sold in excess of quotas. So the more grain a farmer sold to the state, the higher the average sale price he received. Increases to agricultural product prices directly touched off greater incentivization for farmers to increase investments and perform more multi-cropping. A study performed by Lin Yifu in 1992 demonstrated that the contribution rate of increases to agricultural product purchase prices to overall output growth over the years 1978–1984 was 16%.

2.1 Reforms to Markets for Agricultural Products

Over the 25-year span from 1953 to 1978, purchase prices for agricultural products and by-products were extremely stable in every year except 1961, when the purchase price index increased 28% from the previous year. If the base purchase price was 100 in 1950, then from 1961 to 1977, the purchase price index for agricultural products and by-products increased from 201.4 to 209.8, less than an 8% increase over 16 years. In fact, purchase prices even decreased in the years 1962 and 1971. This demonstrates that the state monopoly system was indeed effective at stabilizing prices of agricultural products.

2.1.1 Gradually Shrinking the Scope of the Agricultural State Monopoly

In 1978, there were 113 agricultural products subject to state planning. In 1979, the state pushed reforms to reduce the number of varieties of agricultural products and by-products controlled by the state monopoly, to open rural markets and bazaars, and to restore the system of contract purchasing. In 1980, the state began adjusting the scope of products subject to the monopoly and planned purchasing. All agricultural products excluding grain, oil crops, cotton, sugarcane, tobacco, jute, tea, fruits, meat, eggs, aquaculture products, and wood—all of which remained subject to the state monopoly system—were classified as category three agricultural products and by-products. In 1983, the state continued reducing the scope of agricultural products subject to the monopoly, this time moving fruits from category two, still under state management, to category three. In 1984 the scope of the monopoly grew smaller still when the Ministry of Commerce reduced the number of agricultural products and by-products in categories one and two from 21 to 12, reduced the number of agricultural products subject to the state monopoly to three—grain, oil crops, and cotton—and reduced the number of products subject to the state quota system from 18 to nine, releasing tea, peanuts, beef, mutton, fresh eggs, apples, mandarin oranges, and tangerines from the quota system. In 1985 the state reduced the number of agricultural products subject to state price setting to 38, and again to nine in 1991. By 1993, only markets for cotton, tobacco, silkworm cocoons, and a handful of other agricultural products had not been opened. At this time only about one third of farmer revenues for commercial grain came from state planned grain purchases.

2.1.2 Gradually Reducing the Quantity of State Monopoly Purchases

Shortly after the beginning of Reform and Opening, the state adjusted the quantity of agricultural products purchased under the state monopoly to alleviate the burden on farmers. In 1979, the state reduced the planned grain purchase obligation by 2.5 billion kg. All state purchasing obligations were summarily rescinded for rice-growing regions in which per capita grain rations were 200 kilograms or less and in regions producing grains other than rice or wheat in which per capita grain rations were 150 kilograms or less.

In 1981, the state began promoting the contract purchase and sale system for agricultural products and by-products in an attempt to coordinate agricultural production and state planning. In 1983 and 1984, officials gradually reduced obligations for sale of agricultural products and by-products to the state monopoly system and promoted the development of agricultural products and by-products outside of government-mandated quotas. In 1985, the state ceased issuing quota obligations to farmers on all but a few select products. The state continued setting prices on commodity products such as grain, cotton, oil crops, tobacco, silkworm cocoons, sugar crops, and so on, but now implemented the contract purchasing system for these items. The state fixed prices on grain using the "reverse three-to-seven" ratio (meaning 30% bought at original monopoly prices and 70% bought at higher extra-quota prices). State-purchased cotton was priced at the "reverse three-to-seven" ratio in the North and at the "straight four-to-six" ratio in the South. Any agricultural products not subject to state monopoly obligations, as well as all grain and cotton produced in excess of quotas, could be sold by farmers on the free market. This is what gave rise to the so-called "dual-track system" for the sale and marketing of agricultural products and by-products.

2.1.3 Gradually Developing a Market for Agricultural Products

From 1978 to 1984, the total of policy-dictated subsidies on agricultural products grew from 1.114 billion yuan to 21.834 billion yuan, a 19.6-fold increase. Price subsidies on grain, cotton, and oil crops in particular grew from 1.114 billion yuan to 20.167 billion yuan, an 18.1-fold increase. As these subsidies led to major growth in fiscal expenditures, in 1985 the government pushed out reforms to the circulation system for agricultural products. Between 1991 and 1993, officials opened grain sale prices for urban residents to the market, thus eliminating the fiscal burden of "inversion"—buying high and selling low—between state purchase and sale prices for grain.

Reforms to agricultural product markets went through four stages. In the first, prices were adjusted, and markets were allowed to open. In the second, the planned economy and market-oriented adjustments were integrated. In the third, market mechanisms were allowed to play a fundamental role. In the final stage, market mechanisms were allowed to play a decisive role. The order of reforms was: first an opening of rural markets for agricultural products, and then an opening of urban markets for agricultural markets; first an opening of local markets for agricultural products, and then an allowance of transporting agricultural products long distances for sale. There are three levels of connotation behind gradual reforms. The first is that gradual advancement of such is characterized by "going one step at a time." The second is that the more important a particular agricultural product, the slower it is reformed, and the less important a product, the faster it is reformed, and so these reforms are characterized by being "sometimes fast and sometimes slow." The third is that reforms advance when conditions are good but cease when conditions are poor, and so are characterized by "stopping and starting."

After markets were opened, there was rapid development to all manner of market entities. From 1978 to 1984, the number of rural markets for agricultural products grew steadily from 33,000 to over 50,000. Total grain transactions in rural markets were not staggering, but growth in transactions was rapid, rising from 2.5 billion kilograms in 1978 to 8.35 billion kilograms in 1984, a 3.34-fold increase. By the end of 2004, the number of employees in state-owned grain enterprises dropped by 1.64 million from 1998, a reduction of 49.7%.

2.1.4   Expanding Channels for Circulation of Agricultural Products

Hindrances to the circulation of fresh agricultural products led to problems of overstocking in local production areas and shortages elsewhere. In order to resolve this, in 1983 officials abolished the law requiring all out-shipments of agricultural products and by-products to be approved by local authorities and gave farmers the right to independently manage sales of fresh agricultural products. Farmers were allowed to enter cities and cross both county and provincial lines to sell agricultural products and by-products produced in excess of state quotas, with complete pricing autonomy.

In 1985, the state began reforms specifically targeting the circulation system for agricultural products. This marked a momentous shift in the focus of reforms away from the production and operation system toward the circulation system. The new method was to implement contract purchasing and market purchasing on different agricultural products per their different situations. In China, the scale and degree of market-determined pricing for agricultural products progressed gradually along the lines of the dual-track pricing system of planned prices and market prices.

In 1985, the state monopoly on grain and cotton was abolished in favor of the contract purchasing system. The first 30% of grain sold under the contract system was priced the same as under the state monopoly, and the latter 70% sold at original extra-quota prices (again, the "reverse three-to-seven" ratio). Cotton sold in the South was priced at the "straight four-to-six" ratio, and at the "reverse three-to-seven" ratio in the North. All grain and cotton produced in excess of contractual purchasing requirements could be freely sold on the open market. After the abolishment of the state monopoly system, the "dual-track system" for grain prices formed, combining both state-set prices and market prices.

In terms of real results of these reforms, in 1985 many localities had not implemented reforms to convert from coercive purchasing into contract purchasing, as conditions were not yet ripe. The primary reason for this was that there was a great drop in Chinese grain yields in 1985, and market prices for grain grew over 10%, which caused market prices to be significantly higher than contractually-set prices. Owing to fiscal limitations, the government was not able to promptly increase contractual purchase prices. Farmers were willing neither to fulfil original contracts nor to sign new grain purchase contracts. This situation was remedied only after the bountiful grain harvest of 1987.

In 1992, the state attempted several important measures in making macro-adjustments to grain markets, including the establishment of a grain risk fund, a grain purchase price-protection system, and a state grain reserve system. These measures were not implemented, however, owing to insufficient capital.

With grain purchase and sale prices being regulated by the market, gradual development and stabilization of coordinated relationships between grain-producing and grain-consuming areas, and initial work completed in the establishment of a vertical management system for central grain reserves, the state's ability to make macro-adjustments grew stronger.

In 2001, the central government opened grain markets and allowed for prices to be entirely regulated by markets in the eight key grain-consuming regions of Zhejiang, Shanghai, Fujian, Guangdong, Hainan, Jiangsu, Beijing, and Tianjin. In 2004, the central government completely opened all grain markets in the country, abolishing the institutions requiring licenses to transport and sell grain in different jurisdictions, while also strictly forbidding any regional blockage of free grain trade. Any operator meeting conditions was allowed to purchase and sell grain. This brought about an orderly, standardized nationally integrated grain market of fair competition.

All other purchasing quotas for agricultural products were also abolished. After 1984, large and mid-sized cities gradually withdrew from operations and pricing of fresh agricultural products, eventually giving rise to pricing mechanisms controlled by supply and demand on the market. This further gave rise to a network of markets for fresh agricultural products, with wholesale markets as their core and local markets as their foundation, typified by circulation through multiple channels and competition between a variety of economic entities. The central government completely opened up operations in fisheries products and allowed for market regulation; the market system for fisheries products has improved steadily ever since. Beginning in 1985, the state gradually abolished the state monopoly in edible oil. In 1991, all edible oil in China, except the portion going to urban rations or military use, became subject to supply via negotiated prices and market regulation.

In 1992, pricing in all oil crops except peanuts and rapeseeds, which remained under state control, was completely deregulated. In 1993, the deregulation was extended to all oil crops.

2.2   Agricultural Factor Market Reforms

The dual-track system was also employed in the growth of agricultural factor markets. By "dual-track system," I mean that some pre-existing methods from before the implementation of reforms continue being used to protect the vested interests under the original order while employing new mechanisms for operations for newly added production under the new order. As the vested interests from the old order gradually grow smaller with time, it becomes correspondingly easier to push reforms onto those interests. Agricultural factor markets include labor markets, land markets, and financial markets, of which labor markets are the most dynamic. Financial markets at this time were both insufficiently dynamic and of insufficient scale. Markets for land contracting fell between the other two.

In 2005, rural production factors were 60.6% marketized, reaching the critical point for market economies (60%). Of those factors, labor was 80% marketized, land 52% marketized, and capital 50% marketized.[2] Labor markets grew by gradual advances. At first, urban and rural labor markets were divided, meaning that rural citizens could move about only in between rural industries, hence the term "leaving home without leaving the countryside and entering factories without entering cities." Thereafter, urban and rural labor markets were integrated, giving rise to the ability to "leave home and leave the countryside and enter the factory while also entering the city." Now rural laborers are not just leaving the countryside and entering cities, but the cities themselves are "receiving laborers and their families at the same time." The process of marketizing land factor markets comprises both a gradual elimination of the urban-rural dual structure and the integration of urban and rural economies and societies, and also is a process of rural citizens realizing their property rights to their land. The framework for a pluralistic, competitive rural financial system has finally begun to take shape as financial organs of different kinds of ownership systems have been encouraged in counties; as great efforts have been made in fostering petty loan organizations founded by natural persons, corporate legal persons, or corporate aggregates; as the development of rural household capital mutual aid organizations has been guided; and as private loans have been standardized. Rural production factors have grown increasingly marketized as urban-rural integrated labor markets have gradually been established; as rural land markets have gradually come onto the track of rule-by-law; and as rural capital markets have gradually moved away from monopolies and toward competition.

---

[2]Li Jing and Han Bin, "Report on Rural Marketization in China," Dongfangchubanshe, August 2011.

2.2.1   Reforms to Agricultural Input Markets

Shortly after Reform and Opening, major agricultural production factors such as chemical fertilizers remained under the following administrative mechanisms of the planned economy: integrated monopolistic purchasing and allocation, and hierarchical management. In 1985, the central government made adjustments to the scope of important agricultural production materials under the unified distribution system, including chemical fertilizers. These production materials became subject to a price management mechanism that combined state-set prices, government guided-prices, and market-adjusted prices. This gave rise to a dual-track system for chemical fertilizers and pesticides. State regulation was eventually completely lifted on such production materials as plow animals, small and mid-sized farming implements, pesticides, farm equipment, and others.

In 1994, the central government changed the classification of chemical fertilizers from category one wholesale and category one retail to category one wholesale and category one retail. At the same time, the consignment sale system was promoted; it was not allowable for individuals to sell this product. In 1998, the government rescinded directive-natured production plans and monopolistic purchasing plans for chemical fertilizers, and allowed for manufacturers and companies selling fertilizers to autonomously buy and sell products. Factory prices for fertilizer were no longer state-set, but replaced with a combination of government-guided pricing and open retail pricing. By the end of 1993, 98% of counties (and county-level cities) had ceased to regulate grain prices and had allowed for market regulation of the production and circulation of other agricultural products. As the grain coupon system and state monopoly system were abolished, grain circulation left the "dual-track" system and entered the single track of market guidance.

2.2.2   Reforms to Agricultural Labor Markets

Soon after the founding of New China, there were no restrictions on the mobility of laborers, and most expansion of the urban population resulted from people moving to cities from rural areas, just as in other developing nations. In 1958, the National People's Congress passed the "Regulations on Household Registration of the People's Republic of China" to ensure ample labor for agriculture in the countryside and restrict growth of the urban population, who enjoyed low-priced agricultural products. The household registration system, also known as the *hukou* system, imposed rigorous limitations on the mobility of rural laborers.

2.2.2.1 Policies Restricting Rural Laborers to the Countryside

The Household Responsibility System incentivized the masses of rural citizens to work more hours in agriculture and to seek more opportunities outside of agriculture. In the beginning, most such mobility flowed into the forestry, husbandry, and fishery sectors, but soon began flowing into rural non-agricultural industries. In the late 1970s and early 1980s, educated youths returning to their cities exerted employment pressure on urban centers. At this time the government passed policies restricting rural laborers to the countryside, touching off the "rise of a new army" in rural industry. From 1984 to 1988, the number of rural industrial enterprises in China grew from 4.812 to 7.735 million, an increase of 60.74%. The number of people employed in these enterprises grew from 36.561 to 57.034 million, a growth of 56%.

2.2.2.2 Policies Allowing Rural Laborers to Leave the Countryside

In the mid-1980s, after pressure on urban employment had been alleviated, the government began relaxing restrictions on rural laborers that had prevented them from working in urban areas. This change in policy touched off the surge of migration of rural laborers. Over the three-year span from 1989 to 1991, the state of the macro-economy was poor, and so the central government twice issued urgent notices to place rigorous controls on the "blind migration" of rural laborers, demanding that governments at all levels either clamp down on or completely stop handling procedures allowing rural migrants to work away from home. In 1992, reforms to China's economy came back on track, at which point rural migration picked up in intensity again.

As indicated in Table 2.1, in 1980, 20.28 million rural laborers, 6.37% of all rural laborers, were employed in non-agricultural industries. By 2005, that number had come to exceed 200 million people, an 11-fold increase over 1980, accounting for 40.51% of all rural laborers. In 2014, the figure was again up to 273.95 million, accounting for 50.5% of all rural laborers, which is to say that migrant laborers now account for over half of all rural laborers (Fig. 2.1).

2.2.2.3 The Policy Allowing Migration of Whole Families

The stability of rural migrants finding employment outside of their homes has gradually augmented as the number of years one can work grows. The more stable employment is for migrants, the more likely it is that they will bring their families with them. To meet the demands of these rural migrants, the central government has demanded that local governments in places where laborers migrate provide opportunities for compulsory education to the children of migrants. Table 2.2

Table 2.1 Migration of rural laborers over the years

Year	Absolute			Year	Absolute		
	# of migrant laborers (mn)	% of total rural population	Annual growth		# of migrant laborers (mn)	% of total rural population	Annual growth
1980	20.28	6.37	3.84	1998	138.058	29.73	2.06
1981	19.94	6.10	−1.68	1999	139.847	29.82	1.30
1982	27.14	8.01	36.11	2000	151.646	31.62	8.44
1983	30.447	8.78	12.18	2001	157.780	32.71	4.04
1984	42.826	11.91	40.66	2002	165.360	34.08	4.8
1985	67.136	18.11	56.76	2003	177.110	36.17	7.11
1986	75.219	19.80	12.04	2004	190.990	38.43	7.84
1987	81.304	20.85	8.09	2005	204.120	40.51	6.43
1988	86.110	21.49	5.91	2006	215.584	42.3	5.62
1989	84.983	20.76	−1.31	2007	227.950	44.3	5.74
1990	86.731	20.65	2.06	2008	225.42	43.3	−1.11
1991	89.062	20.67	2.69	2009	229.78	43.7	1.93
1992	97.646	22.29	9.64	2010	242.23	45.5	5.42
1993	109.975	24.85	12.63	2011	252.78	47.1	4.36
1994	119.640	26.79	8.79	2012	262.61	48.8	3.89
1995	127.073	28.21	6.21	2013	268.94	49.8	2.41
1996	130.276	28.77	2.52	2014	273.95	50.5	1.86
1997	135.268	29.43	3.83				

Data source National Bureau of Statistics, *China Statistical Yearbook* (several years); and Ministry of Agriculture, *China Agricultural Development Report* (several years)

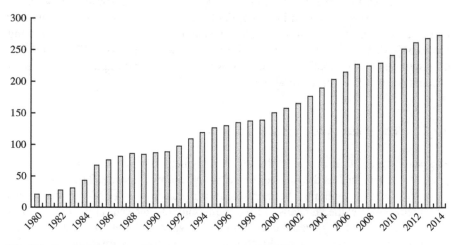

Fig. 2.1 Rural laborer migration figures over the years (million)

Table 2.2 Percentages of rural migrant laborers to total rural laborers over the years

	Total # of rural laborers (mn)	Migrant laborers		Total # of migrants	
		Total # of migrant laborers (mn)	% of total laborers	Leaving home with entire family (mn)	% of total
2008	224.52	140.41	62.5	28.59	12.7
2009	229.78	145.33	63.2	29.66	12.9
2010	242.23	153.35	63.3	30.71	12.7
2011	252.78	158.63	62.8	32.79	13.0
2012	262.61	163.36	62.2	33.75	12.9
2013	268.94	166.10	61.8	35.25	13.1
2104	273.95	168.21	61.3	36.75	13.4

Data source National Bureau of Statistics, migrant laborer surveys conducted over the years

demonstrates that the number of migrants leaving with their entire families grew from 28.59 million in 2008 to 35.25 million in 2013, that latter figure equaling the total amount of rural migrants in 1983.

2.2.3 Reforms to Rural Capital Markets

2.2.3.1 Progress of Reforms

The objective of reforms to rural capital markets is to establish a rural financial system that organically combines commercial financing, policy-based financing, and cooperative financing, on a foundation of cooperative financing. Officials have adopted the following measures to achieve this objective.

One, restoration of rural financial institutions. In December 1978, the third plenum of the 11th Communist Party of China (CCP) National Congress passed the "CCP Central Resolutions on Several Issues Regarding Accelerating Rural Development (draft)," which called for "restoring the Agricultural Bank of China and making great efforts to develop rural credit enterprises." The Agricultural Bank of China (ABC) was thus restored for the third time on March 13, 1979. As compared with previous incarnations of the bank, the scope of oversight over fiscal allocations to the new bank was greatly reduced, while the scope of its credit business was greatly expanded, making it a comprehensive bank responsible for rural financing.

Two, separation of policy-based financing from commercial financing. To this end, the Agricultural Development Bank of China (ADBC) was founded in April 1994. The new bank's major duties were to raise capital for the issuance of agricultural policy-based loans on a foundation of state credit, assume responsibility for state-mandated agricultural policy-based financing, and appropriate agricultural assistance funds on behalf of the state treasury. The bank was specifically responsible for contract purchasing of state grain, cotton, and edible oil reserves as well as other agricultural products, comprehensive agricultural development, policy-based loans for poverty alleviation and other dedicated loan projects, appropriations of agricultural assistance funds on behalf of the treasury as well as oversight of their usage. In May 1998, the ADBC also assumed responsibility for the supply and management of capital for purchasing monopolized agricultural products and by-products in order to assist in nationwide grain circulation system reforms. Responsibility for comprehensive agricultural development, including mountainous regions, water resources, forests, and fields, as well as the issuance of dedicated loans such as poverty alleviation loans with suspended interest, and the issuance of policy-based loans such as those made to grain and cotton processers and accompanying business services was handed over to the ABC. All other policy-based agricultural assistance activities were put under administration of rural credit cooperatives.

Three, separating rural commercial financing from cooperative financing. The direction of reform was for rural credit cooperatives to become cooperative financial organizations and for the ABC to become a commercial bank; rural credit cooperatives and the ABC shirked off their former direct administrative subordination.

Per state policy, rural credit cooperatives could choose to become one of the following: rural commercial banks, rural cooperative banks, incorporated county-level supply and marketing cooperatives, or dual county-and-township-level corporations. The classification chosen by county-level supply and marketing cooperatives was determined by grass-roots credit cooperative delegates on the basis of actual circumstances. It was made mandatory that at least 50% of all loans from such organizations be made to cooperative members, and that all linkages to the ABC be severed by the end of the year. Business management was undertaken by county-level supply and marketing cooperatives, and financial oversight undertaken by the People's Bank of China. Rural cooperative banks were capitalized by legal investments from the treasury of the county (or county-level city) in which they were located, from all manner of companies, and from local residents, and the grade-one corporate system was applied. Their primary loan targets were agricultural service providers, agricultural product processors, and all other kinds of rural enterprises. Fixed asset loans could not exceed 30% of total loans. Although the central government initially wished to turn rural credit cooperatives into cooperative financial organizations, it was clear that they were becoming increasingly commercial and less cooperative over time. For example, most credit cooperatives in developed regions were reformed into rural commercial banks.

Four, establishment of a diversified rural finance system. Central Document Number One of 2004 proposed that rural financial institutions be established to serve the "three rurals"—agriculture, rural areas, and farmers—and an increase in the range of fluctuations on loan interest. Central Document Number One of 2005 then proposed such measures as relaxing entry conditions for rural financial institutions and establishing petty loan organizations founded by natural persons or enterprises closer to rural people and rural needs. Central Document Number One of 2006 then proposed such measures as returning postal reserve capital to the countryside, guiding rural households to develop capital mutual aid organizations, encouraging the establishment of community financing bodies under different ownership structures at the county level, permitting private capital and foreign capital in the purchasing of shares, and standardizing private loans.

2.2.3.2 Standardizing Private Loans and Developing Non-profit Financing

One, guiding financing within rural communities. Central Document Number One of 1984 clearly pointed out the "allowance of free or organized circulation of the capital of rural citizens or collectives." This was the legal basis for fundraising activities within rural communities. Central Document Number One of 1985 then called for "loosening up policies on rural financing and increasing the effectiveness of capital circulation." Central Document Number Five of 1987 then noted: "Some township and village cooperative economic organizations or enterprises have collectively established cooperative funds, and some localities have established trust and investment corporations. These credit activities conform to the demands of the development of commercial production and are beneficial to concentrating idle capital from society and alleviating capital supply shortages of the ABC and credit cooperatives; in principle, we should affirm and support them." In November 1991, the Resolutions of the eighth plenary session of the 13th CCP Central Committee required that all local governments continue to establish rural cooperative funds. In 1996, officials began to clean up and reorganize rural cooperative funds to address issues of illegal financing such as offering nominally high interest rates to attract deposits and the issuing of loans using capital thus raised. The policy specifically called for: merging rural cooperative funds with relatively large amounts of financing activities and loan activities into existing agricultural credit cooperatives or reorganizing them into new rural credit cooperatives after capital verification, and forbidding the attraction of resident deposits by floating shares to them for any fund not willing to be merged into an existing credit cooperative or to be made into a new one. All those without prerequisites for being converted into rural credit cooperatives were made into true cooperative funds. By the end of 2000, all rural cooperative funds were either merged into local credit cooperatives or liquidated and shut down by local governments.

Two, establishment of standards for private loans. There were two government policies regarding private loans. The first severely attacked illegally established financing bodies, the illegal attraction or attraction by ruse of deposits from the general public, and illegal fundraising activities. Financing bodies were not allowed to open accounts, handle accounting, or provide loans for illegal financing bodies or illegal financing activities; those in violation were punished in accordance with the law. The second laid out strict standards for private loan behavior. All capital lent out had to be legally earned and fully owned by the lender. It was strictly forbidden to take money from others to flip to somebody else as a loan. Interest rates were set through consultation between both parties, but interest rates could not be more than five times those established over the same period for similar grades of loans established for financial institutions by the People's Bank of China (excluding fluctuations). All loans exceeding that standard were considered usurious.

Three, support for non-profit petty loans. Officials first allowed and encouraged the development of non-profit petty loans. Petty loans came into practice in China in the mid-1990s. Government organs overseeing financial affairs did not formally approve such financial activities, but out of consideration of the importance of the non-profit nature and effectiveness at poverty alleviation of petty loans, as well as the necessity of developing social poverty alleviation, government officials never took their eyes off of these activities. They further wrote the line "we must summarize and promote the effective method of bringing poverty alleviation capital to households such as petty loans" into the "CCP Central Resolutions on Several Issues Regarding Agriculture and Rural Work" passed in 1998 by the third plenary session of the 15th CCP Central Committee. They then pushed credit cooperatives to develop petty loan services. In July 1999, the People's Bank of China designed the management method of "one loan document per household" and the operational method of "verifying once, issuing loans wherever they are used, controlling balances, and turnover usage" for petty loans to rural households. In January 2000, the People's Bank of China adopted the risk management technique of "mutual guaranteeing of many customers, deposits at set intervals, and loan repayments in stages" for petty loans. Under this technique, the amount of single loans was, in principle, not to exceed the annual income of the borrowing household, and loan terms were not to exceed one year. To encourage credit cooperatives to develop these loans, the People's Bank of China provided agricultural-supporting refinancing capital at interest rates between 2 and 3% while also requiring that rural credit cooperatives issue this refinancing capital to rural citizens in the form of petty loans to be used for agricultural production. They then pushed the postal reserve system to issue petty loans. In December 2005, the China Banking Regulatory Commission (CBRC) established the three provinces of Fujian, Hubei, and Shaanxi as pilots for the issuance of postal reserve petty pledge loans with fixed-interval deposits, in order to establish channels for the return of postal reserves to the countryside, to alleviate pressure from outflows of rural capital, and to smash the monopoly on the loan market of rural credit cooperatives. In December 2006, the State Council authorized the Postal Reserve Bank to issue petty loans everywhere in the nation.

2.2.3.3 Rural Financial Policies Directed at Marketization

One, relaxing controls on interest rates. Formal financial institutions in China had long been making reform explorations into relaxing controls on interest rates. So interest rates on loans issued by financial institutions below the county level had long fluctuated more than those of other financial institutions. In January 2004, the People's Bank of China raised the upper limit on interest rate fluctuations for loans issued by rural credit cooperatives from 2.5 to three times the benchmark rate. In October 2004, the central bank raised the upper limit on interest rate fluctuation on loans issued by urban-rural credit cooperatives to 3.3 times the benchmark. The bottom limit remained at 1.9 times the benchmark rate.

Two, relaxing of entry conditions for financial institutions in rural areas. In December 2006, the CBRC decided to launch pilots in relaxing entry conditions for financial institutions in rural areas in the five provinces and one autonomous region of Sichuan, Inner Mongolia, Jilin, Guizhou, Gansu, and Qinghai. On March 1, 2007, China's first village-and-town bank, the Sichuan YilongHuimin Village-and-Town Bank and Sichuan YilongHuimin Lending Co., Ltd., opened for business. The opening of village-and-town banks, lending companies, and rural capital mutual aid societies in the countryside symbolized the complete opening of rural financial markets in China and effectively ameliorated financial services in the countryside.

Three, development of private commercial petty loan institutions. In 2005, the central bank launched pilots for the development of commercial petty loan bodies in Pingyao, Shanxi; Jiangkou, Guizhou; Guangyuan, Sichuan; Ordos, Inner Mongolia; and Hu County, Shaanxi. On December 27, 2005, the two fully-privately-capitalized commercial petty loan companies Jinyuantai and Rishenglong were allowed to open in Pingyao. In 2006, five other petty loan companies were allowed to open in Sichuan, Guizhou, Shaanxi, and Inner Mongolia. Their upper limit on interest rates was five times the central bank's benchmark rate.

2.2.3.4 Reforms to Formal Rural Financial Institutions

China's formal rural financial institutions include rural credit cooperatives, the ABC, and the ADBC.

Reforms to formal rural financial institutions made progress in the following four areas. First, there was a transition away from solely supporting grain production toward supporting comprehensive agricultural development, including forestry, husbandry, agricultural by-products, and fisheries. Beginning in 1978, the ABC began offering a great measure of loan support to multiple kinds of rural operations, without slacking support for grain production, in order to support adjustments to the agricultural structure. Second, primary loan recipients were no longer collectives but individual rural households. At the end of 1986, the ABC and rural credit cooperatives collectively issued a total of 53.7 billion yuan in agricultural loans, over 60% of which to rural households. Third, the rise of town and village enterprises (TVEs) was supported. Total loans issued by the ABC and rural credit cooperatives to TVEs rose from under 3.3 billion yuan in 1978 to 84.7 billion yuan in 1988. Fourth, the circulation of rural commodities was supported. The total of commercial loans issued by the ABC rose from over 2.60 billion yuan in 1978 to over 230 billion at the end of 1990.

One, reforms to the ABC. In 1979, the ABC was the government department in charge of rural finance. It was effectively a direct subordinate government organ to the State Council, with its own subordinate branches in local governments. In 1984, the ABC was removed from the ranks of other government bodies and made an enterprise, still directly subordinate to the State Council, but it still managed institutional arrangements, personnel decisions, and loan balances of rural credit cooperatives with authorization from the government. Now an enterprise, the ABC underwent enterprise-directed reforms. The first was the reform of its credit management system of "unified deposits and loans," meaning that all deposits and loans in the country were managed by the People's Bank of China alone. In 1980, the ABC implemented a policy of complete responsibility over its own affairs by linking loans with deposits.

This new system of "complete responsibility" was, however, limited to the deposits and loans of commune-and-production-team collectives and individuals, and it was thus referred to as the "little complete responsibility" system. In 1981, the system was expanded to include all lending business, now called "big complete responsibility." In order to benefit maximally from the drive toward increased deposits and increased loans, the system of "contracting once a year" was changed into a fixed big responsibility system that was "fixed for three years." The second was the implementation of a system for retaining profits and responsibility for operations. In 1983, the ABC broke through the fiscal system of "unified deposits and loans" and established a system for retaining profits in order to incentivize all subordinate branches to work harder. The third was the implementation of a capital management responsibility system of "unified plans, graded management, lending out no more than total deposits, and autonomous operations." Officials changed vertical funds regulation into a synthesis of vertical and horizontal funds regulation. The fourth was the bank's taking the lead among state-owned financial institutions in implementing the contracting system. The concrete method for pushing this reform in 1988 was that the ABC pledged to pay 2.45 billion yuan in taxes and profits to the central government, with anything earned in excess of that figure to be divided at the ratio of 10% for the treasury and 90% for the ABC. Per government demands, the bank handed central bank reserves and pooling funds over to the central government and bought treasury and construction bonds stipulated by the state. The bank carried out lending plans that came in the form of directives, completing such indices as deposit growth rates, loan recovery rates, the utilization rate of credit funds, comprehensive fee rates, and capital loss rates. All retained capital on portions not meeting pre-set indicators were deducted at a fixed ratio. In order to reform itself into a commercial bank, the ABC changed its "four-tiered management (bank headquarters—branches—central sub-branches—sub-branches) and single-tiered operations model (sub-branches)" into a "four-tiered operations" model in 1994. Bank officials established the operations department in bank headquarters to handle deposit and accounting services for large enterprises and groups or economic consortiums. Officials implemented a management system of the debt-to-assets ratios at the level of managing credit capital. They also established a risk management system for credit assets and founded a loan approval committee. Finally, they implemented separation between loan issuance and loan approvals, established a risk compensation system, and a system of allowance for doubtful accounts.

Two, reforms to rural credit cooperatives. Reforms to rural credit cooperatives proceeded apace with the goal of restoring their natures as cooperative financial institutions. These reforms were divided into three stages.

In the first stage, the cooperative financing nature of these institutions was restored. In the early 1990s, after establishment of the socialist market economy, the following reform measures were enacted upon rural credit cooperatives in accordance with the demands of developing the market economy. The first was the work of "cleaning up" existing shares—allowing some shareholders meeting conditions to cash out, allowing others to convert their shares into shares of the new company, and the conversion of all other shares into "accounts payable"—and recapitalizing through the issuance of new shares. The second included such measures as implementing increased deposits and increased loans, floating interest rates, debt-to-assets ratio management and so on. The third included the establishment of a congress of cooperative members and a regulatory commission, strengthening democratic management, improving internal job responsibility systems and operations mechanisms, eliminating "iron rice bowl" positions, and bringing about egalitarianism in allocations. The fourth was the establishment of county-level supply and marketing cooperatives for rural credit cooperatives. These were made into the management centers, capital centers, accounting centers, and information service centers of credit cooperatives. The fifth was the establishment of sound institutions at all levels. Management work was institutionalized and standardized. There were five issues in this stage of reforms. The first was that management systems had not yet been completely sorted out, and an effective system for organization and management had not yet been formed. The second was that many administrative measures but few economic and legal measures had been used in the reforms. The third was that credit cooperatives were still subject to control by the ABC and higher-level credit cooperatives, making it difficult to enforce job responsibilities on the part of boards of directors and supervisors. The fourth was that enforcement of credit management laws was lax, and mechanisms to limit lending risks not sound, so many credit cooperatives were still losing money. The fifth was that accounting channels for rural credit cooperatives were obstructed, restricting the development of their business.

In the second stage, reforms were enacted on the operations and management system. The following measures were taken in this stage. First, once original shares were "cleaned up," new shares were sold to individual rural citizens, small businesses, and rural collective enterprises in order to recapitalize the institutions. Second, the People's Bank of China established cooperative finance regulatory bodies and strengthened oversight of rural credit cooperatives. Third, officials founded city (or prefectural-level city) credit cooperative associations to bring about high-level organization of such. Fourth, officials launched pilots in rural credit cooperative work. There were four primary areas of reforms: (1) the establishment of provincial-level credit cooperative associations and reorganization of the credit cooperative organizational system; (2) strengthening of the financial sustainability of credit cooperatives to make them better suited to rural economic development; (3) the reorganization of credit cooperatives in developed areas into rural commercial banks; (4) exploration into ownership systems and corporate structures suitable for credit cooperatives, as well as self-limitations on rural credit cooperatives. Marked reform progress made during this stage was as follows: A major step forward, not a step backward, was taken in the adoption of the shareholding system and the reorganization of credit cooperatives in developed areas into rural commercial banks, and the cooperative nature of these institutions was restored.

In the third stage, innovations were made to the operations and management system. In June 2003, eight provinces (or cities under direct command of the central government), including Zhejiang, were chosen as rural credit cooperative pilots for reforms to management systems and ownership institutions. Specific measures taken include the following. (1) Credit cooperatives were allowed to autonomously select their form of ownership structure, including shareholding systems, shareholding cooperative ownership, straight-up cooperative ownership, and so on, per the principles of shareholding structure diversification and diversified shareholding entities, as well as actual conditions. (2) The central government began paying interest subsidies to protect reserve values of credit cooperatives losing money. The government began exempting or reducing by half corporate income taxes and levying a business tax of only 3% on credit cooperatives in the western region and in pilot areas. The government offered capital support to credit cooperatives in pilot areas through refinancing loans or the issuance of central bank bills and authorized interest rate flexibility in regions with vigorous private lending scenes. In 2004, these reforms to rural credit cooperatives were extended to all regions of the country except Hainan and Tibet.

The course of reforms to rural credit cooperatives went as follows. The costs of reforms to these cooperatives were compensated, and their historical burden was lifted. Shareholding reforms brought about increased investment through purchasing shares, abundant capitalization, clear ownership structures, and increased capacity of credit to withstand risk. Provincial credit cooperative associations were founded. There are still three issues we must resolve: the issue of excessive concentration of power and control by insiders, the issue of incentive and restriction mechanisms on the management stratum of rural credit cooperatives, and the issue of inappropriate administrative interference and management fees on the part of provincial credit cooperative associations.

Three, reforms to the Agricultural Development Bank of China. When first founded in 1994, the ADBC was a policy-based financial institution directly subordinate to the State Council with a vertical leadership management structure. Its primary duties were to oversee policy-based agricultural financing and fiscal agricultural support allocations. Most of its capital came from the issuance of financial bonds to financial institutions, treasury funds intended for agricultural support, and the deposits of enterprises taking out agricultural policy-based loans. The ADBC audited its own accounts and operated autonomously under a corporate governance structure per the principle of neither earning nor losing money. Its activities were guided and supervised by the People's Bank of China. Primarily, it handled state-mandated dedicated reserves, transfer and sale loans, wholesale loans, and loans issued to enterprises processing grain, edible oil, cotton, and jute fulfilling policy-dictated duties, for major agricultural products and by products such as grain, cotton, oil crops, pork, sugar, and so on, with interest discounted by the Ministry of Finance, funds allocated by the People's Bank of China, and projects determined by the State Council. It also issued loans for poverty alleviation, comprehensive agricultural development, small infrastructure projects, and technological transformation projects, as well as agricultural support allocations and the issuance of bonds from the central and provincial governments. In the past two years, the ADBC has also become an agent for multiple kinds of insurance and has developed loans for grain and oil seeds and loans for small agricultural enterprises. The bank has consummated mechanisms for the review and approval of loans, such as its loan approval committee and has established a more independent, authoritative, and effective internal auditing system. It has launched a pilot into a system of placing delegates in charge of the financial committee. It has expanded autonomous operations and commercial activities in which it assumes responsibility for risks, while fully complying with government directives to issue policy-nature loans.

2.2.3.5 Informal Financing in Rural China

Informal financial institutions in rural China can be divided into two categories: traditional rural informal financing and new rural informal financing. The traditional category encompasses four sub-categories: free lending by individuals, small-loan associations, underground private banks, and money backs. Free lending by individuals takes place between family members, friends, and neighbors. Loans amounts are small and terms short. Some such loans are made by strictly oral contract, and some are made by written contract. Most such loans are made without consideration of profits, with interest earned used only to offset some living expenses. Such loans to people other than family members, friends, and neighbors are often conducted in pursuit of profits, and the relatively larger amount of interest payments are used mostly to invest in production. Interest rates on these loans are generally between four and five times those of banks for similar sized loans, and sometimes even higher. Small-loan associations are temporary financial organizations established to achieve ends of mutual aid and cooperation that combine the collection of deposits and the issuance of loans in a single body, and are generally autonomously established by non-professionals and generally held together by bonds of kinship, friendship, or neighborhood. These associations are temporary and can be divided into "monthly associations," "seasonal associations," "semi-annual associations," and "annual associations." They are further divided into "rotating," "determined by shooting the dice," and "drawing lots," to see which member should be the recipient of the new term's loan. Underground private banks are institutionalized or semi-institutionalized financial organizations that operate for profits. Most evolve out of small-loan associations, with the difference between the two being that they attract more deposits from locals and conduct more transactions. Money backs are go-betweens who make arrangements between lenders and borrowers and earn commissions on transactions as well as information fees.

New rural informal financial institutions include rural mutual aid saving societies, rural cooperative funds, rural financial service companies, and so on. First, let's address how new rural informal financial institutions arise. One prominent issue that appeared after reforms to the agricultural micro-base was: capital accumulated by collective economic organizations sat idle for long periods of time, while rural citizens in need of capital were unable to secure loans from credit cooperatives. To resolve this issue, some communities allowed rural households to use their collective shares to access a portion of collective capital (meaning they could receive their portion of dividends but not cash out their shares). These funds were used to establish cooperative funds, which made attempts at capital circulation within the community. By 1988, 80% of townships and towns in Jiangsu, 40% in Hubei, and 28% in Liaoning had established rural cooperative funds, having raised, respectively, 800, 280, and 260 million yuan. Of those three, Liaoning paid out a total of 250 million yuan to individual rural citizens and TVEs. Second, let's address the effects of new rural informal financial institutions. First, they resolved long-standing chaos in collective asset management and issues of inappropriate funds usage, while solidifying and shoring up the collective economy. Second, they expanded rural fundraising channels, alleviated supply and demand imbalances in rural capital, and promoted the growth of both agriculture and the rural economy. Third, they deepened reforms to the rural financial system and drove the formation of a new order in rural finance, with more forms and more levels. Fourth, they suppressed rural usury and drove development of poverty alleviation work and increases to rural incomes. Third, let's address the problems associated with new rural informal financial institutions. The first is the prominence of administrative interference. Although financial organizations within the countryside come in the form of shareholding cooperatives, most have become subordinate to administrative organizations at the township or village level, making it difficult for them to give ample autonomy or benefit to members. Second, the narrow scope of their allowable activities limits their ability to seek opportunities for greater profitability; they have few sources of capital and poor ability to accumulate. Most profit allocations are done per the "two-eight system," meaning that 80% goes to capital owners and 20% goes to daily costs, welfare costs, risk funds, and development funds; only a very limited amount goes to true business development. Third, there is a lack of necessary laws and regulations for capital operations.

2.2.3.6 Scale of China's Rural Finance Market

One, the scale of the formal financial market. By the end of 2005, capital in China's formal rural financial institutions totaled 3.7206 trillion yuan, of which 2.2008 trillion had been issued as loans (10.9% of nationwide loans issued by financial institutions), an increase of 807 billion yuan over 2002, or a 57.9% growth. Total debt of said institutions was 3.5553 trillion yuan, of which deposits totaled 3.2626 trillion yuan (10.8% of total nationwide deposits in financial institutions), an increase of 1.2751 trillion yuan over the end of 2002, an increase of 64.2%. Owners' equity totaled 165.3 billion yuan, an increase of 192.7 billion yuan over the end of 2002. The People's Bank of China had an accumulated total of agricultural supporting refinancing loans of 1.0224 trillion yuan and an ending balance of 59.7 billion yuan, of which over 90% consisted of loans issued to rural households. All rural cooperative financial institutions (including rural credit cooperatives, rural commercial banks, and rural cooperative banks) had issued a total of 1.0071 trillion yuan in agricultural loans, an increase of 449.2 billion yuan over the end of 2002, a growth of 80.5%, higher than the average growth rate of 22.6% for other loan categories over the same period. Of those, a total of 798.3 billion yuan of loans had been issued to rural households, supporting a total of over 71 million rural households. About 60% of rural households applying for loans were granted them. If one includes those rural households who had taken out loans in the past but had no loan balances at the time, the coverage of loan issuance by rural credit cooperatives to rural households was then larger. The amount of poverty-alleviation interest-discounted loans was small. Per statistics from the ABC, by the end of June 2004, the total of petty poverty-alleviation interest-discounted loans made to rural households was 38.1 billion yuan, affecting a total of 11.75 million rural households.

The total of agricultural loans issued by formal rural financial institutions in China grew from 49.70 billion yuan in 1994 to 2.1055 trillion yuan in 2004, a 5.4-fold increase. Of those, short-term agricultural loans totaled 984.3 billion yuan, mid to long-term loans totaled 368.9 billion yuan, and loans made to purchase agricultural products and by-products totaled 652.3 billion yuan, account for, respectively, 46.7, 17.5, and 35.7% of total agricultural loans. The total of short-term loans issued by formal institutions rose and fell, but the proportion of agricultural loans, TVE loans, and individual or small business loans to total short-term loans consistently grew (Table 2.3).

Two, the scale of the informal rural financial market. Per capita rural private lending in China grew from 25.40 yuan in 1984 to 56.64 yuan in 1990, an average annual growth of 14.3%. The nationwide scale of private lending among rural households was between 50 and 70 billion yuan, making it the dominant force in rural lending. It was difficult for formal financial institutions to meet the vigorous demand for rural financing in China. This is an important reason for the development of informal financing and for the dominant role that informal financing came to play in the countryside. Interest rates were high on private loans in regions with highly developed commodity economies. In regions with poorly developed commodity economies, on the other hand, most private loans were made at low or no interest. In economically developed regions, most private loans were used in highly profitable manufacturing operations, but in economically backward regions, most private loans were made to meet urgent life needs or to fund ordinary manufacturing activities. From 1995 to 1999, private loans accounted for about 70% of all rural lending. Zhu Shouyin, the International Fund for Agricultural Development,

Table 2.3 Amounts of various agricultural loans issued by Chinese Financial Institutions, *Unit* billion yuan

Year	Agricultural loans (1)	Loans to purchase ag. products and by-products (2)	Other agricultural loans (3)	Short-term ag. loans (4)	Long and mid-term ag. loans (5)
1990	355.966	231.557	124.409	–	–
1991	453.540	297.303	156.237	–	–
1992	517.841	319.126	198.715	–	–
1993	596.128	356.394	239.734	–	–
1994	496.987	382.602	114.385	114.385	–
1995	698.985	544.506	154.479	154.479	–
1996	878.989	687.077	191.912	191.912	–
1997	1304.291	850.174	454.117	331.464	122.653
1998	1364.515	765.722	598.794	444.424	154.370
1999	1515.892	834.943	680.949	479.239	201.710
2000	1551.082	806.433	744.649	488.899	255.750
2001	1664.244	798.423	865.821	571.148	294.673
2002	1798.154	781.819	1016.335	688.458	327.877
2003	1925.068	728.286	1196.782	841.135	355.647
2004	2105.496	752.316	1353.179	984.311	368.868

Note (1) = (2) + (3); (3) = (4) + (5)

He Guangwen, and others all came to similar conclusions. Loans taken out for life needs accounted for 47.75% of total loans, and 53.29% of all rural private loans were made at no interest. The proportion of loans taken out by rural households from formal financial institutions is increasing, while the proportion of private lending is decreasing (Table 2.4).

In 2003, the capital scale of formal financial institutions was nearly 800 billion yuan. There are four characteristics of private financing. The first is that such lending activities are semi-overt. The second is that there are very few breaches of contract. The third is that a higher proportion of such lending is of a production nature. The fourth is that interest rates are markedly higher.

2.2.3.7 Overall Assessment of Reforms to China's Rural Finance System and Development Thereof

Reforms to China's rural finance system since Reform and Opening have conformed to the demands of deepening financing, have conformed to the demands of transforming the national economy, and have conformed to the demands of the hundreds of millions of Chinese rural citizens for economic development and improvement of life.

Table 2.4 Rural household loan capital sources, 1995–2005 (%)

	Loans from banks or credit cooperatives	Private lending	Other
1995	24.23	67.5	8.02
1996	25.42	69.27	5.31
1997	23.94	70.38	5.68
1998	20.65	74.29	5.06
1999	24.43	69.41	6.16
2000	29.44	68.44	2.12
2001	29.21	68.7	2.09
2002	26.09	71.83	2.08
2003	31.78	63.94	4.28
2004	30.72	62.98	6.3
2005	34.2	58.37	7.43

Following the separation of cooperative finance from commercial finance, the separation of policy-based finance from commercial finance, the relaxing of controls on interest rates, the easing of entry conditions for rural financial institutions, and the continuous innovation in rural financial institutions, financial tools, and financial products, the financial system established by the government with coordination and division of duties between cooperative finance, commercial finance, and policy-based finance, with diversified investment sources, of many kinds, of broad coverage, of flexible administration, and of effective service, is now currently forming.

Rural Chinese citizens have a great deal more opportunity to benefit from financial services, and the coverage of rural financial services is currently expanding and deepening greatly. However, a portion of said credit capital has not played a true role in supporting agriculture. In order to resolve these issues as quickly as possible, we must continue to deepen reforms in the field of rural finance and further amplify financial reforms.

2.3   Reforms to the Agricultural Land System

Before Reform and Opening, China's rural collective land ownership system was "three-tiered ownership with the production team as the foundation." The "three-tier" nature meant some of the land in a given people's commune belonged to the commune, some to the production brigade, and some to the production team. "Production team as the foundation" meant the vast majority of rural land was owned by production teams, which were responsible for management and operation of that land. A small portion of land belonged to communes and production brigades, which were likewise responsible for management and operation thereof.

2.3.1   Progress of Reforms to the Agricultural Land System

2.3.1.1   Promoting Reforms to Allow Farmers the Right
to Operate Contracted Land

By the end of 1983, 99.5% of all production teams in the nation had implemented
the Household Responsibility System, with 97.8% of those implementing the
system of full responsibility for production. The primary source of income for
farmers shifted from the collective toward the household as reforms to the agricultural production and operation system were promoted.

2.3.1.2   Issuing Policies to Uphold the Rights of Farmers
to Contract and Operate Land

After the success of the Household Responsibility System, the state took a series of
measures to protect rural citizens' rights to operate the land they contract. First,
officials extended the terms for which land could be contracted. Before the end of
the first term of land contracting, the central government clearly announced that
land contracting terms were to be extended by 30 years. This made rights to operate
contracted land for rural citizens even more stable in the long term. Second, they
issued certificates of rights to operate contracted land to rural households to limit
the ability of collective economic organizations to redistribute land at will. Once the
process for redistributing land had become stricter, the rights of rural citizens to
operate contracted land became more stable. Third, they rescinded agricultural
planting plans, giving increased autonomy to rural citizens to operate their land as
they saw fit. Fourth, they upheld the rights of rural citizens to transfer land. During
the contracting term, rural households have the legal right to decide whether to
transfer land, and by what process if so. No organization or individual has the right
to coerce rural households into transferring land or to obstruct them from transferring land if that is their wish. Transfers of contracted farmland thus became
increasingly marketized. Fifth, the government made it clear that "increased mouths
do not mean increased land, nor do decreased mouths mean decreases in land" to
prevent local village and township leaders from changing land contracts at will or
distorting the wording of the land contracting policy: "unchanging for 30 years."

2.3.1.3   Improving Laws to Safeguard Rural Citizens' Rights
to Operate Contracted Land

In the beginning, there were issues of disunity of terms for land contracting and
unclear obligations accompanying land contracting rights. This was the root cause
of many disputes over contracted land. To address these issues, the central government in 1998 issued the "Land Management Law," which clearly stipulated that

"the right to contract and operate land is protected by law." The "Rural Land Contracting Law," which went into effect on March 1, 2003, made stringent stipulations for land redistribution, the rights and obligations of contracting land, transfers of contracted land, terms for land contracting, and other areas. This made the right to contract and operate land a right guaranteed by law and allocated directly to rural citizens. The "Property Law" that went into effect on October 1, 2007, clearly stipulated the usufruct and operation rights of contracted land. That means that the rights on farmland contracted out by collective economic organizations, whether it be contracted to a family, obtained via bidding, auction, open negotiations, or any other means, or whether the land is contracted by a collective under the Household Responsibility System, usufruct rights to all such land are now legally protected. Thus the right to operate contracted land has been elevated to a property right now protected by the state's "Property Law."

2.3.2   Developing a Rural Land Market

Shortly after Reform and Opening, the government allowed rural citizens both the right to contract operations rights for land and also the right to transfer those rights to others. However, land transfers proceeded slowly as rural labor transitioned sluggishly. By the end of 1984, only 2.7% of rural households had contracted out part of their farmland, and only 0.7% of all farmland had been transferred by contract. A sampling survey conducted in 1993 indicated that 4.733 million rural households, 2.3% of total rural households, had contracted for a total of 11.61 million μ of farmland, 2.9% of the national total.[3] As the process whereby rural laborers concentrate in urban centers or rural non-agricultural industries has accelerated, a higher percentage of farmland has come to be contracted out. In recent years, the amount of rural land contracted in China has steadily increased. In 2008, the total amount of rural land contracted out broke the 100 million μ mark, up again to 270 million μ, or 21.5% of the national total, in 2012. That number rose again to 340 million μ, 26% of the national total, in 2013, and had reached 380 million μ, or 28.8% of the national total, by the end of June 2014 (Table 2.5).

The process of economic development is one whereby the number of rural households dependent upon farmland for their living grows increasingly smaller. As upgrades are made to the employment structure, the opportunity costs of rejecting agriculture for rural households engaged in multiple enterprises will grow smaller as the share of overall household income from agriculture decreases. Overall incomes of leading rural households are determined primarily by the scale of land operations and not by net income per unit of area of land, and so their ability to pay rent on farmland will increase as the scale of land they operate grows. It is, thus, objectively inevitable that, given the influence of these two trends, more farmland

---

[3]Zhang Hongyu (2002).

Table 2.5 Changes to area of contracted land, *Unit* 100 million μ

	1993	2007	2008	2009	2010	2011	2012	2013	2014
Area	0.12	0.6	1.09	1.51	1.87	2.28	2.78	3.41	3.80
% of total	2.3	5.2	8.9	12.0	14.6	17.8	21.5	26.0	28.8

will be concentrated in the hands of leading rural households. The more stable the rights of rural households to contract land, the easier it will be for land to be transferred, and vice versa. This is the primary reason for emphasizing the stability of land contracting rights.

The advantages of land transfers are the driving of suitably scaled agricultural operations and the development of leading rural households, both of which drive up the overall efficiency of agricultural production operations. Land transfers are beneficial to the centralization of land ownership, thereby reducing the area occupied by roads and paths between farm fields and enabling some abandoned land to be used. The integration of such land can increase total land use efficiency by about 5%. Scaled land operations are also beneficial to increasing the negotiating power of rural households in market transactions, thereby bringing about a certain degree of cost reductions and revenue increases. The primary effects of concentrating grain planting in the hands of a few major households through land transfers are to increase the precision and economic efficiency of investments, to reduce the risks of planting non-grain crops, and to reduce the costs of grain production. Such concentration does not greatly increase grain yields. The specific tasks regarding land transfers are as follows.

One, the scale of farmland operations must be suitable to the level of economic development. Scaled agricultural operations will conform more to reality as gradual advances are made in industry structure upgrading. Agricultural scale is appropriate if the per capita income of leading rural households is not less than the per capita incomes of rural households engaged in multiple industries.

Two, leading rural households should become China's primary agricultural entities. If ever resident incomes reach or exceed the urban-rural resident average income standard of 3000 yuan, or if a smaller amount of leading rural households become the primary force in agriculture determining the country's agricultural competitiveness, we should then adopt policies to accommodate households engaged in multiple industries, even if there are tens of millions of rural citizens engaged in multiple industries who are of no relevance.

Three, land transfers to family farm operations should be given priority. We should give priority to developing family farms, centered on rural households, in rural communities, particularly as the rural social insurance system remains far from perfect. We should add some conditions to the transfer of land to agricultural companies, in order to reduce the occasion of successful operations in non-agricultural operations occupying farmland to the extent possible and to prevent outside capital from occupying farmland for non-agricultural businesses.

Four, scaled land transfer behaviors. We should encourage agricultural operators to sign land transfer contracts. Particularly in cases where piecemeal land parcels are being agglomerated, operators should sign supplemental agreements the original land contractors and clarify all relevant rights.

Five, promotion of shareholding structures in collective land. China is a country where only a minority of localities can set up land shareholding structures. As long as we ensure that land contracting rights remain with rural households, we can quantify the right to contract and operate land into shares and bring about unified operations in tier-one village corporations by reconcentrating contracted land via selling shares in the new company.

The functions of the government in terms of land transfers are as follows. The government should encourage transactions in land shares within the community at the micro scale and rigorously regulate and manage institutions for land usage at the macro scale. The government should eliminate all opportunistic behavior, such as obtaining governmental agricultural subsidies via land transfers, and should stamp out the behavior of some merchants who violate policies stipulating that farmland be used for agricultural purposes. As rents for companies are generally higher than average transfer fees, and as most companies elect to hire those same people who rented the land to them, the farmers themselves benefit doubly. However, as many agricultural companies renting out land use it for purposes other than agriculture, we should be watchful for such abuses.

2.3.3 Scale and Pricing of the Land Market

Prices for transfers of agricultural land are determined by supply and demand of such land. From the perspective of selling land rights, willingness of rural citizens to transfer land rights increases in proportion to annual increases of the costs of operating their land and annual increases to incomes in non-agricultural industries. From the perspective of buying land rights, large specialized households and family farms grow more willing to buy land rights as the level of agricultural mechanization increases and as the benefits from scale operations increase. Relatively speaking, as the degree of differentiation in rural vocations increases, those adept at earning a living from working the land grow more willing to purchase land rights; so there is a degree of rigidity to the price increases of land transfers. One survey indicates that the average per μ annual rental for agricultural land was 293 yuan in 2008, 500 yuan in 2008, 660 yuan in 2012, and 880 yuan in 2013.

Transfer prices of agricultural land correspond to not only the productivity of the land, but also to the location of the land. Prices are higher for land close to urban areas, where there is higher demand for land transfers. In economically undeveloped areas, transfer prices are low, as there is little demand for land transfers. Transfer prices for well-positioned land can run four to five times as much as for poorly-positioned land. Prices are also lower for land fragmented into many small pieces, whereas prices are higher for large swaths of contiguous land. Land suitable for planting grain is priced lower, while land suitable for planting other cash crops is generally priced higher.

2.3.4   Establishing Land Management and Farmland Protection Systems

Over the past 30 years, the central government has used policies and laws to demarcate, standardize, and protect the land rights of rural citizens, including the right to operate contracted land, the right to use collective land intended to be built upon, and the right to use land intended for residential use. At the same time, the government has established a sound system of rules and regulations to manage land usage behavior by instituting a management system for land use and planning, a management system for land use, and a protection system for farmland.

The "Land Administration Law," issued on January 1, 1987, was the beginning of integrated management of urban and rural land. The law laid the conditions for the establishment of a series of rural land administration institutions, including a sound land planning system, a land surveying system, a land usage planning and management system, a system for restricting the usage of land, a system for protecting farmland, and so on. The 1998 revisions to the law as well as the regulations for its implementation, clearly stipulated an overall planning system for land usage. This included the principles for the organization of that planning system, the approvals procedures, changes to authorities, the authority to make changes, and the approvals procedures for establishing overall land usage planning. Thereafter, the central government completed overall land usage planning of five tiers: nationwide, provincial (including autonomous regions and cities under direct command of the central government), provincial-level and provincial capital cities, and townships (and towns), bringing all rural land in the country within the track of centralized planning.

The 1998 revisions to the Land Administration Law brought a system of limitations on land usage within the scope of the law. The state established overall planning for land usage, dividing all land in the country into three categories: agricultural use, construction use, and unused. In order to reclassify agricultural use land as construction use land, one must go through approvals procedures. The revised law clearly stipulated that "construction use" institutions encompassed the system of compensations for occupying farmland and the system for protecting farmland within the prime farmland protection system. The system of compensations for occupying arable land demands that the unit occupying said land be responsible for developing uncultivated land of identical quality and identical area for any occupation of farmland; in cases in which the conditions for cultivating virgin land do not exist or when land thus compensated does not meet requirements, the original unit should pay "wasteland cultivation fees," dedicated funds used to cultivate new arable land. The prime farmland protection system demands that not less than 80% of the farmland in an administrative area be included within prime farmland protection, and that more rigorous administration and control be exerted over such land.

2.4 Reforms to the System and Mechanisms for Agricultural Operations

2.4.1 Reducing the Scope of Administrative Management, Establishing Norms for Administrative Management

China has long taken development of production and protection of supply as the major objectives of agricultural policies. After agricultural development entered a new phase, agricultural policies were expanded from the sole objective of increasing output of agricultural products to also encompass increases to rural incomes, increases to comprehensive agricultural productivity, improvement of the agricultural environment, increases to the quality of agricultural products, and optimization of the agricultural industry structure. Policies were expanded from strategic adjustments based in domestic agriculture to strategic agricultural adjustments based in "the two markets" and "two kinds of resources" and from increasing the prices of agricultural products to protect rural incomes to strategies for using industries, fiscal policy and taxation, and financing to protect rural incomes. This was done to adjust to the demands of agricultural marketization, internationalization, and sustainability.

Agriculture is an industry greatly reliant upon natural endowment and the environment. In order to give rise to regional industry belts with comparative advantages, officials placed focus on the development of high technology and high added value agricultural products in eastern regions and in mid to large cities and their surrounding areas, which were to blaze the trail in modernizing agriculture. Central regions were allowed to maintain comparative advantages in grain production; officials optimized grain varieties planted and the quality structure and drove industrialized production therein. Officials made a great push in allowing grain-planting lands to revert to forests and grasslands, in the development of specialized agriculture, ecological agriculture, and water-conserving agriculture.

Changing government functions; smoothing out interdepartmental relationships; establishing an agricultural administrative management system that integrates pre-production, production, and post-production; and resolving such issues as dispersion of functions, division of industries, monopolization of sectors, and regional blockages. Concrete measures are as follows: eliminate or reduce distortions in production or prices caused by government interference; strengthen such functions as production services, food reserves, direct subsidization of producers, and regionally imbalanced development; strengthen the capacity for public services;

reduce information asymmetry; and preserve market order. Reduce government functions for administrating rural citizens and strengthen management functions over agricultural trade, food safety, and sustainable agricultural development. Reduce governmental interferences in production and trade and increase the support, protection, and comprehensive services the government provides to agriculture.

Promoting agricultural reform pilots. First, select focus industries for reform pilots. For example, establish official veterinary institutions and shore up the veterinary prevention and treatment system. Separate the administrative and executive functions from the service functions of animal husbandry and veterinary stations at every level; also separate executive personnel from service personnel. Second, select focus products for reform pilots; examples include cotton in Xinjiang, soybeans in Heilongjiang, sugar in Guangxi, fisheries in coastal regions, and so on. Third, select focus functions for administrative system reforms. For example, in production bases and wholesale markets implement compulsory quality and safety examinations and establish sound systems for tracing the origins of products. Fourth, select focus regions for reform pilots, implementing, for example, administrative system reforms that integrate agriculture, science, and education; production, processing, and sales; and trade, industry, and agriculture in designated counties and cities. Fifth, on a foundation of summarizing experience, convert more successful methods into laws and regulations and administer such on the basis of the law.

Allocate agricultural resources per the principle of comparative advantages, promote industry upgrading, protect the interests of rural citizens, maintain healthy agricultural development, and increase the international competitiveness of Chinese agricultural products. Strengthen such government functions as market construction, infrastructure construction, development of international markets, food safety, increasing rural incomes, and so on. Increase multilateral cooperation and consultations in agriculture and protect and preserve agriculture on the basis of the law.

Too many links in the administrative chain, or too great a length of such a chain, leads not only to such problems as high costs and low efficiency, but also weakens the regulatory ability of the market. To this end, the government should reduce interventions in agricultural production and markets; decrease such measures as price support through distorting production and trade behavior and marketing loans; strengthen such functions as macro-adjustment and controls, market oversight, and public services; strengthen the implementation of "green box" policies such as ordinary fiscal support of production services, food security reserves, direct subsidization of producers, and regional development plans; and do only things that the market cannot do or cannot do well. The key is to integrate functions, strengthen services, protect the rights of rural citizens, and promote agricultural development.

Clarify the scope of functions of all departments, demarcate administration authorities, establish normal procedures, and bring about symmetry in administrative authorities and administrative responsibilities. Establish a sound execution and oversight system, a support and protection system, a quality standards system, an inspection and licensing system, a market information system, and a marketing services system, in order to strengthen pre-production, production, and post-production public services and protection.

2.4.2 Improving Laws and Regulations, Governing in Strict Accordance with the Law

Revise and improve relevant laws and regulations. Establish laws for agricultural macro-adjustments and controls, agricultural support and protection, market entry, protection of agricultural resources and environments, and so on. Strive to bring about good public services. Earnestly perform such functions as carrying out plans, making adjustments, regulating, and providing services.

Shore up the legal system. Strengthen the dominant position of the market, standardize the economic order on markets, and bring about economic development of markets. Allow markets to play a decisive role in resource allocation and reduce direct intervention into microeconomic activities.

The transparency, stability, and fairness of policies and administrative measures ensure stable expectations for market entities.

Agricultural administration in China has long relied on administrative edicts, and agricultural legislation and execution thereof have begun relatively late. Existing agricultural laws and regulations are skewed toward agricultural production and protection of agricultural resources. We must now take aim at laws in the fields of protecting the dominant position of agriculture, trade of agricultural products, and agricultural investments, and upgrade existing documents and regulations into formal laws and regulations. Consummate the system of agricultural laws and regulations, and bring about administration and protection in accordance with the law.

Expand market entries, reduce domestic support, and abandon export subsidies and special protections per World Trade Organization (WTO) entry protocols. Improve quarantine procedures for animals and plants, health standards, protections of intellectual property rights, and so on. Be proactive in adjusting to and making use of multilateral trade regulations, drive reforms to the agricultural administrative management system, and bring about healthy development in agriculture.

Implement government openness institutions and accountability institutions. Apply administrative and executive accountability into every link and every individual, ensure symmetry of authorities and responsibilities, and see that there are checks on power. Drive increases to the level at which governance is in accordance with the law.

Governance in accordance with the law. Set norms for governmental behaviors per the strategy of ruling the nation in accordance with the law. Strengthen agricultural legislation, increase executive powers, shore up executive teams, and increase the level of legislative execution. Establish sound oversight mechanisms, prevent and reduce "government malfunctions," and promote democratization and scientificization of policymaking.

Establish a sound system of law execution and administration of agriculture that conforms to the demands of the market economy, a market information system for agricultural products, a quality standards system for agricultural products, an inspection and certification system for agricultural products, a safety and oversight system for agricultural production, a system for technical and marketing services for agriculture, a system to oversee the agricultural resources environment, a system to support and protect agriculture, and a system for agricultural product reserves management.

Deepen reforms to the agricultural administrative management system in China, eliminate systemic obstructions impeding development of production, and promote healthy development of agriculture in China. Establish an integrated, efficient administrative system of balanced authorities and responsibilities and that unifies agriculture, science, and education; production, processing, and sales; and trade, processing, and agriculture. Transform government functions and strengthen public services.

Improve the systems for inspections and certifications and for quality standards. The first is self-inspection quality institutions for companies. Improve inspection methods and increase the capacity for inspections. Improve the certifications system at the levels of production environment, inputs, production and processing processes, packaging marks, and so on, as well as the management of certification of agricultural products. Ensure the quality and safety of agricultural products. Promote certifications such as GMP (good manufacturing practices), HACCP (hazard analysis critical control point), ISO9000 (standards for quality assurance and quality management), and ISO14000 (standards for environmental management and protection). Guide producers to develop product certifications. Elevate agricultural standards to coercive technical regulations. Encourage agricultural companies to establish internal control standards to serve as the technical bases for organizing and standardizing production, processing, and sales behaviors.

Clarify executive bodies, standardize the structure of such bodies, improve executive systems, bring about cooperative execution of laws, increase the strength of executive bodies, increase the level of execution, strengthen the fairness and authority of executive bodies, and safeguard the effective implementation of agricultural laws and regulations.

2.4.3 Expanding the Scope of Economic Administration, Improving Economic Management Methods

Establish an administrative system of "complete systemic preparations, reasonable division of labor, symmetric authorities and responsibilities, coordinated operations, and standardized behaviors" that is suited to market economy rules, in line with the thinking of pre-production, production, and post-production integrated management, and in accordance to the demands of stabilizing agricultural product markets, ensuring agricultural product security, increasing rural incomes, and increasing the competitiveness of agriculture, in order to adjust to new opportunities and challenges brought on by globalization.

The main point of reforms is to augment the role that markets play in resource allocation, to reasonably demarcate the scope of functions and authorities between sectors and within sectors, to bolster government functions and the service functions of social organizations, and to improve the government's administrative system.

Agricultural product markets have five basic functions: collection and distribution of commodities, price formation, and information dissemination. Allowing agricultural product markets to fulfill these functions plays an important role in guiding rural citizens to adjust the agricultural structure, vitalizing agricultural product circulation, increasing rural incomes, and accelerating urbanized construction. Establish a unified, open, competitive, orderly agricultural products market system with such modern market circulation measures as distribution chains, electronic trading, and futures trading as the forerunners, wholesale markets as the heart, and retail sales stores, trade and market centers, and supermarkets as the foundations. Build and develop an agricultural product market system at the following seven levels: one, improve service functions; two, drive innovation in circulation systems of agricultural product markets; three, reform the trade methods and operations and management models of wholesale markets for agricultural products; four, accelerate the implementation of market entry institutions for agricultural products; five, improve systems for the collection and dissemination of market information; six, increase the degree of organization of market entities; and seven, strengthen market management.

Implement comprehensive management adapted to the demands of the market economy and establish public organs on the basis of functionality. Two, clarify the positioning of functions and strengthen public services. Integrate the management functions of the quality and safety system and the quality inspection and examination system for agricultural products. Integrate the functions of the construction of market systems and information systems for agricultural products with agricultural products and agricultural input market services as the core. Integrate such services as research and development, marketing, and services for agriculture with increases to agricultural competitiveness as the core. Three, synthesize reforms to public institutions and strengthen such administrative and execution functions as veterinary services, plant protection and quarantine, pesticides and animal medicines, chemical fertilizers, seeds, and so on. Four, continue to transform government functions; convert administrative approvals into such public services as the provision of market information, technological consulting, disaster forecasting, product inspections, marketing services, infrastructure construction, and so on. Improve international cooperation and communication and fulfill the dual duties of protecting China's agriculture and developing international markets.

One, sort out the relationship between sectors and resolve the problems of overlapping and superimposed functions. Two, properly divide responsibilities and increase the reciprocity of the various administrative bodies. Three, protect agricultural resources and the ecological environment and shore up the foundations for eternally sustainable agriculture. Four, establish institutionalized consultation mechanisms for sectors and ensure coordination between agricultural sectors.

2.5   The Experience of China's Rural Reforms

China's economic reforms began in the agricultural sector. The objectives of 30 years of agricultural reforms have been gradual and progressive. Rural reforms in China may be broken into three phases, per changes to the objectives of such reforms. The first phase of reforms was intended to incentivize rural citizens to produce more agricultural products and resolve the issues of widespread rural poverty and insufficient food supply. The most fundamental measure implemented was the Household Responsibility System, which transformed collective agricultural operations into household operations. The second phase of reforms was intended to establish the market economy and bring about economic system restructuring. The specific measures taken in this phase were aimed at developing product markets and factor markets. The third phase of reforms was intended to establish a system and mechanisms that integrated rural and urban planning and to bring about fairness in the rights of rural citizens. The concrete measures taken in this phase were aimed at establishing equality in urban and rural basic public services. During this process, first the government made the transition from doing everything toward only playing an administrative role, and then the government transitioned from administration toward the provision of services.

The Household Responsibility System, created by China's rural citizens in the course of their practical lives, shattered the barriers of the planned economy and brought rural citizens onto the road of growing rich through labor. The process of this mighty reform could be divided into two very clear threads from beginning to end: systemic innovation and the development of markets. The process whereby agriculture and the rural economy in China became marketized was a process where traditional agriculture transitioned into modernized agriculture, and so the experience we gained from these rural reforms was most valuable indeed. This experience is not only of significance for informing our next step in agricultural economic reforms, but is provides lessons for reforms in other economic fields in China and urban centers to draw from.

2.5.1   Enormous Potential for Rural Economic Growth

China's history of revolution and development demonstrates that the power behind both reforms and development lies primarily in the countryside and in the persons of rural citizens. During the era of the New Democratic Revolution, the success of said revolution was won by releasing enormous potential for revolution of the countryside and the peasantry by satisfying the land requirements of the peasantry. In the era of Reform and Opening, China has been led onto the track of rapid development by releasing the potential of incentivizing the countryside and rural citizens by satisfying the needs of rural citizens to have autonomy over their production. In the new stage of development, we must release the enormous potential energy of the countryside and rural citizens by satisfying their demands for a moderately prosperous life, and thus truly alight upon the development path of Chinese characteristics.

Rural citizens comprise the majority of China's population, and rural land accounts for the vast majority of all land in China. This basic national condition demonstrates that if we don't handle rural issues well, then we won't be able to handle China's issues well; if rural citizens are poor, then China cannot become rich and powerful; and if agriculture is backward, then China will not be able to bring about modernization. Thus, during this new stage of development, we should place importance on the countryside, care about the countryside, give full rein to the incentives and innovativeness of rural citizens, and ensure sustainable development of both the countryside and agriculture. This will be the key to China's modernization.

2.5.2   Market Guidance: An Important Factor in Rural Growth

The past 30 years of experience demonstrate that market guidance reforms are one of the most key factors to the rapid growth of China's agriculture. Over the short term, driving up productivity at the individual level has indeed driven growth in agriculture, but this method will maintain the relative advantageousness of rural agriculture, and will lead to the negative result of extending the process of recreating traditional agriculture. A more appropriate choice would be to spur factor fluidity by relying upon market mechanisms and thereby greatly decrease the marginal productivity differences in resource allocation.

Over these past 30 years, as product markets and factor markets have grown, the effect of market mechanisms on agricultural resource allocation has grown more pronounced, and rural microeconomic foundations have grown more adapted to market mechanisms. At the same time, as compared with the objectives of the establishment of the nationwide integrated market system, the countryside requires another series of market-oriented economic reforms.

2.5.3   Non-agricultural Enterprises to Become Mainstay of Rural Development

Over the past 20 years, the rapid rise of TVEs made those enterprises the major sector driving economic growth in China. They not only propelled the industrialization and urbanization of the countryside, but also provided experience for explorations toward a modernization road suited to China's national conditions. From the outset, TVEs faced market competition, and so market mechanisms are naturally adaptable. The economies of scale of non-agricultural industries are quite pronounced. TVEs do not primarily pursue internal economies of scale, but rather external economies of scale formed by the regional agglomeration of many enterprises of the same nature. Their original method of decentralized production but centralized sales drove the development of both wholesale commodity markets and of cities. The method of enterprise spatial aggregation appeared afterward, which has since driven the development of small and mid-sized cities.

The effect of market mechanisms is as follows: they use economic signals to induce rural production toward sectors and regions of high productivity and high rates of return. These in turn drive increases to rural incomes and eliminate disparities in rates of return between industries and disparities in development between urban and rural areas. The effect of government macro-adjustments and controls is as follows: they increase the supply of rural public products and social welfare and rapidly eliminate disparities in the supply of public products and social welfare between urban and rural areas and between regions.

The experience of rural reforms is as follows: the abandonment of high-degree controls on rural citizens enabled rural citizens to autonomously allocate their own resources on the basis of market information, which was advantageous to increasing agricultural production and rural incomes as well as driving rural development. Local governments were encouraged or allowed to actively explore and adopt new regulations and to promote systemic innovation. After new rules and institutions were universally put in place, they were upheld by state policies and laws. China's rural reforms were all pushed by grassroots governments, whether in matters of the Household Responsibility System, TVEs, or village autonomous governance; they were driven forward amid conflicts with preexisting policies. Increases to rural incomes came mostly from increases to agricultural productivity, upgrades to the agricultural industry structure, and shifts in rural labor. The primary contribution of the government was to increase supply of rural public products, thereby laying the foundations for rural citizens to increase incomes and make innovations.

Empowerment is an effective method in further allowing the potential for wealth creation of rural citizens to play an even bigger role, and is also the basic experience of state and rural development in China since Reform and Opening. Rapid growth in agricultural products shortly after Reform and Opening was the result of granting rural citizens autonomy to operate their own land. The rapid rise of non-agricultural industries in rural and urban areas in the mid-1980s was the result of empowering rural citizens to choose their own employment opportunities. Improvements to the relationships between leaders and the masses in grassroots rural communities was the result of empowering rural citizens to choose their own village leaders. Empowering rural citizens is advantageous to increasing the reciprocity of government objectives and the objectives of rural households, which thereby garners widespread support for government objectives among rural citizens. Nevertheless, the process of empowering rural citizens remains incomplete, and as such remains a cardinal focus for deepening rural reforms.

Chapter 3
China's Agricultural Basic Operating System

3.1 Changes to China's Agricultural Basic Operating System

Prior to 1949, China's agriculture operated on a basic operating system of private land ownership and household operations, suited to a natural economy based on sustenance farming. After the founding of New China, a basic agricultural operating system founded upon public land ownership and collectivized operations adapted to the state's industrialization strategy and the ideology of the governing party was gradually established.

The first institution pushed out was that of mutual aid teams (MATs). Agricultural production MATs were reciprocal labor assistance groups founded on the foundation of the individual and per the principles of voluntariness and mutual benefit. There were both provisional and year-round MATs. Provisional MATs were composed of several households who assisted each other with farm work during the busy season and broke up afterward. Year-round MATs were composed of seven or eight households or of several dozen households. In addition to helping each other with farm work, members helped each other with sideline industries and small irrigation projects, and some even owned small amounts of public property. The establishment of MATs inhibited such behaviors as renting land or hiring laborers. In 1950, there were 2.72 million MATs in China; the number of MATs peaked in 1953 at 9.93 million. The MATs represented a basic agricultural operating system at low levels of private ownership of land and common production.

The cooperative system followed the MAT system. In December 1953, CCP Central issued the "Resolutions on Developing Agricultural Production Cooperatives," after which cooperatives quickly replaced MATs. Agricultural production cooperatives were divided into two classes, elementary and high-level, per their degrees of collective ownership of means of production. Elementary cooperatives were established on the foundation of private ownership of primary means of production, but all land, draft animals, and large and mid-sized farm

© Social Sciences Academic Press and Springer Nature Singapore Pte Ltd. 2017
Z. Li, *Reform and Development of Agriculture in China*,
Research Series on the Chinese Dream and China's Development Path,
DOI 10.1007/978-981-10-3462-6_3

equipment were assessed for value and sold to the collective for shares. All such items were for the collective use of the cooperative, but all members shared in dividends. Labor compensations for collective members was often higher than their remuneration for means of production like land. Labor was recorded in the form of work points. The degree of public ownership of agricultural means of production was higher for collectives than for MATs. High-level cooperatives were established on a foundation of public ownership of primary means of production. All privately held land of collective members was appropriated to the collective with no compensation. All draft animals and large and mid-sized farm equipment were purchased by the collective, but members did not share in dividends. Income was allocated to collective members per the principle of "each receiving according to work done," after deductions of taxes, production costs, accumulation funds, and public welfare funds. The degree of public ownership of agricultural means of production was higher in high-level cooperatives than in elementary cooperatives. In 1954, there were over 114,000 cooperatives in the country, of which only 200 were high-level and the rest elementary. By 1956 the total was 750,000, of which 210,000 primary and 540,000 high-level. At this time, 88% of all rural households in the country were members of collectives. Cooperatives represented a basic agricultural operating system of a relatively low degree of public ownership of land and a relatively small amount of collective production.

Next came the people's commune system. The method of establishing "big collectives" (precursors to communes) had already appeared during the era of agricultural collectivization. In winter 1957 and spring 1958, "united bodies" were promoted to meet the needs of building farm irrigation works. In March 1958, the CCP Politburo's Chengdu Conference passed the "Opinions on Appropriately Merging Small Agricultural Collectives into Local Big Collectives," after which local governments around the country began the work of merging small collectives into big collectives. In some places, people's communes were established. In August of that year, the CCP Politburo Beidaihe Conference passed the "CCP Central Resolutions on the Issue of Establishing People's Communes in the Countryside." After the Resolutions were promulgated in early September, a nationwide movement for establishing people's communes erupted. In only a little over a month, most of the nation had been converted into communes. Early the next year, over 740,000 agricultural production collectives around China had been pared down to a little over 26,000 people's communes, with 120 million member households, accounting for over 99% of all rural households in the nation. The basic agricultural operating system in place during the early phase of people's communes was one of public land ownership and collective production with the administrative village (or township or county) as the basic unit. Very soon thereafter, a series of ills, all of which difficult to mitigate, were exposed in this system. The central government used the opportunity of the three years of natural disasters beginning in early 1960 to adjust the system to a basic agricultural operating system based on public ownership of land and collective production but with the natural village as its base unit.

Even though such adjustments were effective, they did not totally resolve all existing issues. Twenty years later, the central government took the opportunity of promoting the Household Responsibility System to implement a new basic agricultural operating system based in public ownership of land, with the natural village as its base unit, and with the rural household as the base unit of agricultural production. In 1980, the Household Responsibility System had been extended to only 5.0% of the total of basic accounting units of rural land, but that number jumped to 80.9% in 1982 and again to 99.1% in 1984.[1] This demonstrates that the limitations of ideology on the selection of a basic agricultural operating system are first gradually strengthened and then gradually relaxed. Public ownership of land and collectivization of production were first gradually expanded and then gradually relaxed.

After comprehensive implementation of the "Household Responsibility System" in 1984, how to drive construction of a basic agricultural operating system through organizational innovation became a major focus of deepening agricultural reforms. To promote such explorations, the state established a slew of rural comprehensive reform pilot zones. In 1994, the Central Rural Work Commission issued a document formally proposing the task of "constructing a basic agricultural operating system."

3.2 Environmental Changes Facing Construction of the Basic Operating System

Over 30 years of development, major changes occurred in the environment facing the construction of China's basic agricultural operating system. The most striking such change was: the super small scale agricultural resource allocation method, which had played a major role in resolving the hunger and warmth issues of the masses of peasantry, been founded upon household operations, and typified by a complete unity of contracting rights and operating rights, came to be ever less suited to the objective needs of agricultural development.

3.2.1 Sustenance Fields Less Important

The robust development of agricultural products, marked improvements to infrastructure such as road networks, and increases to the diversification of rural income sources all led to increases in the quantity of rural households purchasing food on

---

[1]Ministry of Agriculture Rural Cooperative Economy Guiding Bureau, *Agricultural Collectivization in Contemporary China* editing bureau: *Materials on Rural Cooperative Economic Organizations and the Development of Conditions for Agricultural Production* (1950–1991).

the market. Sustenance fields, which had long been the places where rural citizens grew all the food required for their families, but once household responsibility fields became concentrated in the hands of a few adept families, these sustenance fields became less suitable and important.

3.2.2 Gradual Increases to Opportunity Costs of Agriculture

As industrialization and urbanization picked up speed, the proportion of rural citizens engaged in non-agricultural work gradually increased. As employment in non-agricultural industries became more stable and incomes in such fields grew more quickly, agricultural income grew increasingly less important for rural households. The opportunity costs for engaging in agriculture for rural citizens thus grew gradually greater.

3.2.3 Using Land to Provide for Old Age Less Important

Although land remains an important resource for rural citizens to provide for themselves in old age, social methods for old age care have replaced resource-based methods. This is the inevitable result of economic development and is furthermore the inevitable result of gradual improvement to the rural social security system. The rural social senior care system remains weak at present, but is growing stably. It is not difficult to see that the growth of that system will allow it to replace the method of providing for old age through land, and that latter method will only grow less important with time.

3.2.4 Differentiation in Production and Capital Functions of Agricultural Land

Shortly after Reform and Opening, contracting and operating rights for agricultural land, as well as the production and capital functions of said land (its physical form and its asset form) were completely integrated. As the amount of agricultural land transferred by contract grew steadily greater, the rights to contract and operate agricultural land, and the two aforementioned functions gradually grew apart. The simplest method for adjusting to this change was to allow rural households to materialize their land rights. A government that opted for laissez faire policies would do well to choose this method. The advantages of this method are that it is not easy for disputes over land rights to arise, nor any careless mistakes. Its downfalls are that it is not advantageous to promoting integration of land and increases to agricultural competitiveness. Another method is to allow rural households to convert their land rights into shares. Table 3.1 demonstrates that despite 30 years of changes to the collective economy, in 2012 the collective economy still controls a large quantity of collective assets. A question we cannot avoid is how to manage these assets best.

China is one of few countries in the world with a historical legacy of collective ownership of agricultural land but which still possesses the conditions for issuing rights to said land as shares. This is an appropriate choice for a government that adopts active policies. The upsides of this method are that it is advantageous to bringing differential income to leading rural households who agglomerate parcels of

Table 3.1 Estimated net rural assets in China, 2012

	Asset type	Area (bn μ)	Asset valuation (bn yuan)	% of total
Net nationwide rural assets			127307.47	100
State owned, collective operated	Grassland	2.261	1742.58	1.37
State owned, operated by contract	Grassland	2.739	2110.98	1.66
Collective owned and operated			13187.43	10.36
Of which	Farmland	00.54	1084.28	
	Forest land	0.310	208.90	
	Grassland	0.450	346.82	
	Business-use construction land	0.042	9147.43	
	Other business assets		2400.00	
Collective owned, individual operated			74167.10	58.26
Of which	Farmland	1.756	35058.51	
	Forest land	2.430	1659.40	
	Grassland	0.550	423.89	
	Homestead land	0.170	37025.30	
Individual owned and operated			36099.38	28.35
Of which	Agricultural fixed assets		1998.30	
	Non-ag. fixed assets		850.97	
	Residences		24027.09	
	Net deposits		7583.23	
	Cash and other financial assets		1639.79	

land together and to optimizing the land resource allocations of leading households and increasing their agricultural competitiveness. The downfalls of this method are that there may be disputes over land rights or possibly large mishaps if land added value evaluations are unfair, if regulation mechanisms at the village or commune level are inappropriate, or if the government's power to protect agreements is insufficient. Rural citizens should be given final say in which method to choose, and the government should not have to make an across-the-board policy decision. The government is responsible for strengthening administration over land value added appraisals, supervising village and commune level regulation, and protection of relevant agreements.

3.2.5 Differentiation Between Rural Citizens

Shortly after the dawn of Reform and Opening, rural citizens were both the operators of contracted land as well as the owners of the usufruct rights to contracted land, meaning that the identities of landlord and peasant were embodied in them simultaneously. In recent years, as there have been upgrades to the employment structure and income structure of rural households, there has been separation between the two identities of "peasant" and "landlord." These separations come in one of two forms. Under the first, contracted land is transferred to other rural households for profit, and the original party does not engage in agricultural production. Under the second, a household outsources the agricultural production activities on its contracted land to another household, remunerates that household, and assumes responsibility for daily supervision and maintenance of cash crops. In order to pay dual attention to both maximizing income and seeing to the household (and its contracted land), the best choice is for strong laborers to leave home to earn money and for the weaker laborers to remain home and watch over household assets. All the "weak laborers" left at home can perform some amount of agricultural work, but not many can see to all of a family's farm work, with the number growing smaller daily. With fewer and fewer weak laborers left at home, but with more and more land for them to administer, we have reason to make a judgment on the differentiation happening between these rural citizens.

Another way that rural citizens diverge is that some reduce their labor and increase their leisure time. A question I often ask when conducting surveys in the countryside is: Since it doesn't take a lot of labor to pull weeds, why do you prefer to buy weed killer and spend time shooting the breeze in the village instead of doing this work? Their answer is usually as follows: the amount you save by spending an entire day pulling weeds is equal to the amount one of our children can earn in one hour working elsewhere. Our children would rather work for one extra hour than spend an entire day pulling weeds, and so they prefer leisure to performing the extra labor.

3.2.6 Diversification of Organizational Market Entry Methods for Rural Citizens

There are many organizational methods by which rural citizens enter markets, but the government tends to prefer the rural cooperative. In truth, there is a strong negative correlation between the importance of rural cooperatives and the degree of perfection of the market economy. The worse the market economy, the more flaws the market has, and vice versa for the more important cooperatives are. This is also the primary reason that the importance of rural cooperatives tends to decrease proportionately to the level of perfection of the market economy. China should place the focus on deepening reforms and accelerating improvements to the market economy, and should not promulgate rural cooperatives to adapt to an imperfect market economy.

In a market environment of ample competition, rural households can choose to join rural cooperatives, or align with agricultural companies, or transact with agents. It is precisely this diversification of the choices available to rural households that has driven competition between the various kinds of organizations, and so diversification of choices is essential. Given that understanding, now what we must build is a basic agricultural operating system that is advantageous to spurring competition between different types of organizations, and not a system that is advantageous only to the development of rural cooperatives.

To summarize, the crux of the basic agricultural operating system prior to 1980 was to concentrate agricultural surpluses and accelerate industrialization. After Reform and Opening, the crux shifted to incentivizing the masses of rural citizens to produce and resolving insufficient food supply. The crux of the system we should build at present is in driving competition between the various organizations. We should place primary attention on resolving restrictions on the application of agricultural technology imposed by over-small scales of agricultural operations and the restrictions on the incentives for rural citizens to engage in agriculture imposed by low relative profitability of agriculture.

3.3 The Development of New Agricultural Operators in China

New agricultural operations entities include leading farms,[2] specialized rural households, rural specialized cooperatives, agricultural companies, and so on. These entities must simultaneously meet three conditions. The first is that per capita

---

[2]Family farms are a very broad concept. Even in the US, with its bountiful per capita allotment of arable land, family farms are defined as those for which production or sales of agricultural products exceeds USD $1000. At present in China, the family farms we advocate for are leading farms that correspond to the registered rural household system. To make this concept easier to understand and

net incomes of rural households must not be lower than those of rural households engaged in multiple industries.[3] The second is that they must have viability. Production operations must not be reliant upon government subsidies (not including compensations in the form of added value from the provision of ecological services). The third is that they must adhere to all institutions and rules. In other words, production operations must conform to and adhere to relevant laws and regulations and uphold the market and social requirements of adhering to agreements.

3.3.1 Leading Farms

At present, 229 million households in China are operating contracted farmland, and of those, 85% operate a total of 10 μ or fewer of land. It is difficult for such households to develop modernized agriculture on less than 10 μ of land except in such labor-intensive, capital-intensive, and high added value industries as vegetables, flowers, and fruit. So many such households opt to engage in non-agricultural enterprises,[4] first at home in the countryside, and then later move to cities to engage in the same. As more rural citizens make this choice, and as their employment stabilizes, there are corresponding increases to the quantity of farmland rights transferred away by contract. At first, most such transfers were made between friends and relatives, usually at low costs. In recent years, however, demand for farmland has outstripped supply, and costs have consistently risen. Most land has been transferred to leading farms and other new micro-operation entities, which can afford to pay more for said land, which has driven the rise of such entities.

(Footnote 2 continued)

accept for foreign academics, I suggest replacing use of the term "family farm" with the term "leading farm".

[3]Existing research divides rural households engaged in multiple industries into two categories, with those earning most of their income from agriculture in category I and those earning most of their income from non-agricultural enterprises as category II. In truth, there is also a need to categorize specialized rural households, with those earning less per capita income than category I multiple-industry households as category I and those earning not less per capita income than multiple-industry rural households as category II. Category I specialized rural households are traditional rural households, and category II specialized rural households are leading households. Leading rural households from other nations or regions should be used to measure levels of agricultural development.

[4]As urban reforms trailed rural reforms, and as there were many issues to be resolved regarding the tens of millions of educated youths returning to cities following the Cultural Revolution, it was nearly impossible for urban centers to absorb rural laborers during the mid-1980s. This gave rise to the state policy allowing rural citizens to engage in non-agricultural enterprises without leaving the countryside. This marked a major advance over the state policies during the era of the people's commune, when rural citizens were forbidden to work at anything except agriculture. The state policies of the 1990s allowing rural citizens to both engage in non-agricultural enterprises and leave the countryside were an even bigger advance. All this demonstrates that reforms in China are enacted gradually.

The leading farm survey conducted by the Ministry of Agriculture in March 2013 indicates the following: As of the end of 2012, there were 877,000 leading farms in 30 provinces, autonomous regions, and cities under direct command of the central government of China (Tibet excluded), operating a total area of 176 million μ of land, 13.4% of total arable land in China. Each leading farm employed an average of 6.01 laborers, on average 4.33 of which were family members and the remaining 1.68 hired labor. Of all leading farms, 409,500, or 46.7%, were engaged in planting, while 393,300, or 45.5%, were engaged in animal husbandry and/or aquaculture. Another 52,600, or 6%, were engaged in both, and the remaining 15,600, or 1.8%, were engaged in other industries. Of all leading farms, 484,200, or 55.2%, operated a total of less than 50 μ of land, and 189,800, or 21.6%, operated between 50 and 100 μ. Another 170,700, or 19.5%, operated between 100 and 500 μ, while 15,800, or 1.8%, operated between 500 and 1000 μ. A final 16,500, or 1.9%, operated more than 1000 μ. Nationwide total annual revenue for leading farms in China was 162 billion yuan in 2012, with an average annual per farm revenue of 184,700 yuan.[5]

3.3.2   Specialized Households

Many households of laborers working in urban enterprises are unwilling to transfer their land rights away, and so many opt to hire specialized households to handle some or all of the following on their contracted land: plowing, planting, fertilizing, spraying pesticides, and harvesting. This demand has driven the development of specialized rural households. Specialized households generally focus on one link of the agricultural chain and typically earn 80% more of total household income from such agricultural activities. At present, five percent of all Chinese rural households are specialized households, and most of those are also leading rural households. As indicated in Table 3.2, total nationwide revenue for mechanized farming households was 59.3 billion yuan in 1990, up to 260.6 billion in 2005 and again up to 477.9 billion in 2012. The average annual increase over the first 15 years was 13.4 billion yuan, up to 26.8 billion yuan over the last seven. Growth in this sector is accelerating markedly.

Since 1996, the average amount of time that specialized households owning combine harvesters use said machines has increased from seven to 10 days a year to over a month, working from south to north as wheat in different regions matures. Marked increases to the amount of time that agricultural machinery is used have enabled specialized households to increase operational efficiency without increasing harvest costs. At present, the cross-regional harvesting model has been extended to such crops as rice and corn, as well as to other links of the production chain. In

---

[5]Dong Jun, "Nationwide Leading Farm Total Now 877,000," Xinhua Online, accessed June 5, 2013, news.xinhuanet.com/xiangtu/2013-06/05/c_124814602.htm.

Table 3.2 Revenues of
mechanized farming
households since 1990, *unit*:
billion yuan

Year	Revenue	Year	Revenue	Year	Revenue
1990	59.30	2003	226.97	2008	346.65
1995	103.68	2004	242.15	2009	389.41
2000	200.00	2005	260.61	2010	424.79
2001	204.00	2006	281.10	2011	450.90
2002	215.00	2007	298.60	2012	477.90

Data source Ministry of Agriculture

2013, over 70,000 corn harvesters were employed in such harvesting across the grain regions of the nation, harvesting an average of 915 μ of corn per harvester. The average fee for mechanized harvesting is between 80 and 100 yuan/μ, yielding total profitability of more than 40,000 yuan.[6] A lack of area to sun-dry grain has limited the ability of grain farmers to increase the scale of their operations, and so demand for grain drying machinery is growing rapidly. Mechanized grain drying will become a new area for research, development, and application of agricultural machinery.

3.3.3   Specialized Farmer Cooperatives

As of the end of 2013, there were 950,700 farmer cooperatives in China, including legally registered specialized cooperatives and shareholding cooperatives, with membership of 72.21 million households, accounting for 27.8% of all rural households. There were also over 56 million coalitions and 2554 federations. As of the end of February, 2014, there were 1.0388 million specialized farmers cooperatives, capitalized with a total of 2.04 trillion yuan.[7] With support from state policies, cooperation between farmers cooperatives became widespread, and the establishment of coalitions of such cooperatives gave rural citizens greater ability to resist market risks, increase incomes, and grow rich.

3.3.4   Agricultural Companies

There are three agricultural domains suitable to company operations. The first is the planning and execution of planting as well as scaled animal husbandry and aquaculture. Agricultural products and commodities produced by such companies are more standardized and more capital-intensive, and also make better use of scale

---

[6]Zhao Jie, "Amount of Corn Harvested by Machine in China Increased by Over Six Percent Over Five Consecutive Years," *Nongminribao*, December 4, 2013.

[7]Data from the State Administration of Industry and Commerce (SAIC).

economies and have more room for growth. The second is the agricultural product processing industry. This includes edible oil processing, processing of livestock, fowl, and fish, fruit and vegetable processing, and specialized product processing. This is an important channel for increasing the added value of agricultural products. The third is the production services industry. The focuses of this industry are improvement of seed varieties, chain stores for agricultural supplies, modern logistics for agricultural products, agricultural information services, and so on. These industries have great prospects for growth and are also focus recipients of state policy support.

As pork production accounts for 64% of all meat production in China, I shall focus on the pork industry to demonstrate the growth of the scaled husbandry industry, primarily led by specialized companies. Up to the end of the 20th century, over 90% of pigs in China were raised in small numbers by individual households. Over the past 10-plus years, the scaled pork industry has grown rapidly. In 2005, 38% of all pigs produced in China were raised by specialized husbandry households with 50 or more pigs; that figure increased to nearly 65% in 2010[8] and again to approximately 79% in 2013. The same held true in the dairy cow industry. In 2012, the market share of households pasturing 100 or more cows had risen to 40%, and up to nearly 30% for households with 300 or more cows. The scaled fowl raising industry has also grown rapidly.

There are presently over 300,000 agricultural production and operation organizations in China, most of which are leading enterprises. These affect 120 million rural households and achieve average annual per household income increases of over 2800 yuan for agricultural operations. Agricultural industry demonstration bases are developing at accelerated rates, and the cluster and agglomeration effects are becoming more evident; this has gradually become a growth pole driving economic growth in the countryside. With over one million agricultural service organizations in China, the influence of such in areas such as mechanized agriculture, prevention and treatment of pest insects and crop diseases, prevention of animal epidemics, and so on, has grown more pronounced daily.

3.4   The Thinking Behind Fostering Leading Rural Households

Profound changes are currently taking place in rural China. Under the influences of marketization, specialization, de-agriculturalization, urbanization, and others, agricultural operations models that have been passed down for several thousands of years have basically disintegrated, and the "three replacements" have taken hold in the agricultural operations system. The first was the replacement of sustenance

---

[8]Xu Mengqin, "A New Era for the Pork Raising Industry in China," *Zhongguoxumushouyibao*, September 23, 2013, 9th edition.

agriculture with commercial agriculture. The second was the replacement of labor arrangements between villagers who knew each other by labor arrangements between strangers. The third was the replacement of community rules with market rules. This means that over the past few decades of rapid economic growth, the fundamental conditions for the development of modern agriculture have already been laid. Corresponding adjustments must be made to agricultural operations institutions and the agricultural operating system in light of the aforementioned three replacements.

It was, from an objective standpoint, inevitable that the total quantity of farms would decrease amid the processes of industrialization and urbanization. One must also note that the total quantity of farms tends to stabilize once the processes of industrialization and urbanization are basically complete. In the US, for example, the number of farms decreased from 5.7 million in 1900 to 2.2 million in 1990, with an average annual decrease of 168,500 in the 1950s, 101,300 in the 1960s, 51,000 in the 1970s, and 29,400 in the 1980s. The total number of farms in that country basically stabilized in the 1990s. The total number of farms in the US has held at around 2.20 million from the 1990s to present. China's process of shifting agricultural laborers remains far from complete. Given such conditions, it is only reasonable that the number of farmer households should decrease. This is also a basic condition for the expansion of the average agricultural scale of operation and for rapid growth of farmer incomes.

China should go to great lengths to develop leading farms and form them into the primary entities driving growth in agriculture. However, small farms shall continue to exist for a long time. In the US, for example, most agricultural supply is met by large farms, but a large amount of agricultural products in that country still come from small farms totaling net agricultural product sales of between USD $1000 to 10,000 per year.[9] We must remain soberly aware of this fact, lest we make mistakes stemming from overzealousness.

I included the above analysis to demonstrate the following: only a portion of rural households—not all—will become new agricultural operation entities. So in order to establish a new agricultural operation system, we must place our focus on that portion of rural households with the capability of becoming new agricultural operation entities, and cause them to be beneficial to the development of the new agricultural operation system to the greatest extent possible.

---

[9]Analysts have demonstrated that there are three reasons that a large number of American agricultural products still come from small farms with sales revenues of between USD $1000 and $10,000. The first is that many households owning small farms earn most of their income from non-agricultural work; in 2004 the per household non-agricultural income of such households was USD $74,000, several times their agricultural income. The second is the American income tax law that allows individuals to exempt losses from farm operations from their taxes. The third is support from such government programs as the Conservation Reserve Program (CRP) and the Wetlands Reserve Program (WRP). The data indicate that from 2002 to 2008, the CRP paid out a total of USD $12.8 billion, with over 80% of that total going to small farms. Over the same period, the WRP paid out an annual average of USD $180 million, with over 82% going to small farms.

The report of the CCP's 18th National Congress proposed persisting in and improving basic rural operating institutions and erecting a new rural operations system that combines intensification, specialization, organization, and socialization.[10] Central Document Number One of 2013 and the third plenum of the 18th CCP National Congress both established the creation of a new agricultural operations system and the fostering of new agricultural operation entities as the foundation upon which to develop modern agriculture. Central Document Number One of 2014 elaborated further on this issue. In order to encourage the transfer of land operation rights to new operation entities and develop a wide variety of scale operations, we must grow the market for land rights transfers, explore the establishment of a risk guarantee fund system for agricultural land transferred to commercial and industrial enterprises, and provide subsidies for land transfers in places that meet appropriate conditions. We must innovate in the creation of a market-oriented agricultural services system, push such service models as cooperatives, orders, and trusteeships, and improve the production and sales service market system for agriculture. In order to encourage the development of major mixed ownership agricultural production enterprises, the central government should establish a certain proportion of supporting facilities accompanying construction to new agricultural operations entities in its annual indexes for construction land. The central government should also encourage local governments and private citizens to invest in joint venture guarantor companies, in order to provide loan underwriting services to new agricultural operations entities. The government should ramp up education and training of management personnel for new professional rural citizens and new agricultural operations entities. The government should also support qualified for-profit service organizations in their provision of agricultural services for the benefit of the public through such means as government purchasing of services, and so on.

The primary tasks involved in creating a new agricultural operations model are the growth of markets, the improvement of institutions, and the fostering of leading rural households. There are four primary reasons for this. First, opportunities for growth in modern agriculture should be left to those leading rural households who steadfastly remain in the countryside; we should avoid to the extent possible attracting outside capital and thereby selling the opportunities for growth in modern agriculture on the cheap to entrepreneurs who earned their first pot of gold in non-agricultural sectors, and then allowing these entrepreneurs to hire local rural citizens in their development of modern agriculture. Second, leading rural households are those which have adopted corporate operations, have entered the market system, and are viable thereupon; they are just as efficient as any other entrepreneurs. Third, establishing leading rural households as the core of this system helps to increase the level of organization of agricultural production, helps to promote standardization, scale operations, and branded operations in agriculture, and helps

---

[10]In my opinion, socialization is not sufficiently accurate to express this concept; marketization is a better expression.

to preserve economic and social stability in the countryside. Fourth, the level of agricultural development of a country or region—including agricultural product security, international competitiveness in agriculture, and sustainability of agriculture—is determined by the conditions of the leading rural households of that country or region. I have the following concrete suggestions for the fostering of leading rural households:

1. Promote a separation of land operation rights and land contracting rights and promote the development of leading households through such means as land transfers and the selling of shares for farmland operation rights.
2. The government should provide services to leading rural households in areas such as technology, information, personnel development, cooperation between households, and so on, to lay the conditions for growth of leading rural households. The government should also develop markets for pre-production, production, and post-production services, reduce the production costs of leading rural households, and increase the productivity of leading rural households.
3. Innovate in the rural operations system and provide the conditions for intensification, specialization, scale operations, and organization of leading rural households; allow the comparative advantages of leading rural households—in scale, efficiency, technology, markets, and so on—to play as big a role as possible.
4. Allow companies and social organizations to engage in a wide variety of activities in the countryside, in order that they may lend effective support to the development of leading rural households.

3.5 Summarizing Comments

The changes that have taken place in China's basic agricultural operations system demonstrate that the restrictions imposed upon said system by ideology first grew gradually stronger but then were gradually relaxed. Public ownership and collectivization of land likewise first gradually grew stronger but then were gradually relaxed.

The aim of the basic agricultural operations system prior to 1980 was to consolidate agricultural surpluses and accelerate industrialization. The aim of said system in the years since 1980 has been to provide incentives for increased production to the masses of rural citizens and to resolve their warmth and food issues. The aim of the system at present is to drive competition among the various different entities and eliminate the restrictions on the application of agricultural technology imposed by overly small scales of agricultural operations and the restrictions on the incentives for rural citizens to engage in agricultural production imposed by overly low relative profitability of agriculture.

The methods of farmland allocation with the household as their foundation, in which contracting and operation rights are inseparable, and of extremely small scales will grow increasingly less suited to the demands of agricultural development as the importance of sustenance and old age support fields drops, as the production functions and capital functions of farmland are separated, as farmers and landlords become differentiated, and as opportunity costs for engaging in agriculture grow greater. In this chapter, we explored the three criteria for leading farms, analyzed the challenges facing leading farms, and made suggestions for accelerating the fostering of leading farms, having proven that leading farms are the most important new agricultural operations entities.

Chapter 4
The Development of Agriculture in China

4.1 China's Natural Agricultural Resources

4.1.1 Low Per Capita Quantities of Land

China's per capita endowment of arable land is 1.5 μ, coming in at one third the global average, and making China one of the nations with the smallest amount of per capita arable land. China's per capita endowment of forested land is approximately 1.8 μ, one seventh of the global average, and its per capita endowment of grasslands is a little over three μ, again one third of the global average.

4.1.2 Big Regional Differences in Available Water

China's north-south span exceeds 5500 km and crosses over 50° of latitude. The majority of China's land falls within the middle latitudes between 20° N and 50° N. We separate the nation into two halves, the southeast and the northwest, with each region accounting for approximately half of the nation's land, using the dividing line of 400 mL of annual precipitation. Rainfall is abundant in the southeast, which is subject to monsoon weather patterns from the Pacific Ocean. Most of the year's rain falls during the hot months, with over 80% of precipitation coming during the time that primary crops are grown. This is the primary reason that over 90% of China's agricultural regions are located in the southeast. The northwest is comprised of semi-arid and arid environments. Most areas in the northwest receive less than 400 milliliters of annual precipitation, with precipitation figures for some areas in the double or even single digits of milliliters. The drought index in most of the region is above 1.5, and in excess of 20 in some places, limiting agricultural development. These regions are endowed with broad expanses of grassland and are the pastoral heartlands of China.

© Social Sciences Academic Press and Springer Nature Singapore Pte Ltd. 2017
Z. Li, *Reform and Development of Agriculture in China*,
Research Series on the Chinese Dream and China's Development Path,
DOI 10.1007/978-981-10-3462-6_4

4.1.3 Discoordination in Water and Land Resources

The annual average runoff from China's rivers is 2.7115 trillion m^3 of water, equivalent to an annual average runoff depth of 285 mm, less than many other countries. The per capita share of runoff is 2558 m^3, only about a quarter of the global average of 10,800 m^3. Arable land in the Yangtze River basin and regions south of the Yangtze account for 37.8% of total nationwide arable land, but these lands receive 82.5% of total nationwide runoff. Arable land in the basins of the Yellow, Huai, and Hai Rivers accounts for 38.4% of total nationwide arable land, but these lands receive only 6.6% of total runoff. The time distribution of water is also extremely imbalanced, with great year-to-year fluctuations.

4.2 Agricultural Inputs

4.2.1 Labor

In 1952, there were 173.17 million laborers engaged in agriculture in China, accounting for 83.5% of total employment in China. In 1991, there were even more agricultural laborers, 390.98 million, 3.26 times the 1952 figure, but now such laborers accounted for only 59.7% of nationwide employment. In 2000, 360.43 million laborers were engaged in agriculture, forestry, or fisheries, but now they accounted for only 50% of nationwide employment. In 2014, that same figure dropped to 230.76 million, now accounting for only 29.9% of nationwide employment (see Fig. 4.1). Aside from the marked changes to the number of agricultural laborers, there were also great changes to the composition of this labor

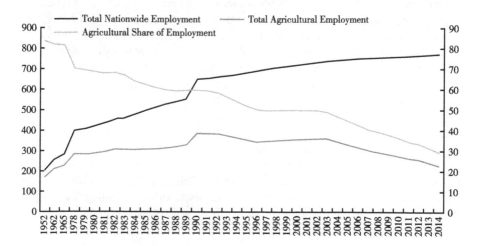

Fig. 4.1 Changes to China's agricultural labor pool (million)

pool, as the share of people 45 years and younger had grown quite low indeed. One must note that as more and more rural households opted to contract agricultural services, the amount of agricultural production tasks that could be completed by the elderly and infirm remaining in the countryside became limited. That is to say that their "farmer characteristics" diminished while their "landlord characteristics" became more prominent (Table 4.1).

Reductions to the amount of labor required per unit area of land is the primary reason for the drop in agricultural laborers. From 1978 to 1985, the number of man-days required per μ of rice, wheat, corn, and soybeans fell from, respectively, 38.1–21.9, 30.7–14.5, 31.1–16.3, and 22.2–11.6, for respective drops of 42.5, 52.7,

Table 4.1 Agricultural laborers and their proportion to nationwide employment in China, *unit* million people

	No. of laborers in agriculture, forestry, husbandry, and fisheries			No. of laborers in agriculture, forestry, husbandry, and fisheries			No. of laborers in agriculture, forestry, husbandry, and fisheries	
		%			%			%
1952	173.17	83.5	1973	288.57	78.7	1994	366.28	54.3
1953	177.47	83.1	1974	292.18	78.2	1995	355.30	52.2
1954	181.51	83.1	1975	294.56	77.2	1996	348.20	50.5
1955	185.92	83.3	1976	294.43	75.8	1997	348.40	49.9
1956	185.44	80.6	1977	293.40	74.5	1998	351.77	49.8
1957	193.09	81.2	1978	283.18	70.5	1999	357.68	50.1
1958	154.90	58.2	1979	286.34	69.8	2000	360.43	50.0
1959	162.71	62.2	1980	291.22	68.7	2001	363.99	50.0
1960	170.16	65.7	1981	297.77	68.1	2002	366.40	50.0
1961	197.47	77.2	1982	308.59	68.1	2003	362.04	49.1
1962	212.76	82.1	1983	311.51	67.1	2004	348.30	46.9
1963	219.66	82.5	1984	308.68	64.0	2005	334.42	44.8
1964	228.01	82.2	1985	311.30	62.4	2006	319.41	42.6
1965	233.96	81.6	1986	312.54	60.9	2007	307.31	40.8
1966	242.97	81.5	1987	316.63	60.0	2008	299.23	39.6
1967	251.65	81.7	1988	322.49	59.4	2009	288.91	38.1
1968	260.63	81.7	1989	332.25	60.0	2010	279.31	36.7
1969	271.17	81.6	1990	389.14	60.1	2011	265.94	34.8
1970	278.11	80.8	1991	390.98	59.7	2012	257.73	33.6
1971	283.97	79.7	1992	386.99	58.5	2013	241.71	31.4
1972	282.83	78.9	1993	376.80	56.4	2014	230.76	29.9

Data source Multiple years of the *China Statistical Yearbook*, published by the National Bureau of Statistics. The 2014 figure of 226.69 million is an estimate from Wang Chuanjing *Analysis and Forecasts of Economic Conditions in Rural China* (*2015 Edition*), Chinese Academy of Social Sciences Rural Development Institute and National Bureau of Statistics Rural Socioeconomic Survey Office, (Shehuikexuewenxianchubanshe, 2015), 54

47.6, and 47.7% (see Fig. 4.2). Changes to labor inputs over this period are primarily the result of increases to labor productivity and were brought on by the reform from collective operations into household operations. Thus agricultural usage of labor has been typified by rapid decreases per unit of area. In 2011, man-days of labor required per μ of rice, wheat, corn, and soybeans fell to, respectively, 7.6, 5.6, 7.2, and 3.1, respective drops of 65.3, 61.4, 55.8, and 73.3% from 1985 (see Fig. 4.2). Changes to labor requirements during this time were closely related to the application of farming machinery; in other words, they were primarily the results of machinery replacing laborers. There was a slow reduction to the number of agricultural laborers owing to the gradual replacement of such laborers by farming machinery (Table 4.2).

4.2.2 Farmland

Statistics on the area of farmland—land under cultivation (LuC) in statistical terms—in China over the past 60 years are in a state of relative disorder. Although these data may be used to analyze agriculture during a given time period, they cannot reflect the true state of changes to the area of LuC in the nation. We must reconstruct such statistics in order to accurately reflect the state of development of agriculture in China over the past 60 years.

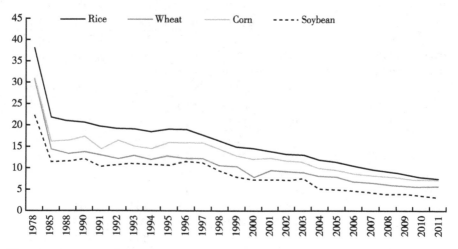

Fig. 4.2 Changes to rice, wheat, corn, and soybean labor requirements per μ since 1978 (man-days/μ)

Table 4.2 Labor requirements per μ for rice, wheat, corn, and soybeans, *unit* man-days/μ

	Rice	Wheat	Corn	Soybeans		Rice	Wheat	Corn	Soybeans
1978	38.1	30.7	31.1	22.2	2000	14.6	7.9	12.4	7.4
1985	21.9	14.5	16.3	11.6	2001	14.1	9.5	12.4	7.4
1988	21.1	13.5	16.5	11.6	2002	13.3	9.3	11.7	7.2
1990	20.6	14	17.3	12	2003	13.1	9	11.3	7.5
1991	19.9	13	14.6	10.4	2004	11.9	8.1	10	5.2
1992	19.3	12.2	16.4	10.7	2005	11.4	7.9	9.5	5.1
1993	19.2	13	15.3	11.1	2006	10.4	7	8.7	4.7
1994	18.6	12	14.7	11	2007	9.7	6.6	8.3	4.5
1995	19	12.7	16	10.7	2008	9.1	6.1	7.9	3.9
1996	19	12.4	16	11.4	2009	8.4	5.8	7.5	3.9
1997	17.8	12.2	15.9	11.2	2010	7.8	5.6	7.3	3.4
1998	16.4	10.8	14.2	9.3	2011	7.6	5.6	7.2	3.1
1999	15.1	10.5	12.8	7.9	2012				

Data source Several years of *Compiled Data on Costs and Profits of Nationwide Agricultural Products*, National Development and Reform Commission Pricing Bureau

4.2.2.1   The Reasons for Reconstructing LuC Area Statistics in China

There are three reasons for this situation, as follows:

First, the sources of base numbers for LuC area in the various stages are all different, and it is not possible to link the data they provide. There have been two government organs responsible for releasing LuC area in China. The first was the National Bureau of Statistics (NBS), which compiled this data from 1949 to 1995, and the second is the Ministry of Land Resources (MLR), which compiled this data from 1996 to 2012. The MLR data can be broken into two sub-sets: years 1996 to 2008 and years 2009 to 2012. As can be seen in Fig. 4.3, it is impossible to accurately deduce the true state of changes to the area of LuC in China over the past 60 years by comparing these three groups of data.

Second, different indexes were used to measure changes to the area of LuCin the three different stages, and data on net changes to area are not comparable. Since 1998, net changes to the area of LuC in China have been calculated based on the four indicators of farmland occupation of non-agricultural construction, structural adjustments, return of farmland to nature, and ruination by disaster, as well as by a fifth indicator of newly added arable land. In 1997 and all years prior, net changes to the area of LuC were calculated based on additions and reductions to land under cultivation. In some years, net changes to the area of such land were not calculated.

Third, in some stages, there were only reductions, and no additions, to the area of LuC. This is the primary reason that there were sustained decreases to the area of LuC in China from 1958 to 1994. Over the 20-plus years from 1958 to 1985, the people's commune system was in place in China. The greatest advantage of this system was that organized rural citizens were able to accomplish things that

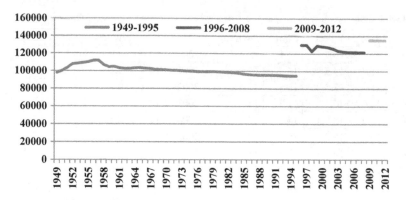

Fig. 4.3 Land under cultivation area data issued by the NBS and MLR from 1949 to 2012 (kha). *Note* Data from 1949 issued by the NBS, and data from other years issued by MLR

individual rural households could not, including the cultivation of virgin land that would have been difficult for individual households. On the basis of that logic, it seems reasonable that there should have been increases to the area of LuC in China during this period. There are three reasons that the area of LuC fell rather than increasing. The first was that the government ceased issuing land certificates (also known as land deeds), killing the incentives for peasant collectives to report increases to LuC. The second was that peasant collectives were unwilling to proactively increase their grain requisitioning burdens. Government grain requisitioning orders were made on the basis of the area of LuC. Should a peasant collective ever report increases to LuC, their grain requisitioning burden would grow correspondingly. The third was that newly added LuC became the basic method for reaching government-set objectives for grain production (such as the Outlines on Grain Production). Grain production per μ were calculated based on the total production capacity and total land under cultivation reported to higher authorities. It was advantageous not to report newly added land under cultivation to achieve or reduce the government-established production targets. Thus most peasants referred to newly added LuC as "helping fields".

For the same reasons, peasant collectives promptly reported any land occupied for construction in order to reduce their grain requisitioning burdens while not affecting actual grain production. This was done to reduce government-established requisitioning targets by reducing the amount of LuC which the government used to calculate such targets. This is the primary reason one sees progressive yearly decreases in the area of LuC as reported by the NBS over this period.

4.2.2.2 Conditions for Reconstructing Data for Area of LuC in China

Beneficial conditions are now in place for reconstructing data for China's area of land under cultivation.

First, LuC data for the period 1949–1957. Over this period, local governments issued land certificates for LuC. In order to receive rights to their land, rural households actively cultivated virgin land and reported such to the government, and so there were sustained increases to the amount of LuC on the books of land management bureaus. Relevant research demonstrates that the total area of LuC in 1957 was 1.997 billion μ, of which 209 million μ were newly added since 1949. The data for newly added land, stemming from the records of the issuance of government land certificates, are doubtlessly accurate. One can thus assume that data for the entire period 1949–1957 were on the whole accurate.

No nationwide surveys of LuC in China were performed prior to 1949, nor were any nationwide land measurement data available. Local governments measured LuC during the 1950s in order to issue land certificates, and in 1957 authorities arrived at the figure of 1.977 billion μ. We also know that over the years 1949–1957, peasants cultivated a further 209 million μ of virgin land. We can thus calculate, based on these two figures, that the area of LuC in China in 1949 was 1.768 billion μ, which is likely to be more or less accurate.

Second, data from 2009 to 2012. In 2013, the MLR issued LuC area data for the period 2009–2012 based on remote sensing data of changes to such area. As compared to the US-performed remote sensing survey of Chinese LuC in 1995, the remote sensing data used for the issuance of this data made detections at the level of each individual village, and overcame the previous deficiency of such surveys of not including tea plantations, fruit orchards, greenhouses, and other such agricultural occupations of land within the scope of LuC. These are the most accurate data on LuC in China to date. This is also an important reason that this survey arrived at a larger figure for area of LuC than the American survey of 1995. We must note that analysis of remote sensing data is performed on the basis of whether there are marked changes to the amount of organisms on LuC. It is difficult for such surveys to include LuC which is being left fallow for a year or upon which there are no striking changes to growing organisms within the data pool, and so there is always the possibility of underestimating the area of LuC with such surveys. This is also the primary reason that the MLR report includes the technical term "area of planted arable land".

Third, data for changes to the area of LuC from 1998 to 2008. We have relatively accurate data for changes to usage of LuC over this period (see Table 4.3). With data for the area of LuC from 2009 to 2012, we can deduce the area of LuC in each individual year over the period 1998–2008.

There are four reasons that we are able to accurately assess changes to usage of LuC over this period. First, the government subsidized returns of LuC to nature. In order to receive said subsidies, rural households would not have under-reported any return of farmland to forest, grassland, or lake. There were limited funds available for such government subsidies, and so officials would not have tolerated over-reporting by rural households, and so we assume that these data are accurate. Second, there was a great disparity in compensation standards for LuC occupied for construction and LuC occupied for non-agricultural uses. In order to receive a maximum of government subsidies, rural households would not have

Table 4.3 Changes to area of LuC in China, 1998–2008, *unit* kha

		Returned to nature	Structural adjustments	Occupation for construction	Ruined by disaster	Newly added
1998	254.6	164.6				
1999	436.6	394.6	107.1	205.3	134.7	405.1
2000	962.3	762.8	265.6	163.3	61.7	291.1
2001	627.3	590.7	45.0	163.7	30.6	202.6
2002	1686.2	1425.5	274.6	196.5	56.4	266.8
2003	253.7	223.7	33.1	22.9	5.0	31.1
2004	80.0	73.3	20.5	14.5	6.3	34.6
2005	361.6	390.3	12.3	212.1	53.5	306.7
2006	306.8	339.4	40.2	258.5	35.9	367.2
2007	40.7	25.4	4.9	188.3	17.9	195.8
2008	19.3	7.6	24.9	191.6	24.8	229.6

Data source Several years of the MLR's *Land Resources Report* and *Nationwide Statistical Results of Changes to Land Usage*

under-reported the area of LuC occupied for construction, nor would the government have tolerated any over-reporting, and so we can assume that these data are also accurate. Third, the government supported restoration of LuC ruined by disaster. Although statistics for LuC ruined by disaster were not compiled as stringently as those for the previous two categories, there was still very little space for under-reporting by rural households or toleration of over-reporting by the government, and so we assume that these data as well are on the whole accurate. Fourth, newly added LuC was closely linked to government land management policies; large disparities in reported quantities were not likely, and so we assume that these data as well are accurate. Most doubts surrounding newly added LuC revolved around the quality, and not the quantity, of such land. We must note three things here. First, poor quality of newly added LuC was the norm, and not an abnormal circumstance intentionally arrived at. Second, we must note not only that it is impossible to compare the quality of newly added LuC with LuC that had been occupied for other purposes over the short term, but also that such disparities in quality gradually disappear over time. Third, in order to accelerate this process, it was necessary to adopt comprehensive policies for increasing the fertility of newly added LuC.

Fourth, estimates for the years in which increases to LuC area turned into decreases. A major issue in reconstructing LuC area data is establishing which years LuC area in China decreased instead of increasing. I think that total LuC area in China increased during the era of the people's commune. Shortly after the beginning of the Household Responsibility System, LuC area was still increasing. The reason is that when we were making estimates for the middle of the period of returning farmland to forests, we discovered that some such returned land had been initially cultivated from virgin land after the implementation of the Household Responsibility System, and not land contracted from collectives. Here we must make a generalization about what drove farmers to cultivate virgin land in different time periods. I think that increases to the area of LuC during the 1950s were linked to the impulse of peasants to own land rights. Increases to LuC area during the era of the people's commune were linked to the drive to meet or reduce government-set grain requisitioning targets. Increases to LuC area shortly after Reform and Opening were linked to the drive of rural households to retain more grain to sell privately for increased income.

Per this logic, it was my initial belief that the years in which LuC area decreased rather than increased came after 1984, and I came to accept the opinion that 1984 was the year in which the area of LuC in China was at its peak, for the following reason: there is a strong negative correlation between the potential for cultivating virgin land and the wealth of a given production team. That is to say that most production teams with the potential to cultivate virgin land were poor and located in western or mountainous regions, while most production teams lacking potential for cultivating virgin land were wealthy and located in eastern or plains regions. Nearly all production teams that implemented the Household Responsibility System in 1983 and 1984 were wealthy and lacked potential for cultivating virgin land, but those poor teams that implemented the Household Responsibility System relatively early had already exploited all potential for cultivating virgin land by 1984. Thus I accept the opinion of many academics that China reached peak area of LuC in 1984.

Fifth, estimates for years lacking data for changes to LuC area. The last task remaining is to estimate data for LuC area over the 40 years from 1958 to 1997. I think that the purpose of reconstructing these data is not to reflect fluctuations to the area of LuC, but rather to iron out such fluctuations, in order to give an outline of the trends of LuC area over these 40 years. In concrete terms, that is to say that I take 1984 as the inflection year and draw an outline of progressive additions to LuC area prior to 1984 and progressive decreases thereafter on the basis of the limited available information. My assumption is that leading up to 1984, the rate of increase to LuC area in China progressively fell, meaning that the amount of area added in each year was less than the year prior. After 1984, there were first progressive increases to the amount of LuC area lost, meaning that the amount of area lost was greater than the year prior. After a certain point, the progressive increases switched to progressively smaller amounts of LuC area lost, meaning that the amount of area lost in each year was less than the year prior. Eventually, the rate of decrease dropped to zero, and total LuC area in China stabilized. There are four reasons for the stabilization of the area of LuC in China. First, the management system for LuC is growing increasingly stringent, and execution of regulations is growing stronger. Second, the rate of urbanization as determined by markets in China has reached 56% (greater than the 20% rate of urbanization determined by the household registration system), and we are already past the peak of annual occupation of farmland for urbanization. Third, changes to usages of rural land are now concentrated in the rezoning of rural land for construction purposes, making this usage the present focus of state repurposing of rural land. Fourth, the per capita area of construction-use land in China has already exceeded the average level for developed nations. This has greatly increased the potential for land to be constructed upon and urbanized. This should further serve as another focus for increasing potential land usage in China.

4.2.2.3   The Results of Reconstructing LuC Area Data

I made three assumptions when reconstructing LuC area data. The first is that the data backing the government issuance of land certificates from 1949 to 1957 is reliable and not in need of reconstruction. The second is that 1984 was the inflection point where LuC area ceased increasing and began decreasing. The third is that the newer the data, the more sophisticated the methods and technology employed in data collection, and thus the closer to reality that data must be. Per these three assumptions, my so-called reconstructed LuC area data for 1958–2008 was calculated based on the figures for 2009–2012 released by the MLR. The concrete steps taken were as follows. (1) I deduced data in each individual year from 1998 to 2008 based on usage [zoning] changes to LuC over the same period. (2) The amount of LuC area reduced from 1985 to 1997 is equivalent to the difference between LuC area in 1998 and the area in 1984. (3) LuC area in 1984 minus LuC area in 1957 equals the total amount of LuC area added between 1958 and 1984. (4) LuC data for the period 1958–1997 can be calculated based on the above suppositions. The results of my reconstruction of China's LuC area data are as follows (see Table 4.4 and Fig. 4.4).

4.2.3   Water Resources

Agriculture consumes a much greater share of national water resources than it does land resources, and so we must pay attention to the amount of water being used for agriculture. Figure 4.5 demonstrates this. Total water consumption for agriculture in China ballooned from 100.1 billion m^3 in 1949–479.0 billion m^3 in 1995, but then gradually fell to 232.1 billion m^3 in 2011. There were small additions to water consumption for agriculture in 2012 (245.6 billion m^3) and 2013 (254.8 billion m^3), but such short-term changes do not affect the general long-term trend of decreasing water usage for agriculture; these changes may very well be the result of more accurate measurement of water usage. The primary reason for increases to water consumed for agriculture is growth of total area under irrigation. In regions with relatively sparse water resources, farmers do not lightly abandon their rights to water usage, and so increases in irrigation efficiency are often connected to increases to the total area under irrigation. To change this situation, we must develop a market for exchanging water rights. Again from 1949 to 2011, the share of water used for irrigation to total water resources fell from 97.1 to 62.0%. One must note that a portion of water used in irrigation can be recaptured and reused;

Table 4.4 Reconstructed data for LuC area in China

Year	Area	Year	Area	Year	Area	Year	Area	Year	Area
1949	11786.67	1962	13466.55	1975	14185.37	1988	14566.31	2001	14028.13
1950	11960.00	1963	13523.18	1976	14239.13	1989	14540.77	2002	13934.03
1951	12133.33	1964	13579.58	1977	14292.68	1990	14514.14	2003	13681.10
1952	12306.67	1965	13635.76	1978	14346.01	1991	14486.18	2004	13655.72
1953	12486.67	1966	13691.71	1979	14399.13	1992	14456.61	2005	13647.72
1954	12660.00	1967	13747.44	1980	14452.05	1993	14425.13	2006	13593.48
1955	12833.33	1968	13802.95	1981	14504.75	1994	14391.37	2007	13547.46
1956	13006.67	1969	13858.24	1982	14557.24	1995	14354.93	2008	13541.36
1957	13180.00	1970	13913.31	1983	14609.52	1996	14315.29	2009	13538.46
1958	13237.77	1971	13968.15	1984	14661.59	1997	14295.73	2010	13526.83
1959	13295.31	1972	14022.78	1985	14638.43	1998	14276.16	2011	13523.86
1960	13352.62	1973	14077.19	1986	14614.95	1999	14237.97	2012	13515.85
1961	13409.70	1974	14131.39	1987	14590.97	2000	14172.48	2013	

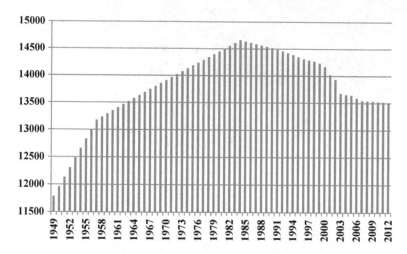

Fig. 4.4 Changes to LuC area in China based on reconstructed data (kha)

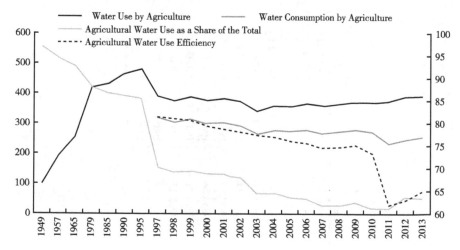

Fig. 4.5 Changes to agricultural water usage and share of water used in China (billion m³)

this is why agricultural water consumption rates are lower than water usage rates (Table 4.5).

The above analysis demonstrates that the resource factor inputs into agriculture of labor, land, and water resources shifted from increases to decreases. The reliance of agriculture on natural resources has gone from ever higher to ever lower; this is the result of a transformation in agriculture away from growth and toward development.

Table 4.5 Changes to the agricultural water usage and the share of agricultural water usage to total water usage in China

	Agricultural water usage (bn m³)	Agricultural water usage share (%)	Agricultural water consumption (bn m³)	Agricultural water consumption share (%)
1949	100.1	97.1		
1957	193.8	94.6		
1965	254.5	92.7		
1979	419.5	88.0		
1985	432.3	86.7		
1990	466.4	86.2		
1995	479.0	85.4		
1997	392.0	70.4	319.1	81.4
1998	376.6	69.3	305.0	81.0
1999	386.9	69.2	311.8	80.6
2000	378.4	68.8	301.2	79.6
2001	382.5	68.7	301.4	78.8
2002	373.8	68.0	291.9	78.1
2003	343.1	64.5	265.2	77.3
2004	358.4	64.6	276.0	77.0
2005	358.3	63.6	273.0	76.2
2006	366.2	63.2	277.2	75.7
2007	360.2	61.9	268.7	74.6
2008	366.4	62.0	273.7	74.7
2009	372.2	62.4	279.5	75.1
2010	369.1	61.3	271.7	73.6
2011	374.4	61.3	232.1	62.0
2012	389.9	63.6	245.6	63.0
2013	392.0	63.4	254.8	65.0

Data source Several years of the *China Water Resources Yearbook* and *Water Resources Report*, both published by the Ministry of Water Resources

4.2.4 Capital Inputs

Since Reform and Opening, the effects of capital production factors such as farm machinery, farming infrastructure, chemical fertilizers, and pesticides on agriculture have been different from those of resource production factors such as arable land, fresh water, and labor. Their contribution rate to agricultural growth displays a rising trend. As it is difficult to produce a clear figure for the absolute degree of change effected by the influence of capital inputs on agricultural development, I have chosen the four indicators of comprehensive mechanization rate, irrigation rate, commodization rate of seeds, and rate of soil fertilization based on testing—all of which have the potential to replace labor inputs, land inputs, and fertilizer inputs and the greatest value of such for each is 100%—to reflect changes to the amount of influence exerted by capital inputs on agricultural development.

4.2.4.1   Comprehensive Mechanization Rate

The comprehensive mechanization rate of agriculture is a weighted average of the rates of mechanization of tilling, seed broadcasting, and harvesting. The formula is $0.4 * C_1 + 0.3 * C_2 + 0.3 * C_3$, where all three C values are mechanization rates, C_1 being the tilling rate, C_2 being the seed broadcasting rate, and C_3 being the harvesting rate. All three C values are the percentage of LuC upon which said practice is mechanized (land not requiring tilling has been excluded from calculations of the tilling mechanization rate). As demonstrated in Fig. 4.6, from China's comprehensive mechanization rate of agriculture rose from 18.8 to 61.0%, a 3.2-fold increase, from 1978 to 2014. The rate increased 10.2% over the 22-year span from 1978 to 2000, an average annual increase of 0.46%, but it increased 32% over the 14-year span from 2000 to 2014, an average annual increase of 2.29%. The average annual increase rate over the latter 14 years was nearly six times that of the former 22, which demonstrates that growth of China's comprehensive mechanization rate of agriculture accelerated markedly in the 21st century.

4.2.4.2   Irrigation Rate

The irrigation rate is the percentage of LuC which is effectively irrigated. Hydrothermal synchronization in China's agricultural regions is not very good, and so in most regions irrigation is employed to resolve this problem. For several thousand years, Chinese rural households have consistently placed emphasis on the

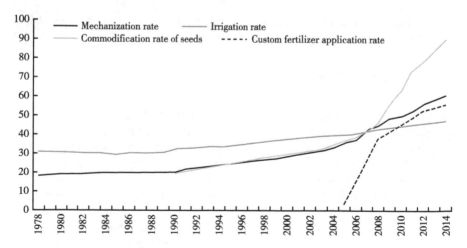

Fig. 4.6 Changes to agricultural capital inputs

construction of irrigation works, and so China's irrigation rate was already 31.3% at the outset of Reform and Opening. As can be seen in Fig. 4.6, the irrigation rate grew from 31.3% in 1978 to 47.5% in 2014, an increase of 16.2%. The rate increased by 6.7% over the 22-year span from 1978 to 2000, for an average annual increase of 0.30%. The rate increased a further 9.5% over the 14-year span from 2000 to 2014, for an average annual increase of 0.68%. The latter 14 year period thus experienced 3.23 times the growth in this rate of the former 22 year period. This demonstrates that growth to China's irrigation rate has accelerated markedly in the 21st century.

4.2.4.3 Rate of Seed Commoditization

The quality of seeds determines the fertilizer tolerance and photosynthesis rates of crops. Seed quality further determines the foundations upon which crop yields and crop quality are based. Therefore, the development and promulgation of improved varieties is the fundamental means of improving crop yields and quality. That said, different varieties work better in different stages of agricultural development. During the stage in which "every family farmed, and every household reserved seeds", individual rural households were responsible for their own crop variety improvement. The quality of improved varieties was relatively low, and so disparities were relatively great. During the stage of "four selfs and one supplement" (namely self-breeding, self-selection, self-retaining, self-using, and supplementary compounds), there emerged a specialized seed breeding industry and different compounds used to supplement improved varieties from region to region. When the quality of improved varieties rose, disparities reduced, but there were no major breakthroughs made in variety improvement. During the period of "four-ations and one supply" (namely production specialization, processing mechanization, quality standardization, and distribution regionalization), production, processing, and sales of improved varieties grew into an independent industry within agriculture. It was at this time that breakthroughs were made in the quality of improved varieties. During the stage of "seed engineering" (including testing, production, processing, promulgation, sales, and management), a further breakthrough was made in the quality of improved varieties, and there were increases to all of the four aforementioned "-ations". Per the changes that have transpired across the stages of improved variety development, I proffer that the commoditization rate of seeds is the best indicator for comparability and additive nature of the usage of improved varieties. As is demonstrated in Fig. 4.6, China's rate of seed commoditization was only around 20% in 1990, but rose to 30% by 2000, 84% by 2014, and is estimated to hit 90% in 2015, thus meeting the state-set objectives for the "seed engineering" program.[1]

---

[1]The target set by this program was to reach a seed commoditization rate of 90% by 2010, which would bring China close to the rates of developed nations. This target is expected to be reached five years later than stipulated by the program.

4.2.4.4   Rate of Soil Fertilization Based on Testing

The rate of soil fertilization based on testing is the percentage of total area of seed broadcasting upon which the technology of testing the soil in order to administer proper amounts of fertilizer is applied. This technology was first applied in China in 2005. In 2014, this technology had been spread to over 1.4 billion μ of LuC, affecting over two thirds of nationwide rural households. This technology allows for data collected during soil surveys to be used to maximum effectiveness. During the course of my research, I discovered that government administration departments that have mastered soil surveys publicly display spatial positioning maps divided into numbered sections of each village under their administration within the corresponding villages. These departments further promise that rural households need only call their local land management bureau with the spatial positioning numbers of their land in order to receive all fertilization data collected on said land. The results of a sampling survey of rural households indicated that yields of wheat, rice, and corn increased by 3.7, 3.8, and 5.9%, respectively, and that incomes increase by 30 yuan/μ, when this technology is used. Per μ income increases can go up to 100 yuan or higher on fields planted with vegetables and fruits. This method has decreased the amount of unnecessary fertilizer usage by an average of over one million tonnes per year.

On the whole, although China's irrigation rate dropped slightly during the period of transition from collective operations to household responsibility, all three of these indicators have experienced more or less steady increases. Hydrothermal synchronization and the match between allocations of water and land resources in China are not good. Much farmland in China's western regions lack the water resources necessary for irrigation; this is the primary reason for the relative sloth in increases to the irrigation rate. Some of China's farmland is located on steep slopes in mountainous regions, divided into very small plots, making mechanization inappropriate; this is the primary reason that China's agricultural mechanization rate is still not extraordinarily high. The usage of chemical fertilizers usually needs to be accompanied by a corresponding amount of water resources. Chemical fertilizers are not suitable on farmland where water is particularly scarce; this is the primary reason that the rate of soil fertilization based on testing has not been extended to all LuC. I emphasize these points in particular to demonstrate that it is not practical to expect any of these indicators to reach 100%.

4.2.4.5   Agricultural Plastic Sheeting

Covering fields with plastic sheeting is an important measure for maintaining stability of agricultural production in dry areas. In 1979, the total area of LuC covered by such sheeting in China was only 44 ha. That figure rose from 2040.7 kha in 1988 to 27,575.7 kha in 2014 (see Table 4.6), a 13.5-fold increase. In addition, there are also several million μ of LuC in China meeting irrigation conditions that are covered by raised sheeting (greenhouses). In order to avoid counting such land

Table 4.6 Changes to agricultural capital inputs, *units* %, kilotonnes, and kha

	Comprehensive mechanization rate	Irrigation rate	Commoditization rate of seeds	Rate of soil fertilized per testing results	Chemical fertilization rate	Area of farmland covered by agricultural sheeting
1978	18.8	31.3			8840.0	
1979	19.0	31.3			10863.0	
1980	19.3	31.1			12694.0	
1981	19.4	30.7			13349.0	
1982	19.5	30.3			15134.0	
1983	19.6	30.6			16598.0	
1984	19.8	30.3			17398.0	
1985	20.0	30.1			17758.0	
1986	20.1	30.3			19306.0	
1987	20.2	30.4			19993.0	
1988	20.3	30.5			21415.0	2040.7
1989	20.5	30.9			23571.0	2776.9
1990	20.7	32.7	20.0		25903.0	3513.2
1991	22.1	33.0	21.0		28051.0	4249.4
1992	22.8	33.6	22.0		29302.0	4985.7
1993	23.5	33.8	23.0		31519.0	5721.9
1994	24.2	33.9	24.0		33179.0	6244.3
1995	24.9	34.3	25.0		35937.0	6494.0
1996	25.6	35.2	26.0		38279.0	7449.0
1997	26.3	35.8	27.0		39807.0	9150.0
1998	27.0	36.6	28.0		40837.0	10034.0
1999	27.7	37.3	29.0		41243.2	10114.6
2000	29.0	38.0	30.0		41464.1	10602.8

(continued)

Table 4.6 (continued)

	Comprehensive mechanization rate	Irrigation rate	Commoditization rate of seeds	Rate of soil fertilized per testing results	Chemical fertilization rate	Area of farmland covered by agricultural sheeting
2001	30.0	38.7	31.0		42537.6	10960.7
2002	31.0	39.0	32.0		43393.9	11701.1
2003	32.0	39.5	33.0		44115.6	11966.9
2004	33.5	39.9	35.0		46365.8	13063.2
2005	35.9	40.3	37.0	4.3	47662.2	13538.4
2006	38.0	41.0	39.0	15.8	49276.9	14144.4
2007	42.5	41.7	42.0	27.8	51078.3	14938.4
2008	45.0	43.2	47.0	38.4	52390.2	15308.1
2009	48.8	43.8	56.0	42.0	54044.0	15501.1
2010	50.0	44.6	63.0	45.6	55616.8	15595.6
2011	52.3	45.6	73.0	49.3	57042.4	19790.5
2012	56.0	46.2	78.0	53.0	58388.5	23333.3
2013	59.0	47.0	84.0	54.7	59118.6	25454.5
2014	61.0	47.5	90.0	56.3	59709.8	27575.7

Data source Data provided by the National Bureau of Statistics and Ministry of Agriculture

twice, greenhouse covered land was not included in the area of LuC covered with on-the-ground sheeting. That is to say that I counted only land in dry regions covered with on-the-ground sheeting here, and did not include any greenhouse-covered land, including those in regions that require irrigation.

4.2.4.6   Chemical Fertilizers

From 1978 to 2014, the total amount of chemical fertilizers employed in Chinese agriculture grew from 8840 to 59,710 kilotonnes, a 6.75-fold increase. Average chemical fertilizer usage in China was in 1993 less than the established standard of 225 kg/ha; excessive use of chemical fertilizers began in 1994. Average per hectare use of chemical fertilizers in 2014 was 442.3 kilograms, nearly double the allowable standard. On the one hand, rapid increases to chemical fertilizer use have played a positive role in increased agricultural yields in China, but on the other hand, this has exerted an egregious negative impact on China's water and soil. At present, reducing quantities of chemical fertilizers used has become a focus of China's agricultural policies.

4.2.5   Adjustments to the Agricultural Structure

As indicated in Fig. 4.7, if one divides agriculture in China into two stages, pre-Reform (and Opening) and post-Reform, one can see striking differences in the agricultural structure between these two stages. In the pre-Reform stage, the agricultural structure in China was relatively stable, but adjustments were made rapidly in the post-Reform stage.

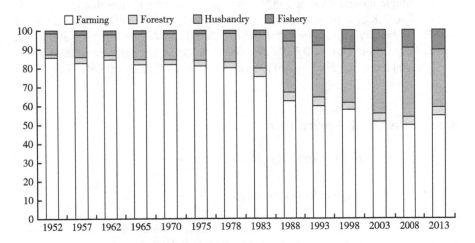

Fig. 4.7 Changes to China's agricultural structure

Table 4.7 Changes to China's agricultural structure

	Planting	Forestry	Husbandry	Fisheries
1952	85.9	1.6	11.2	1.3
1957	82.7	3.3	12.2	1.9
1962	84.7	2.2	10.9	2.2
1965	82.2	2.7	13.4	1.8
1970	82.1	2.8	13.4	1.7
1975	81.0	3.1	14.2	1.7
1978	80.0	3.4	15.0	1.6
1983	75.4	4.6	17.6	2.3
1988	62.5	4.7	27.3	5.5
1993	60.1	4.5	27.4	8.0
1998	58.0	3.5	28.6	9.9
2003	51.7	4.3	33.1	10.9
2008	50.1	3.8	36.8	9.3
2013	55.1	4.2	30.4	10.3

Data source Data published on the website of the National Bureau of Statistics

Over the 26 years from 1952 to 1978, the share of total agricultural output attributable to the planting industry fell from 85.9 to 80.0%, a reduction of 5.9 percentage points, for an average annual drop of 0.23%. The share attributable to forestry, on the other hand, rose from 1.6 to 3.4%, a total increase of 1.8%, an average annual growth of 0.07%. Husbandry's share grew from 11.2 to 15.0%, a total increase of 3.8%, an average annual growth of 0.14%. The share attributable to fisheries increased from 1.3 to 1.6%, a total growth of 0.3%, and an average annual growth of 0.01%.

Over the 30 years from 1978 to 2008, the share of total agricultural output attributable to the planting industry fell from 80.0 to 50.1%, a total drop of 29.9%, for an average annual drop of 1.00%. Over the same period, forestry's share grew from 3.4 to 3.8%, a total increase of 0.40%, and an average annual increase of 0.01%. Husbandry's share grew from 15.0 to 36.8%, a total growth of 21.8% and an average annual increase of 0.73%. The fisheries industry's share grew from 1.6 to 9.3%, a total increase of 0.73% and an average annual increase of 0.26% (Table 4.7).

4.3   Growth of Agriculture

4.3.1   Material Productivity of Agriculture

4.3.1.1   Primary Agricultural Products

Yields of agricultural products grew rapidly in China shortly after the enactment of Reform and Opening. Once we entered a stage of balanced total yields and annual agricultural surpluses in the late 1990s, the rate of increase to yields of primary agricultural products fell off, but overall speed remained high. Now, over 30 years later, the greatest advance in Chinese agriculture is the marked increase to the stability of agricultural product yields. As indicated in Fig. 4.8, over the two periods 1978–1980 and 1996–2000, the average annual grain yield grew from 319.15 to 496.31 million tonnes, an average annual growth of 2.23%. Over the same period, average annual cotton yields grew from 2.36 million tonnes to 4.31 million tonnes, an average annual growth of 3.06%. Average annual cotton yields grew from 6.45 million to 24.48 million tonnes, an average annual increase of 6.90%. Average annual vegetable yields grew from 257.27 million tonnes over the years 1991–1995 to 379.12 million tonnes over the period 1996–2000, an average annual increase of 8.06%. Since entry into the 21st century, average annual grain yields have increased from 496.31 to 592.46 million tonnes, an average annual increase of 1.27%. Over the same period, average annual cotton yields have increased from 4.31 to 6.47 million tonnes, an average annual increase of 2.94%. Oil crop yields have grown from 24.48 to 34.44 million tonnes, an average annual increase of 2.47%. Average annual vegetable yields have grown from 379.12 to 718.00 million tonnes, an average annual increase of 4.67% (Table 4.8).

4.3.1.2 Per Capita Share of Primary Agricultural Products

Under the dual effects of stable growth to grain yields and steady slowing of population growth, China's 2012 per capita grain yield of 435.4 kg was 116.4 kg higher than the 1978 figure and 69.3 kg higher than the 2000 figure. The 2012 yield of pork, beef, and lamb was 45.5 kg higher than in 1978 and 17.0 kg higher than in 2000. The 2012 fisheries products yield was 38.7 kg higher than in 1978 and 14.2 kg higher than in 2000. The 2012 cow's milk yield was 27.7 kg higher than in

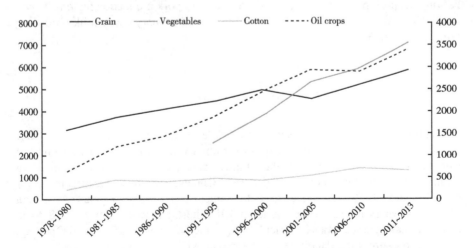

Fig. 4.8 Yields of grain, cotton, oil crops, and vegetables in China since reform and opening

Table 4.8 Yields of grain, cotton, oil crops, and vegetables in China since reform and opening, *unit* mn tonnes

	Grain	Cotton	Oil crops	Vegetables
1978–1980	319.15	2.36	6.45	
1981–1985	370.64	4.32	12.05	
1986–1990	408.47	4.05	14.46	
1991–1995	449.23	4.61	18.65	257.27
1996–2000	496.31	4.31	24.48	379.12
2001–2005	458.78	5.43	29.43	533.66
2006–2010	521.13	7.00	29.09	593.14
2011–2014	592.46	6.47	34.44	718.00

Data source Several years of the *China Statistical Yearbook*, published by the National Bureau of Statistics

1978 and 21.1 kg higher than in 2000. The 2012 yield of oil crops was 20.2 kg higher than in 1978 and 2.3 kg higher than in 2000. The 2012 cotton yield was 2.8 kg higher than in 1978 and 1.6 kg higher than in 2000. The per capita share of agricultural products in China has already reached the global average in all but a few particular products, and China's per capita food share is already at the average level of East Asian economies.

4.3.1.3 Production Concentration of Primary Agricultural Products

The share of nationwide grain yields of the 13 primary grain producing regions increased from 69.21% from 1959 to 1959 to 77.78% from 2010 to 2012, for an increase of 8.57% (this despite the fact that the former period included Chongqing and not the latter period). The general state of affairs now is soybeans and corn in the Northeast, peanuts and wheat in the Huang-Huai-Hai region, rapeseeds in the Yangtze River Basin, and cotton in the Yellow River Basin and the Northwest. The nationwide pork production share of the 13 primary pork production regions is over 75%. The nationwide cow's milk share of the seven primary cow's milk producing regions is over 60%.

4.3.2 Value Productivity of Agriculture

Agricultural productivity can be expressed in terms of land productivity and labor productivity, where land productivity is the output value of planting per area unit of LuC, and labor productivity is the output value per unit of labor required in planting, forestry, husbandry, and fisheries. Chinese statistical departments commonly employ 1952 fixed prices to make comparisons across the years. As a span of over 60 years now separates us from 1952, here I have employed 1978 fixed prices to make comparisons in agricultural productivity since Reform and Opening, in order to express the data in terms the reader will more easily relate to.

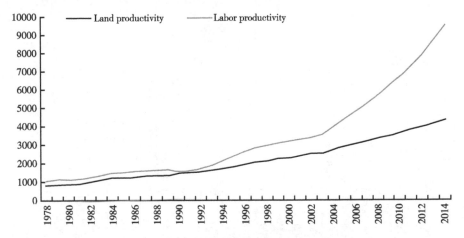

Fig. 4.9 Land and labor productivity in Chinese agriculture since reform and opening

4.3.2.1   Land Productivity

As indicated in Fig. 4.9, over the 36 years of Reform and Opening, China's LuC productivity and agricultural labor productivity have both been highly progressive and stable. Despite fluctuations to LuC productivity and a slight dip in agricultural labor productivity during the period of adjustments from 1989 to 1991, there have been no subsequent major drops or rises like those prior to Reform and Opening. In concrete terms, LuC productivity in China rose from 779 yuan/ha in 1978–4296 yuan/ha in 2014, a 5.5-fold increase, and an average annual increase of 4.86%.

4.3.2.2   Labor Productivity

Agricultural labor productivity grew from 1017 yuan in 1978 to 9483 yuan in 2014, a 9.3-fold growth, and an average annual growth of 6.40%. Elasticity of demand for agricultural products is extremely low, and so it was no easy task for Chinese agriculture to maintain annual growth of five to six percent over 36 years (Table 4.9).

4.3.3   Technological Productivity of Agriculture

4.3.3.1   Increasing Contributions of Agricultural Total Factor Productivity

Our research demonstrates that over the period 1985–2010, agricultural total factor productivity (TFP) in China increased approximately one percentage point per year (see Table 4.10). Data issued by the Ministry of Agriculture indicate that the

Table 4.9 Land and labor productivity in Chinese agriculture since reform and opening, *units* yuan/kg, yuan/person

	Land productivity	Labor productivity		Land productivity	Labor productivity		Land productivity	Labor productivity
1978	779	1017	1991	1452	1558	2004	2746	3962
1979	828	1082	1992	1517	1671	2005	2860	4362
1980	823	1079	1993	1599	1854	2006	3026	4814
1981	876	1124	1994	1654	2071	2007	3155	5197
1982	968	1206	1995	1789	2368	2008	3307	5643
1983	1046	1288	1996	1934	2644	2009	3435	6113
1984	1162	1459	1997	2024	2820	2010	3577	6603
1985	1162	1496	1998	2126	2959	2011	3780	7244
1986	1196	1541	1999	2224	3045	2012	3948	7842
1987	1274	1609	2000	2265	3131	2013	4124	8696
1988	1293	1642	2001	2371	3232	2014	4296	9483
1989	1327	1643	2002	2480	3369			
1990	1436	1510	2003	2526	3546			

Table 4.10 Growth rate of Chinese agricultural TFP and breakdown (1985–2010)

Year	Technological efficiency	Technological progress	TFP	Year	Technological efficiency	Technological progress	TFP
1986/1985	0.964	1.086	1.048	2001/2000	0.986	1.027	1.012
1987/1986	0.997	1.000	0.996	2002/2001	1.006	0.990	0.996
1988/1987	0.978	1.077	1.053	2003/2002	0.976	1.092	1.066
1989/1988	1.008	1.039	1.047	2004/2003	0.997	1.125	1.122
1990/1989	1.007	1.025	1.033	2005/2004	0.970	1.055	1.023
1991/1990	0.972	1.014	0.986	2006/2005	1.208	1.050	1.269
1992/1991	0.939	1.052	0.987	2007/2006	0.808	1.074	0.868
1993/1992	0.988	1.165	1.150	2008/2007	0.997	1.103	1.100
1994/1993	0.979	1.120	1.097	2009/2008	1.021	1.030	1.052
1995/1994	1.047	1.096	1.147	2010/2009	0.992	1.028	1.020
1996/1995	0.989	1.061	1.049	1989/1985	0.983	1.058	1.036
1997/1996	0.954	1.030	0.982	1995/1990	0.988	1.077	1.064
1998/1997	0.992	0.952	0.944	2003/1996	0.987	1.015	1.001
1999/1998	1.025	0.970	0.994	2004/2010	0.993	1.066	1.059
2000/1999	0.966	1.008	0.973	2010/1985	0.988	1.051	1.038

Note Nationwide figures calculated per geometric mean of data from each individual province

contribution rate of technological advances to agricultural growth was 54.5% in 2012.

4.3.3.2 Gains in Agricultural TFP Stem from Technological Advances

From 1985 to 2010, average annual growth of agricultural TFP in China was 3.8%. Of that total, the average annual growth to agricultural technology was 5.1%, while the average annual growth of agricultural technological efficiency was negative 1.2%. Technological advances drove growth to China's agricultural TFP, while a drop in technological efficiency detracted from overall growth to the figure.

The results are the same whether one divides the period studied into four sub-periods (1985–1989, 1990–1995, 1996–2003, and 2004–2010), or divides the data between primary grain-producing regions and non-grain-producing regions, or between east, center, and west. This demonstrates that growth to agricultural TFP over this period was technologically induced.

4.3.3.3 Room for Gains in Technological Efficiency Greater Than Room for Gains in Scale Efficiency

As indicated in Table 4.11, China's grain production technological efficiency is 0.795, which leaves a great deal of room for improvement. China's grain production scale efficiency, on the other hand, is 0.957, leaving little room for improvement. The research of Xu Qing et al. demonstrates that there is nearly no marked scale efficiency in wheat, rice, and corn. Increasing the scale of land operations has a pronounced impact on reducing production costs, as every μ of increased scale can reduce costs between two and 10%. That is to say that increases to the scale of agricultural operations has a pronounced effect on increasing the incomes of rural citizens.

4.4 Development in Other Agricultural Sectors

There have been two pronounced changes in the forestry, husbandry, and fisheries industries since Reform and Opening. The first is that growth in these industries has outstripped that of the planting industry (see Table 4.7 and Fig. 4.7). The second is that the transition from priority on production to priority on the environment of these industries has been more marked than in the planting industry. The faster growth in these industries is primarily the result of market demand. In addition, the replacement of the strategy of "taking grain as the key" by comprehensive development of agriculture, forestry, husbandry, and fisheries has also played a positive role. The transition from priority on production to priority on the environment in the forestry, husbandry, and fisheries industries has been the result of a strengthening of

Table 4.11 Economic efficiency of Chinese grain production

Region	Technological efficiency	Scale efficiency	Region	Technological efficiency	Scale efficiency	Region	Technological efficiency	Scale efficiency
Beijing	0.766	0.999	Anhui	0.786	0.878	Sichuan	0.861	0.810
Tianjin	0.745	0.980	Fujian	0.795	0.940	Guizhou	0.708	0.940
Hebei	0.748	0.907	Jiangxi	0.834	0.995	Yunnan	0.574	0.998
Shanxi	0.570	0.984	Shandong	1.00	0.905	Tibet	1.00	1.00
Inner Mongol.	0.719	0.951	Henan	1.00	0.831	Shaanxi	0.524	0.985
Liaoning	0.868	0.993	Hubei	0.864	0.954	Gansu	0.536	0.974
Jilin	1.00	1.00	Hunan	0.908	0.971	Qinghai	0.623	0.960
Heilongjiang	1.00	1.00	Guangdong	0.796	0.951	Ningxia	0.625	0.997
Shanghai	1.00	1.00	Guangxi	0.698	0.966	Xinjiang	0.954	0.957
Jiangsu	0.989	0.938	Hainan	0.648	0.961	Nationwide	0.795	0.957
Zhejiang	0.917	0.969	Chongqing	0.596	0.980			

Data source Yang Tianrong et al., "Analysis of the Efficiency of Specialized Production in Chinese Grain Producing Regions", *Southwest Agricultural University Journal (Social Sciences Edition)*, (2009) 6

the consciousness of environmental protection on the part of the people as well as economic development. The upsurge in enthusiasm for environmental protection and ecological balance first emerged shortly after the beginning of Reform and Opening, but for the first 20 years thereafter, the influence of such thought on national policies and the thinking of Chinese people was very limited. The major floods in the Yangtze River Basin in 1998 marked an inflection point in the transformation of the forestry, husbandry, and fisheries industries. To reverse the continued loss of forests and grasslands and the shrinking of wetlands, the state rolled out a series of focus environmental projects for protection of natural forests, returning farmland to forests, returning pasture land to grasslands, and returning fields to lakes. The implementation of these environmental projects effectively promoted the protection and construction of the three major ecological systems of forests, grasslands, and wetlands. After over 10 years of efforts, we began to see initial reversals in the trends of these three major systems. One should note that the formerly established objectives were merely initial objectives; in order to increase the sustainability of the forestry, husbandry, and fisheries industries, we must continue to increase development goals and push growth in these three industries, with priority on the environment, toward higher levels of development.

4.4.1 Forest Protection and Construction

The proportion of China's terrain covered by forests increased from 12.7% at the beginning of Reform and Opening to 21.63% at present, an increase of 8.93%. Over the same period, the area of forested land increased from 121.86 to 208.00 million ha, an increase of 70.7%. The total volume of live trees and forest volume in China increased from 9.532 billion and 8.856 billion m^3 to 16.433 billion and 15.137 billion m^3, respectively, for respective increases of 72.4 and 70.9%. Growth rates for live wood volume and forest volume were nearly identical, demonstrating that China's forests are not at all the way some describe them: increases only to forested area without related increases to forest volume (Table 4.12).

To eliminate the negative environmental impact of logging in natural forests, China launched the natural forest protection program in 1998. This program affected forest resources in the focus state-owned forest areas of the upper reaches of the Yangtze River, the upper and middle reaches of the Yellow River, the Northeast, and Inner Mongolia. Stage one of the program was divided into two segments, the first (2000–2005) aimed at halting logging in natural forests, constructing ecological public welfare forests, and making arrangements for newly unemployed workers. The second segment (2006–2010) was aimed at protecting natural forest resources, allowing regrowth of forests and grasslands, and promoting sustainable development of the economy and society. Total investment in the program was 96.2 billion yuan. This program effectively protected 56.00 million ha of natural forests, planted 15.267 million ha of public welfare forests, and caused a net increase to forest volume of 460 million m^3.

Table 4.12 Changes to total forested area and forest volume in China

	1st Forest resources survey	2nd Forest resources survey	3rd Forest resources survey	4th Forest resources survey	5th Forest resources survey	6th Forest resources survey	7th Forest resources survey	8th Forest resources survey
	73–76	77–81	84–88	89–93	94–98	99–03	04–08	09–13
Forest coverage (%)	12.7	12	12.98	13.92	16.55	18.21	20.36	21.63
Total volume of live wood	95.32	102.61	105.72	117.85	124.88	136.18	149.13	164.33
Forested area	12186	11528	12465	13370	15894	17500	19545	20800
Forest volume	88.56	90.28	91.41	101.37	112.67	124.56	137.21	151.37
Natural forest area						11576	11969	12200
Natural forest volume						105.93	114.02	122.96
Man-made forest area					4667	5326	6169	6900
Man-made forest volume					10.1	15.05	19.61	24.83

In 2011, the natural forest protection program entered its second stage, with a total investment of 244.02 billion yuan. Primary objectives were to, by 2020: increase the area of public welfare forests by 115.50 million μ, increase forested area by 78.00 million μ, increase forest volume by 1.1 billion m³, add 416 million tonnes of carbon sinks, drive pronounced growth in biodiversity, and bring about harmony and stability in forest areas.

The programs for returning farmland to forests and grasslands are the ecological construction programs that have had, to date, the largest investments, the broadest affected area, the most onerous duties, and the most public participation in China. Investment in stage one of this program was 224.5 billion yuan. A total of 364 million μ of new forest was added, and two percent or more of additional forest coverage was achieved in program areas, via the returning of farmland to forest, the creation of forests on desolate mountains, and the enclosing of mountains to grow forests. In 2007, upon the expiry of the state subsidies in grain for farmland returned to forests and living expenses, the state recapitalized the project with 206.6 billion yuan, to continue the payment of subsidies to rural families affected. The total investment in both stages of the program has been 431.1 billion yuan.

China has also implemented a program for construction and protection of the forest system, a program for sandstorm prevention in the area around Beijing, a program for establishing protection areas for protecting wild animals and nature, and a program for rapidly growing high-yield forests. Driven by these programs, the speed of forestry construction in China has increased greatly. If one compares the results of the first and seventh forest resource surveys, one will note that the total area of forested area in China has increased from 121.86 million μ to 195.45 μ, an increase of 60.4%. Over the same period, the volume of live wood has increased from 9.53 billion m³ to 14.91 billion m³, a growth of 56.45%, and the percentage of forested area has increased from 12.70 to 20.36%.

The implementation of these six major forestry programs has achieved an annual carbon sequestration of 338.22 million tonnes, of which newly added forests are responsible for 175.00 million tonnes, accounting for over half of annual carbon sequestration. This has been a major contribution to alleviating the negative effects of climate change (Table 4.13).

4.4.2   Grassland Protection and Construction

Since the beginning of Reform and Opening, we first transitioned from a strategy of "dual contracting of grass and livestock", which aimed to increase only the quantity of livestock products, into a strategy of "more grass and more livestock, increases to both quality and efficiency". We then transitioned into a strategy of "removing livestock and regrowing grassland, enclosing and moving". This marked an initial transition from sole focus on economy toward focus on the environment and also marked the beginning of placing priority on the environment.

Table 4.13 Carbon sequestration contributions of China's six major forestry programs

	Total forest area in program		Newly added forest in program	
	Total area (km^2)	Annual carbon sequestration (mn tonnes)	Total area (km^2)	Annual carbon sequestration (mn tonnes)
Returning farmland to forests program	319,800	73.46	273,000	71.08
Beijing area sandstorm control program	49,400	11.13	31,700	7.13
Natural forest protection program	388,800	94.99	83,900	18.99
Forest protection program	344,000	95.46	142,700	37.60
Rapid growth of high-yield forests program	133,300	40.20	133,300	40.20
Natural forest area protection program	97,400	22.98	0	0
Total	1.3327 mn	338.22	664,600	175.00

From 2003 to 2010, the total investment in the "returning pastures to grasslands" program was 14.3 billion yuan, of which 10 billion yuan came from central government subsidies and the remaining 4.3 billion came from local governments. Concrete measures taken were as follows. The government paid 5.5 kg of feed (4.95 yuan) per μ of pasture on which grazing was now forbidden per year. The government paid a further subsidy of 1.375 kg (1.2375 yuan) per μ of land per year for seasonal recuperation of grasslands, calculated at a rate of three months of feed per year. The limitation on all these subsidies was five years. Subsidies for enclosed grasslands were 16.5 yuan/μ per year.

To fortify environmental protection of grasslands, convert the development mode of the livestock industry, promote sustained income increases for herders, and maintain national ecological security, beginning in 2011, the central government laid out 13.6 billion yuan for the establishment of grasslands environmental protection subsidies and reward mechanisms in the eight major grassland provinces (or autonomous regions) of Inner Mongolia, Xinjiang, Tibet, Qinghai, Sichuan, Gansu, Ningxia, and Sichuan. Concrete measures taken were as follows:

1. Subsidies paid on grasslands forbidden for pasturing use. Subsidies of 90 yuan/ha were paid for grasslands on which pasturing was strictly forbidden to promote grassland regrowth.
2. Rewards paid for promoting balance between grassland and livestock. Subsidies of 22.5 yuan/ha were paid to herders raising a reasonable amount of livestock on a given area of grassland, outside of those areas forbidden to pasturing, to reward their not exceeding the land's carrying capacity.

3. Subsidies for herder production. Subsidies paid for improved livestock varieties were increased, and the scope of subsidies was increased from only meat cattle and sheep to include yaks and goats. The government paid a standard subsidy of 150 yuan/ha on 6 million ha of man-made pastureland in the eight provinces (or autonomous regions) for improved varieties of grass. Comprehensive means of production subsidies were paid at a standard of 500 yuan per household to nearly 2 million herder households in the eight provinces (or autonomous regions).

The program to return pasturelands to grasslands has effected pasturing bans on 440 million μ of grasslands. Reports from the China Grassland Monitoring and Supervision Center indicate that in areas affected by the program, coverage rates, height, and grass yields are, respectively, 29, 64, and 78% higher than in non-program areas.

Beginning in 2005, grasslands management departments of the Chinese government conducted nationwide grasslands surveys and published annual reports thereof. The data contained in these reports indicate that (see Table 4.14) from 2005 to 2013, total grass yields on natural grasslands in China increased from 937.84 million tonnes to 1.02220 billion tonnes, an increase of 6.9%. The livestock overload rate fell by 18.8% from 34.0% in 2006 to 15.2% in 2014. Due to the encouragement of raising livestock in pens and purchasing straw and feed from agricultural areas, a portion of the excessive quantity of livestock in pasture areas was sold to agricultural areas to be fattened there, and so the actual overcapacity rate will continue to decrease somewhat. These data demonstrate that China's grassland ecological systems are stably improving. Analysis indicates that the elimination of the livestock tax has killed local governments' incentives to develop livestock husbandry on grasslands, while increases to alternative means of earning a living have caused continuous reductions to the amount of herders willing to raise

Table 4.14 Changes to primary productivity of the grasslands ecological system

	Grass yield on natural grasslands (mn tonnes)	Converted to straw (mn tonnes)	Livestock carrying capacity (mn sheep)	Livestock overloading rate (%)
2005	937.84	294.21	230.31	–
2006	943.13	295.87	231.61	34.0
2007	952.14	298.65	233.69	33.0
2008	947.16	296.27	231.78	32.0
2009	938.41	293.64	230.99	31.0
2010	976.32	305.50	240.13	30.0
2011	1002.48	313.22	246.20	28.0
2012	1049.62	323.88	254.57	23.0
2013	1055.81	325.43	255.79	16.8
2014	1022.20			15.2

Data source China Grassland Monitoring and Supervision Center reports, 2005–2014

Table 4.15 Changes to the grades of grassland in China

	Grades 1 and 2 (%)	Grades 3 and 4 (%)	Grades 5 and 6	Grade 7 (%)	Grade 8 (%)
1970s	9	18	33	18	22
2009	7	12	19	22	40
2010	8	13	26%	20	33
2011	7	15	29%	19	30
2012	7	18	31%	17	27
2013	6	16	34%	18	26

Data source China Grassland Monitoring and Supervision Center reports, 2009–2014, and grassland surveys from the 1970s

livestock in natural grasslands. As the husbandry industry on grasslands gradually reduces, the impact of husbandry on grasslands will continue to decrease.

As indicated in Table 4.15, there is a degree of difference in the quality of China's grasslands from the 1970s to 2013. There was a three percent reduction to share of grasslands rated grade one[2] and two, and a reduction of two percent to the share of grasslands rated grade three and four. There was a one percent increase to the share of grasslands rated grade five and six, and a the share of grasslands rated grades seven and eight remained steady, with a gain of four percent for the share of grade eight grasslands. In particular, when one looks at all these data together, one can see that the trend for reduced quality of grasslands has come under control.

4.4.3 Wetlands Protection and Construction

From the 1950s to the 1970s, a great area of lakes and wetlands in China were reclaimed as farmland. Once basic food self-sustenance was achieved in the mid-1980s, the state began implementing the "returning fields to lakes" policy. This program brought about a historical transition overturning the thousands of years during which Chinese reclaimed land from lakes and wetlands and began returning farmland to lakes at a great scale.

The State Council approved "Nationwide Wetlands Protection Program Plan (2002–2030)" includes objectives for effective protection of 90% or more of nationwide wetlands by 2030, allowing full effects of the wetlands ecological system, and bringing about sustainable use of wetlands resources.

The results of the second nationwide wetlands resources survey conducted over the years 2009–2013 indicate a total nationwide wetlands area of 53.6026 million ha, a reduction of 3.3963 million ha from the first survey, an 8.82% reduction. However, the area of wetlands under official protection increased by 5.2594 million

---

[2]Note: Grade one is the most superior grade of grassland, and grade eight is the poorest.

ha between the two surveys, for an increase from 30.49% to 43.51% of total wetlands protected. China's wetlands contain a total of about 2.7 trillion tonnes of fresh water, 96% of China's total usable water resources. Wetlands are extremely effective at purifying water and increasing water quality. Every hectare of wetlands can eliminate over 1000 kg of nitrogen and over 130 kg of phosphorous per year.

Chapter 5
Transformations to Agriculture and Agricultural Policies in China

Since 1949, and particularly since the launch of Reform and Opening in the late 1970s, changes to agriculture and agricultural policies in China have increased agricultural productivity to a great degree and have enabled China to meet the food demands of one fifth of the world's population with only one ninth of the world's arable land. To explain this phenomenon, in this chapter I shall systematically describe the changes to agriculture and agricultural policy in China and briefly assess the experience obtained and lessons learned therefrom.

5.1 Changes to the Agricultural Operations Model

5.1.1 Transition from Collective to Household Operations

During the era of the people's commune, rural citizens often distrusted collective operations. Particularly when there were great losses to agricultural yields, affected rural citizens often asked for a restoration of household operations to tide them through, and some leaders tacitly permitted them to do so. Government officials, under the influence of the ideology of the times, would immediately correct this deviation from public ownership as soon as yields improved slightly. In the late 1970s, rural citizens again adopted the method of household operations. The difference this time was that the central government tolerated this method as an exception, although it was still not openly endorsed. Thereafter, the government gradually came to acknowledge and affirm this method in its policies. Thereafter, household operations in agriculture were quickly promulgated everywhere in the Chinese countryside. Concrete changes to policies were as follows.

The "Resolutions on the Several Issues of Accelerating Agricultural Development," issued by the CCP Central Committee in September 1979, clearly noted: "there shall be no production contracted to households" "except in cases of

© Social Sciences Academic Press and Springer Nature Singapore Pte Ltd. 2017
Z. Li, *Reform and Development of Agriculture in China*,
Research Series on the Chinese Dream and China's Development Path,
DOI 10.1007/978-981-10-3462-6_5

particular need for production in some sideline industries and for isolated households located in remote areas where transportation is not convenient." This was the first time that a CCP Central Committee document formally announced that the Household Responsibility System could be employed in some exceptional cases in a policy document; the effects of this cannot be underestimated. CCP Central Document Number 75, issued in September 1980 under the title "Some Issues Related to Further Accelerating and Improving the Responsibility System for Agricultural Production," further noted: "in those isolated mountainous, impoverished, and backward regions," "when there is a demand for production to be contracted to households, the demand of the masses should be supported; either production or all work may be contracted to households." Per the spirit of this document, production teams around the nation began contracting either production or all work responsibility to households, and the percentage of production teams with one form or the other (production or all work) of the Household Responsibility System in place grew very quickly from 1.1% at the beginning of 1980 to 20% by the end of that year. At this time, all of the nation's poorest production teams put one form of the Household Responsibility System into place. The CCP Central Committee documents that relaxed and then rescinded restrictions on household agricultural operations, of 1981 and 1982, caused 30% of lower-middle production teams and then 30% of lower-upper production teams, respectively, to put one form of household responsibility in place. CCP Central Document Number One of 1983 further noted that the responsibility system of contracting with remuneration linked to output was the "operations method that combined disperse operations and unified operations" under a socialist collective ownership economy, and "under such an operations method, household operations divided by individual contracts to individual families is only one level of operations within a cooperative economy, and is a new kind of household operations. There is an essential difference between this and the small private individual economy of the past; the two should not be confounded." The Document went on to note that the Household Responsibility System of contracting with remunerations linked to output "is suitable to both the status quo centered on manual labor and to the characteristics of agricultural production, as well as to the demands of productivity development required for our process of modernization." At this time a further 15% of relatively good production teams came onto the track of household responsibility. CCP Central Document Number One of 1984 proposed solidifying and improving the methods and measures of the Household Responsibility System, at which point four percent of the best production teams also put the system in place. This demonstrates that the Household Responsibility System, either of production only or of all work, was a bottom-to-top decision made by individual rural citizens, but its rapid promulgation across the nation was the result of a gradual top-to-bottom abandonment of the traditional people's commune system on a foundation of continuous successful experiences.

The data demonstrate that from 1978 to 1984, the average annual increase to agricultural yields in China was 7.7%. If we calculate using a production function, then 46.89% of those gains came from increases in productivity brought about by the revolution of the Household Responsibility System (Lin Yifu's figure was 42.2%). Over the same period, grain yields grew from 304 million tonnes to 407 million tonnes; rural per capita net incomes grew from 133.6 to 355.3 yuan; the absolute number of rural citizens living in poverty fell from 250 to 130 million; and the incidence of poverty fell from 30.7 to 15.1%.[1]

5.1.2 Transition from Scattered to Scale Operations

The effects of this systemic transformation hit all at once. It was the same for the effects of household operations' replacing collective operations. In 1984, household operations in agriculture were put in place nearly ubiquitously in China, and the contribution of household operations to agriculture peaked. In 1985 and thereafter, the task of agricultural development became to develop new agricultural operators and gradually push changes from traditional agriculture toward modern agriculture, given the prerequisite of maintaining household operations. This transformation proceeded slowly in the last century, but gradually accelerated upon entry into this century; it remains, however, far from complete.

5.1.2.1 Developing Household Farms via Land Transfers

By the end of 2011, 228.80 million rural households in China were participating in land contracting operations. Of those, 85% operated a total of 10 μ or less land. It is very difficult for rural households to develop modern agriculture on land of area less than two thirds of a hectare, except in labor-intensive, capital-intensive, high-value-added projects such as vegetables and flowers. This led many rural citizens to engage in non-agricultural industries in the countryside,[2] and thereafter to enter urban areas to engage in non-agricultural industries. As this segment of the rural population grew, and in particular as their employment became increasingly

---

[1]The definition of poverty in China is as follows. Nutritionists formulate food lists per the most basic nutrition requirements, and then then the food costs necessary to meet these requirements are calculated. That number is divided by Engel's coefficient (0.65) to arrive at the minimum amount of income necessary to maintain warmth and adequate nutrition. Anybody whose income falls below this level is considered to be in poverty.

[2]As urban reforms lagged behind rural reforms, in addition to the need to solve the problems of the tens of millions of educated youths returning to urban areas after the Cultural Revolution, urban centers in the mid-1980s had nearly zero capacity to employ rural citizens. So at the time, the state issued a policy allowing rural citizens to engage in non-agricultural enterprises, but not to leave the countryside. This was a marked step forward from the policies enacted during the era of the people's commune that forced all rural citizens to remain in the countryside and engage in agriculture. The policies enacted in the 1990s allowing rural citizens to both leave the countryside and engage in non-agricultural enterprises was thus an even greater step forward. This demonstrates the gradual nature of reforms in China.

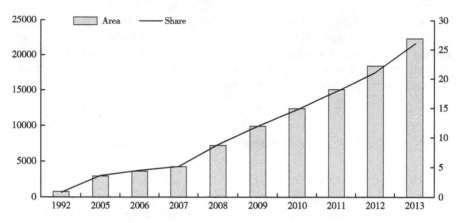

Fig. 5.1 Changes to the area of land under contracted operations and the share of such to total contracted farmland in China

stable, rural citizens began to transfer away their land rights. As demonstrated in Fig. 5.1, in 1992, less than one percent of farmland in China was subject to land transfers. Over the 13 intervening years up to 2005, that figure grew 2.7%, an average annual growth of 0.2–3.6%. By 2013, the figure was up to 26%, meaning a total increase of 22.4% over eight years, for an average annual increase of 2.8%; this demonstrates a pronounced acceleration in land transfers. The transfer rate of farmland in eastern developed regions was high: 60.1% in Shanghai, 48.2% for Jiangsu and Beijing, and 42.9% for Zhejiang.

At the outset, most land transfers took place between family members and friends, and transfer fees were low. In recent years, as transfer prices have continued to increase, most land transfers began being made to household farms[3] and other new micro-operations entities, thus promoting the development of household farms. The results of a household farm survey conducted by the Ministry of Agriculture in March 2013 indicate that there were 877,000 household farms in 30 of the nation's 31 provinces, autonomous regions, and cities under direct command of the central government (Tibet excluded) as of the end of 2012; these farms operated a total of 176 million μ of farmland, accounting for 13.4% of nationwide farmland. The average household farm employed 6.01 laborers, of whom 4.33 were family members, and 1.68 were long-term employees. Of all household farms, 409,500 engaged in planting, accounting for 46.7% of the total. Another 393,300, or 45.5%, engaged in husbandry. Another 52,600, or 6% engaged in a combination of both planting and husbandry, while 15,600, or 1.8%, engaged in other industries. Of the total, 484,200, or 55.2%, operated a scale of 50 or fewer μ. Another 189,800,

---

[3]The basic criteria for household farms are as follows: The operators of the farm must hold rural household registration. The primary source of labor on the farm must be household members. Primary income of the household must come from agriculture. Scale stability of operations must meet standards set by agricultural departments at the county level or higher.

or 21.6%, operated a scale between 50 and 100 μ, while 170,700, or 19.5%, operated a scale of between 100 and 500 μ. A further 15,800, or 1.8%, operated a scale of between 500 and 1000 μ, while the remaining 16,500, or 1.9%, operated a scale of 1000 or more μ. Total operations revenue for all nationwide household farms in 2012 was 162.0 billion yuan, for an average annual perform income of 184,700 yuan.

5.1.2.2   From Division of Labor in Production to Developing Specialized Households

In practice, many households whose primary laborers have left home to work elsewhere are unwilling to transfer away their land rights. These households instead opt to hire specialized rural citizens to help them plow, plant, spread fertilizers and pesticides, harvest, and perform other production activities on their land. This demand has driven the development of specialized households. In 1990, the total operating revenue of nationwide mechanized rural households was 59.3 billion yuan, up to 260.6 billion in 2005 and again to 447.9 billion in 2012. That marks an average annual increase of 13.4 billion over the former 15 year period and 26.8 billion over the latter seven year period (Table 5.1).

Survey data demonstrate that since 1996, specialized rural households owning combine harvesters have begun adopting a method of harvesting wheat first at the northernmost end of their territory and then moving southward. This has enabled them to extend their average duration of harvesting from the previous average of seven to 10 days to over a month's time. Marked increases to the use of farming machinery have enabled them to greatly increase operating efficiency while continuously increasing the amount of harvesting fees collected. At present, this cross-regional method of harvesting has been extended to crops like rice and corn, and these principles have also been applied to other links of the production chain. In 2013, there were over 70,000 corn harvesters in grain-producing regions across the nation engaged in cross-regional harvesting, with the average area harvested per harvester being 915 μ.

Table 5.1   Changes to operations revenues of mechanized rural households since 1990

Year	Business income of mechanized agricultural households	Year	Business income of mechanized agricultural households	Year	Business income of mechanized agricultural households
1990	59,300	2003	226,968	2008	346,650
1995	103,680	2004	242,150	2009	389,409
2000	200,000	2005	260,610	2010	424,790
2001	204,000	2006	281,100	2011	450,900
2002	215,000	2007	298,600	2012	477,900

Data source Ministry of Agriculture

As the scale of planting has increased, there has been rapid growth in the demand for machine-drying of grains. The application of this technology will greatly reduce the amount of rural land required for sun-drying of grains. The problem now is that at present, machine drying technology that preserves the quality of final products remains immature.

5.1.2.3 Developing Agricultural Companies Through Industry Upgrading

Generally, the household farm model is suitable for field crops that require intensive land use. Capital-intensive industries, and industries of agricultural products that produce roughly the same amount of product daily, such as livestock, fowl, aquaculture, vegetable planting, fruit planting, and flowers, are better suited to company operations. There are, on the whole, three agricultural areas suited to company operations. The first is mechanized or scaled husbandry. The products of this industry are more standardized than field crop products. This area is more investment-intensive, its scale economies more pronounced, and has higher potential for growth and profitability. The second is the industry for processing agricultural products. There is great room to increase the added value of these agricultural products, including edible oils, aquaculture products, fruits, vegetables, and distinctive agricultural products. The third is the production services industry. The focus here is on improved variety seed services, means of agricultural production chain-store operations, modern logistics for agricultural products, cross-regional mechanized agricultural operations, agricultural information services, and so on. This is an industry with great prospects for growth and is a focus of state policy support.

The development of agricultural companies is advantageous to improving resource allocations in the planting industry, to expanding the scale of the planting industry, to increasing the business productivity of the planting industry, to driving technological advances in agriculture, to building industry chains, and to building cooperation in agriculture. Agricultural companies will necessarily comprise replacements for small agricultural production. So long as the rural social security system remains unsound, such a replacement will cause adverse effects on the employment and opportunities to increase incomes of small agricultural operators.

5.1.3 Transition from Coercive to Inductive Administration

Prior to Reform and Opening, emphasis was placed on controlling the activities of rural citizens. Both the household registration system, which prevented rural citizens from leaving the countryside, and the employment control system, which forced rural citizens to work in agriculture, constituted controls on the activities of rural citizens. Emphasis now is placed on inducing desired activities on the part of rural citizens. In concrete terms, that means: using ecological subsidies to induce rural citizens to return farmland to forests, return pastureland to grassland, and return fields to lakes; using the self-administration system for rural citizens to put democratic elections and democratic policies in place; using the systems of openness of village government and finances to put democratic oversight in place; and replacing the voluntary labor system and accumulation of labor point systems guided by officials with the "one matter, one discussion" system guided by village citizens in order to put democratic administration in place.

The primary responsibilities of grassroots rural governments prior to Reform and Opening were to collect taxes, requisition grains, enforce planned birth, and so on: the achievement of government-set objectives. The primary responsibility of grassroots rural governments at present is service. They ensure education for all rural citizens and their children through the free compulsory education system and the training system. They provide medical care to rural citizens through the rural cooperative medicine system. They ensure aid to impoverished rural citizens through the minimum living standard guarantee system. They ensure care of senior rural citizens through the rural senior care system.

5.2   Changes to the Agricultural Structure

5.2.1   Transition from Reliance on Rainwater to Irrigation

Throughout the history of agriculture in China, laying down proper conditions for irrigation has been an important task during the slack farming season. However, as of 1949, only 15.929 million ha of land in China was effectively irrigated, accounting for only 13.5% of nationwide LuC. This meager 13.5% figure was the result of thousands of years of efforts on the part of the Chinese peasantry. The area of effective irrigation in China as of 2013 was 63.473 million ha, now accounting for 47% of nationwide LuC, an increase of 33.5% over the short period of a little over 60 years. As productivity on irrigated land is markedly higher than on dry land, most of China's agriculture is now irrigation-dominated, per calculations of agricultural added value. Development trends indicate that the percentage of nationwide LuC under effective irrigation will continue to grow as the area of irrigation grows, and the irrigation-dominated nature of Chinese agriculture will grow increasingly more pronounced (Fig. 5.2 and Table 5.2).

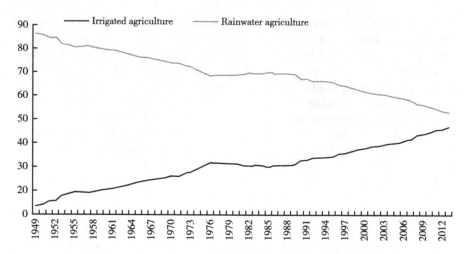

Fig. 5.2 Changes to irrigated agriculture and rainwater agriculture in China

Table 5.2 Changes to area under effective irrigation in China

Year	Area	Year	Area	Year	Area	Year	Area	Year	Area
1949	15,929	1962	28,697	1975	43,284	1988	44,376	2001	54,249
1950	16,707	1963	29,810	1976	44,981	1989	44,917	2002	54,355
1951	18,541	1964	30,923	1977	44,999	1990	47,403	2003	54,014
1952	19,335	1965	32,036	1978	44,965	1991	47,822	2004	54,478
1953	22,251	1966	32,829	1979	45,003	1992	48,590	2005	55,029
1954	23,223	1967	33,622	1980	44,888	1993	48,728	2006	55,751
1955	24,690	1968	34,414	1981	44,574	1994	48,759	2007	56,518
1956	24,848	1969	35,207	1982	44,177	1995	49,281	2008	58,472
1957	25,005	1970	36,000	1983	44,644	1996	50,381	2009	59,261
1958	25,743	1971	36,441	1984	44,453	1997	51,239	2010	60,348
1959	26,482	1972	38,005	1985	44,036	1998	52,296	2011	61,682
1960	27,220	1973	39,223	1986	44,226	1999	53,158	2012	62,491
1961	27,958	1974	41,269	1987	44,403	2000	53,820	2013	63,473

5.2.2 Transition from Planting-Based to Husbandry-Based Agriculture

China long ago accomplished the transition from migratory agriculture to fixed-location agriculture. Migratory agriculture calls for methods of crop rotation and nomadic herding. Fixed-location agriculture, on the other hand, calls for continuous cultivation methods that combine agriculture and herding. The so-called "combination of agriculture and herding" means to use the waste materials from the planting industry as feed for the husbandry industry, and to use the waste materials

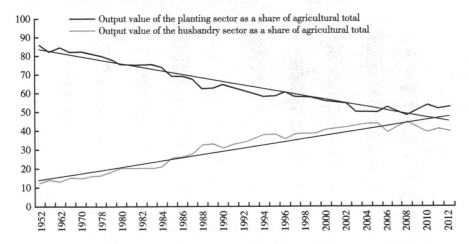

Fig. 5.3 Changes to the shares of agricultural industry output of planting and husbandry in China

from the husbandry industry as fertilizer for the planting industry. As demonstrated in Fig. 5.3, the planting industry accounted for 85.9% of China's total agricultural output value, and the husbandry industry accounted for only 12.5%, in 1952. By 2012, the planting industry share of agriculture was down to 52.5%, while the husbandry share was up to 40.1%. The year of the greatest change was 2008, when planting accounted for 48.4%, and husbandry for 44.5%. The development trend demonstrates that soon the husbandry industry's share will exceed that of the planting industry, at which point agriculture in China will become husbandry-dominated.

5.2.3 Transition from Dispersed to Concentrated Husbandry

A particularly striking change in agriculture in the 21st century has been the replacement of production methods in individual households by scaled livestock raising operations. As pork accounts for 64% of all meat consumed in China, I shall use the pork industry as an example of scaled husbandry operations. At the end of the 20th century, over 90% of pigs in China were raised by individual rural families. In recent years, the scaled pork raising industry in China has grown rapidly, with some companies emerging capable of producing 100,000 or more pigs per year, and the Guangdong Wens Group Co., Ltd., produces over a million pigs per year. The share of scale pork raising operations producing 500 or more pigs annually rose from 22% in 2007 to 46% in 2014, more than doubling. That figure is expected to hit 50% by 2015. The same is true in the dairy industry. As of 2014, scaled dairy operations with 100 or more producing dairy cows accounted for 41% of the nationwide industry (Fig. 5.4).

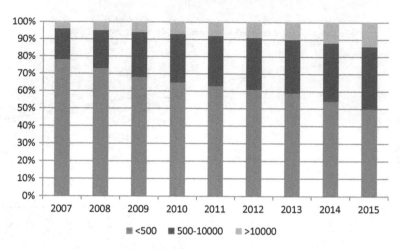

Fig. 5.4 Changes to the pork-raising structure in China since 2007

5.2.4 Transition from Wild Catching to Farming in Fisheries

In 1978, China's total production of fisheries products was 4.6534 million tonnes, of which 67.59% was wild caught at sea, 9.66% farmed in seawater, 6.37% wild caught in freshwater, and 16.38% farmed in freshwater. In 2012, total production was up to 59.0767 million tonnes, of which 44.67% was farmed in freshwater, 23.52% wild caught at sea, 27.83% farmed in seawater, and 3.88% wild caught in freshwater.

As demonstrated in Fig. 5.5, seawater farming grew the fastest, from 449,500 tonnes in 1978 to 16.4381 million tonnes in 2012, an average annual increase of 11.16%. Next came freshwater farming, increasing from 762,300 tonnes in 1978 to 26.4454 million tonnes in 2012, an average annual increase of 10.99%. Next was freshwater wild caught production, increasing from 296,400 tonnes in 1978 to 2.2979 million tonnes in 2012, an average annual growth of 6.21%. Growth was slowest in ocean wild caught production, increasing from 3.1452 million tonnes in 1978 to 13.8953 million tonnes in 2012, an average annual growth of 4.47% (Table 5.3).

5.2.5 Transition from Net Exports to Net Imports of Agricultural Products

From 1953 to 1978, agricultural products accounted for over 70% of China's total exports, making them China's dominant international trade product and primary

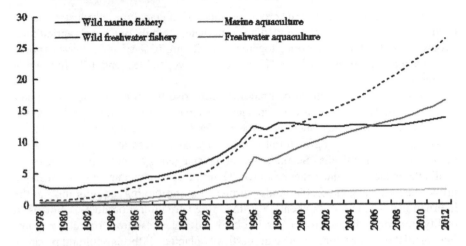

Fig. 5.5 Changes to the production structure of fisheries in China (mn tonnes)

Table 5.3 Fisheries output in China *Unit*: Tonnes

	Total (mn)	Seawater wild catching (mn)	Seawater farming	Freshwater wild catching	Freshwater farming
1978	4.6534	3.1452	449,500	296,400	762,300
1981	4.6058	2.7743	458,000	359,500	1.014 mn
1991	13.5078	6.0964	1.9046 mn	914,900	4.5919 mn
2001	37.9593	12.4412	9.8938 mn	1.8623 mn	13.762 mn
2011	56.0321	13.5672	15.5133 mn	2.2323 mn	24.7193 mn
2012	59.0767	13.8953	16.4381 mn	2.2979 mn	26.4454 mn

Data source Ministry of agriculture

source of foreign exchange. These products made a positive contribution to driving the development of China's foreign trade.

As indicated in Table 5.5, although total trade, total exports, and total imports of agricultural products have all grown since 1980, their share of total foreign trade, exports, and imports has steadily fallen, from 27.8, 34.4, and 21.7%, respectively, in 1980, to 4.5, 3.5, and 5.4%, respectively, in 2013. The scale of China's trade in agricultural products grew rapidly after accession to the World Trade Organization (WTO) at the end of 2001. In 2002, China's total trade in agricultural products was USD $30.6 billion, with a positive trade balance of USD $5.6 billion, a historic record. Since 2004, however, China has maintained a trade deficit in agricultural products, hitting a high of USD $51.04 billion in 2013. This means that China has now transitioned from being a net exporter of agricultural products to being a net importer.

Labor-intensive agricultural products such as aquaculture products, garden products, and animal products ended up comprising the bulk of China's agricultural exports, with the three categories together constituting 65% of agricultural exports: 25% for aquaculture products, 23% for fruits and vegetables, and 17% for animal products.

Land-intensive agricultural commodities comprise the bulk of China's agricultural imports. There are many advantages to increases to the quantity of imported agricultural commodities, such as soybeans. First, this is advantageous to China's maximum benefit from agricultural comparative advantages and to increasing the incomes of rural citizens. Second, this is advantageous to reducing pressure on available arable land and water resources. Third, this is advantageous to restricting growth of China's favorable trade surplus and promoting equilibrium in the international balance of payments. By importing agricultural products, China is in reality importing the usufruct of arable land and water resources of other nations. Per calculations, for China to have domestically planted all the agricultural products it imported in 2010, we would have needed 870 million μ of agricultural land, equivalent to 36% of the total planted area of the nation in that year (Table 5.4).

Table 5.4 Basic situation of International Trade of Chinese Agricultural Products

	Agricultural product trade (bn US$)				Share of total (%)		
	Total	Exports	Imports	Net exports	Imports and exports	Exports	Imports
1980	10.59	6.24	4.35	1.89	27.8	34.4	21.7
1990	18.42	10.65	7.77	2.88	16.0	17.2	14.6
1997	24.89	14.93	9.96	4.97	7.7	8.2	7.0
1998	22.14	13.81	8.33	5.48	6.8	7.5	5.9
1999	21.63	13.47	8.16	5.31	6.0	6.9	4.9
2000	21.86	12.66	9.2	3.46	4.6	5.1	4.1
2001	27.9	16.07	11.38	4.69	5.5	6.0	4.7
2002	30.59	18.04	12.44	5.6	4.9	5.5	4.2
2003	40.36	21.43	18.93	2.5	4.7	4.9	4.6
2004	51.42	23.39	28.03	−4.64	4.5	3.9	5.0
2005	56.29	27.58	28.71	−1.13	4.0	3.6	4.4
2006	63.02	31.03	31.99	−0.96	3.6	3.2	4.0
2007	78.1	37.01	41.09	−4.08	3.6	3.0	4.3
2008	99.16	40.5	58.66	−18.16	3.9	2.8	5.2
2009	92.13	39.59	52.55	−12.96	4.2	3.3	5.2
2010	121.96	49.41	72.55	−23.14	4.1	3.1	5.2
2011	155.62	60.75	94.87	−34.12	4.3	3.2	5.4
2012	175.77	63.29	112.48	−49.19	4.5	3.1	6.2
2013	186.69	67.83	118.87	−51.04	4.5	3.5	5.4
2014	194.50	71.96	122.54	−50.58	4.5	3.1	6.3

Data source Published data from the Ministry of Agriculture

5.3 Changes to Agricultural Policies

5.3.1 Transition from Concentrating Agricultural Surpluses to Supporting Agricultural Development

Prior to rural tax reforms,[4] of the approximately 150–160 billion paid by rural citizens to grassroots governments and village committees—coming from agricultural taxes, husbandry taxes, agricultural specialty taxes, the "three deductions," the "five fundraisings," and annual apportioning—about a third came from taxes. The abolishment of the agricultural tax and elimination of the foundations and platforms upon which "hitchhiking fees"—raising the price of some unlisted goods by taking advantage of the government's price readjustment power—were established the conditions necessary to eliminate the dual urban-rural structure, adjust the income allocation structure, change the functions of grassroots governments and village autonomous organizations, downsize town and township organs, and reduce the amount of people living off of government funds.

Since 2004, the central government and provincial governments have issued a series of policies to benefit rural citizens, including direct grain subsidies, improved variety subsidies, subsidies for purchasing large agricultural machinery, and comprehensive subsidies for agricultural means of production. This has been universally welcomed by rural citizens across the country.[5] As indicated in Table 5.5, investments in all subsidies have grown continuously, except direct grain subsidies, which have held steady.

---

[4]The Chinese government began comprehensive reforms to rural and agricultural taxes in 2003. The primary tasks of said reforms were mostly completed by the end of 2004.

[5]In order to understand the opinion of rural citizens on direct grain subsidies, in 2005, the Ministry of Finance conducted a questionnaire survey on 1809 rural citizens growing grain in the 13 primary grain producing provinces (or autonomous regions). The survey's results indicate that 98.34% of respondents "understand the direct subsidy policy" and only 1.66% "know a little." No respondent answered "don't know." Among the respondents, 1677, or 93%, responded "satisfied" with the direct subsidy policy. Only 85, or 5%, responded "somewhat satisfied." Ninety-nine percent of respondents, 1782 in total, responded that they thought the direct subsidy policy "increased" their incentives to plant grain. Ninety-five percent, or 1722 respondents, answered that they "preferred the direct grain subsidy policy" to the previous policy of price-protected purchasing. That price-protected purchasing policy was considered a "yellow box policy," but the direct subsidization of farmers planting grain was considered a "green box policy," more advantageous to allowing China's grain products to be competitive on international markets. At the same time, this policy created favorable conditions for marketization reforms of grain purchasing and sales. (cited from the research report into direct grain subsidies in the 13 primary grain producing provinces of Zhu Zhigang et al. accessed from http://www.mof.gov.cn/pub/jinjijianshesi/zhengwuxinxi/diaochayanjiu/200806/t20080619_47083.html).

Table 5.5 Central Government Agricultural Subsidies, Unit: bn yuan

Year	Total	Comprehensive agricultural means of production subsidies	Direct grain subsidies	Improved variety subsidies	Agricultural machinery subsidies
2003	13.00	–	–	–	–
2004	14.52	–	1.16	2.85	0.07
2005	17.37	–	1.32	3.87	0.30
2006	30.95	1.200	1.42	4.15	0.60
2007	51.36	2.760	1.51	6.66	2.00
2008	103.04	7.160	1.51	12.34	4.00
2009	127.45	7.950	1.51	19.85	13.00
2010	122.59	7.059	1.51	20.40	16.50
2011	140.60	8.600	1.51	22.00	17.50

Data source Ministry of Finance

Table 5.6 Fiscal Outlays for Central Direct Rewards of Major Grain Planting Counties

	2005	2006	2007	2008	2009	2010	2011
Funds (bn yuan)	5.5	8.5	12.5	14.0	17.5	21.0	22.5

Data source Ministry of Finance

5.3.2 Transition from Comprehensive Support to Focus Support

Initially, the government adopted agricultural policies that affected all equally without discrimination. In order to promote the rise of primary agricultural production areas, the government enacted focus support policies, while retaining a foundation of general support policies. For example, the government in 2005 enacted the policy for rewarding major grain planting counties (see Table 5.6), in 2007 enacted the policy for rewarding major pork producing counties (1.5 billion yuan per year), and in 2008 enacted the policy for rewarding major edible oil producing counties (2.5 billion yuan per year). Guided by industry policies, agricultural products gradually became concentrated in comparatively advantageous production regions, and division of labor in agricultural production regions became increasingly pronounced. At present, regionalized production has become the norm in planting regions. The 13 primary grain producing provinces account for over 70% of nationwide grain production and provide over 80% of nationwide commercial grain. The Northeast is now China's soybean and corn belt. The 13 primary pork producing provinces now account for over 75% of nationwide pork production. The seven primary dairy provinces now account for over 60% of nationwide dairy production. This change is primarily the result of market mechanisms being allowed to play a role, but the adoption of agricultural policies doubtlessly accelerated this process.

Table 5.7 The development of pollution-free agricultural products in China

	Certified pollution-free agricultural products (No.)	Production volume of pollution-free agricultural products (mn tonnes)
2010	56,500	276
2009	50,765	264
2008	41,249	220
2007	34,184	206
2006	23,636	144
2005	21,627	104

Data source Ministry of Agriculture

5.3.3   Transition from Quantity Security to Quality Security

As problems related to the security of food quantity came to be resolved, China began enacting policies to bring about food quality security. With motivation from said policies, there was rapid growth to the amount of agricultural products meeting quality standards. By the end of 2010, there were 56,500 certified pollution-free products in China, with total production of 276 million tonnes (see Table 5.7). There were 38,370 agricultural production areas certified pollution-free. Of those, 26,276 were engaged in planting, covering a total area of 31.62 million ha, or 24% of nationwide LuC. Another 7547 were engaged in husbandry, raising a total of 3.415 billion animals. Another 4547 were engaged in fisheries, covering an area of 2.6511 million ha. Total domestic sales of "ecological products" hit 300 billion yuan.

5.3.4   Transition from Expanding Production to Protecting the Environment

In the past 20 years, China has placed an increasing amount of importance on environmental protection and construction, and has issued policies for the protection of the ecological systems of forests, grasslands, and wetlands.

5.3.4.1   Policies for the Protection of Natural Forests

To eliminate the negative environmental impact of logging in forests, China launched the natural forest protection program in 1998. This program affected forest resources in the focus state-owned forest areas of the upper reaches of the Yangtze River, the upper and middle reaches of the Yellow River, the Northeast, and Inner Mongolia. State one of the program was divided into two segments, the first (2000–2005) aimed at halting logging in natural forests, constructing ecological public welfare forests, and making arrangements for newly unemployed workers. The second segment (2006–2010) was aimed at protecting natural forest resources, allowing regrowth of forests and grasslands, and promoting sustainable development of the economy and society. Total investment in the program was 96.2 billion yuan. This program effectively protected 56.00 million ha of natural forests, planted 15.267 million ha of public welfare forests, and caused a net increase to forest volume of 460 million m^3.

In 2011, the natural forest protection program entered its second stage, with a total investment of 244.02 billion yuan. Primary objectives were to, by 2020: increase the area of public welfare forests by 115.50 million μ, increase forested area by 78.00 million μ, increase forest volume by 1.1 billion m^3, add 416 million tonnes of carbon sinks, drive pronounced growth in biodiversity, fundamentally solve the issues of re-employing newly unemployed persons, and bring about harmony and stability in forest areas.

5.3.4.2 Policies for Returning Farmland to Forests

The program for returning farmland to forests and grasslands is the ecological construction program that has had, to date, the largest investments, the broadest affected area, the most onerous duties, and the most public participation in China. Investment in stage one of this program was 224.5 billion yuan. A total of 364 million μ of new forest was added, and two percent or more of additional forest coverage was achieved in program areas, via the returning of farmland to forest, the creation of forests on desolate mountains, and the enclosing of mountains to grow forests. This also brought about a certain degree of water and soil conservation. Corresponding policy measures include the following: (1) Provision of grain subsidies to households returning farmland to wilderness. Annual grain subsidies in the Yangtze River Basin totaled 2250 kg of unrefined grain per hectare, and 1500 kg of unrefined grain per hectare in the Yellow River Basin, converted to an official rate of 1.4 yuan/kg of grain, all paid from central government fiscal outlays. Limitations on these subsidies were eight years for ecological forests, five years for economic forests, and two years for grasslands. The proportion of ecological forests to economic forests was 4:1. (2) Provision of cash subsidies to households returning farmland to wilderness. Within the term limit of the subsidy program, households were paid 300 yuan/ha. (3) Provision of free seedlings to households returning farmland to wilderness. The standard for this program was 750 yuan/ha. (4) The condition for rural citizens to receive subsidies was that they had to fulfill the duty of forest creation or grass planting on desolate land suitable for forest planting on an area not less than that on which they were receiving subsidies. (5) Rural households received their grain and cash subsidies on the strength of "relinquished farmland duty" cards and certificates proving fulfillment of associated duties.

In 2007, upon the expiry of the state subsidies in grain for farmland returned to forests and living expenses, the state recapitalized the project with 206.6 billion yuan, to continue the payment of subsidies to rural families affected. The annual

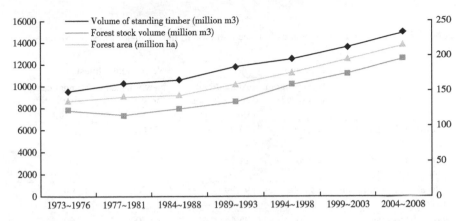

Fig. 5.6 Changes to the area and volume of forests in China

subsidy standard was 1575 yuan/ha in the Yangtze River Basin and the South, and 1050 yuan/ha in the Yellow River Basin and the North. The government also paid living subsidies of 30 yuan/ha, linked to protection duties. Limitations on the subsidy program are eight years for ecological forests, five years for economic forests, and two years for grasslands. The total investment in the program has so far been 431.1 billion yuan.

In addition to the natural forest protection program and program for returning pastureland to grassland, China has also implemented a program for construction and protection of the forest system, a program for sandstorm prevention in the area around Beijing, a program for establishing protection areas for protecting wild animals and nature, and a program for rapidly growing high-yield forests. As indicated by the data from China's seventh nationwide forest resources survey contained in Fig. 5.6, the speed of forestry construction in China has increased greatly, as a result of these programs. If one compares the results of the first and seventh forest resource surveys, one will note that the total area of forested area in China has increased from 121.86 million μ to 195.45 μ, an increase of 60.4%. Over the same period, the volume of live wood increased from 9.53 billion m^3 to 14.91 billion m^3, a growth of 56.45%, and the percentage of forested area has increased from 12.70 to 20.36%. The seventh forest resources survey demonstrates that the area of man-made standing forest is 61.6884 million ha, and the volume of man-made forests 1.961 billion m^3, putting China in first place globally for man-made forest area. The plan for forestry construction in China is as follows: increase the area of forests by 40.00 million ha and the volume of forests by 1.3 billion m^3 over the 2005 levels by 2020.

Table 5.8 contains the total areas affected and annual carbon sequestration achieved by the six major forestry programs over the past 10 years. The data in this table demonstrate that the six major forestry programs have made a contribution to alleviating the negative impact of climate change.

Table 5.8 affected area and annual carbon sequestration of the six major forestry programs from 2000–2010

	Total forest		Newly added forest	
	Total program area (km2)	Annual carbon sequestration (mn tonnes)	Newly added forest (km2)	Annual carbon sequestration (mn tonnes)
Returning farmland to forests program	319,800	73.46	273,000	71.08
Beijing area sandstorm control program	49,400	11.13	31,700	7.13
Natural forest protection program	388,800	94.99	83,900	18.99
Forest protection program	344,000	95.46	142,700	37.60
Rapid growth of high-yield forests program	133,300	40.20	133,300	40.20
Natural forest area protection program	97,400	22.98	0	0
Total	1.3327 mn	338.22	664,600	175.00

Data source State Forestry Administration

5.3.4.3 Policies for Returning Pastureland to Grassland

Since the beginning of Reform and Opening, we first transitioned from a strategy of "dual contracting of grass and livestock" that aimed to increase only the quantity of livestock products into a strategy of "more grass and more livestock, increases to both quality and efficiency." We then transitioned into a strategy of "removing livestock and regrowing grassland, enclosing and moving." This marked a gradual transition from sole focus on economy toward "dual focus on the environment and the economy, but with priority given to the environment."

China implemented such policies as the "returning pastureland to grassland" policy and others for prohibiting pasturing, allowing pastureland to recover, and rotating pasturing in order to address the dangers of sandstorms, caused by desertification of grasslands, as quickly as possible. Since 2003, total investment in the "returning pastureland to grassland" program has been 14.3 billion yuan, of which 10 billion yuan were central government subsidies and the remaining 4.3 billion came from local governments. The program concentrated on 66.70 million ha of pastureland in China's West, accounting for 40% of the region's grasslands suffering badly from deterioration. During the "Eleventh Five-year Plan" period, the program affected an area of over 30.00 million ha, of which nomadic pasturing was prohibited and replaced by pen raising on 16.799 million ha, and partial-year bans on nomadic pasturing replaced by partial pen raising on 15.60 million ha. Grass seeds were planted on another 10.409 million ha. The policy was implemented as follows. The government paid for 5.5 kg of feed (4.95 yuan) per μ of pasture on which grazing was now forbidden per year. The government paid a further subsidy of 1.375 kg (1.2375 yuan) per μ of land per year for seasonal recuperation of grasslands, calculated by three months of feed per year. The limitation on all these subsidies was five years. Subsidies for enclosed grasslands were 16.5 yuan/μ per year, with 70% coming from the central government and 30% coming from local governments. In 2004, the feed cost assumption for the grain subsidy under the returning pastureland to grassland policy was changed to 0.9 yuan/kg of feed grain, but the subsidization standards did not change.

To fortify environmental protection of grasslands, convert the development mode of the livestock industry, promote sustained income increases for herders, and maintain national ecological security, beginning in 2011, the central government laid out 13.6 billion yuan for the establishment of grasslands environmental protection subsidies and reward mechanisms in the eight major grassland provinces (or autonomous regions) of Inner Mongolia, Xinjiang, Tibet, Qinghai, Sichuan, Gansu, Ningxia, and Sichuan. Concrete measures taken were as follows:

1. Subsidies paid on grasslands forbidden for pasturing use. Subsidies of 90 yuan/ha were paid for grasslands on which pasturing was strictly forbidden to promote grassland regrowth.
2. Rewards paid for promoting balance between grassland and livestock. Subsidies of 22.5 yuan/ha were paid to herders raising a reasonable amount of livestock on a given area of grassland, outside of those areas forbidden to pasturing, to reward their not exceeding the land's carrying capacity.
3. Subsidies for herder production. Subsidies paid for improved livestock varieties were increased, and the scope of subsidies was increased from only meat cattle and sheep to include yaks and goats. The government paid a standard subsidy of 150 yuan/ha on 6 million ha of man-made pastureland in the eight provinces (or autonomous regions) for improved varieties of grass. Comprehensive means of production subsidies were paid at a standard of 500 yuan per household to nearly 2 million herder households in the eight provinces (or autonomous regions).

The program to return pasturelands to grasslands has effected pasturing bans on 440 million μ of grasslands. Reports from the China Grassland Monitoring and Supervision Center indicate that in areas affected by the program, coverage rates, height, and grass yields are, respectively, 29, 64, and 78% higher than in non-program areas.

5.3.4.4   The Policy for Returning Fields to Lakes

Returning fields to lakes and wetlands protection are two focus areas for environmental protection and construction of wet ecologies in China as well as an important component of China's program for natural protection and ecological restoration. These both exert a profound impact on national environmental security.

A great volume of lakes and wetlands were converted to agricultural purposes between the 1950s and 1970s. After basic food self-sufficiency was attained in the mid-1980s, the central government began implementing the policy for "returning fields to lakes." This policy brought about a historic transition in China, reversing the millennia of reclaiming land from lakes and wetlands into a wide-scale return of such land to lakes. By the end of 2006, there were a total of 473 wetlands natural protection areas, covering an area of 43.46 million ha. Thirty wetlands areas, including Dongting Lake, Poyang Lake, and Zhalong were included on the national register of important wetlands. The total area of these programs was 3.46 million ha.

The "Nationwide Wetlands Protection Program Plan (2002–2030)," approved by the State Council, demanded effective protection of 90% or more of China's natural wetlands by 2030. It also called for allowing full functionality wetlands ecological systems, and for bringing about sustainable usage of wetlands resources.

5.3.5　Transition from Economic Development to Social Development

In the past 20 years, the Chinese government has not only continued to place emphasis on economic construction, but has also placed an ever greater amount of importance on social development in its policies. The government has rolled out a series of systems in this area, including the free compulsory rural education system, the new rural cooperative medicine system, equality in infrastructure provision, protection for minimum living standards of rural residents, and rural pension insurance.

5.3.5.1　Free Compulsory Rural Education

In 2006, China began implementation of a policy for free compulsory rural education, divided by project and proportion of funding between the central and local governments. The concrete measures of this policy are as follows: complete abolishment of tuition for the compulsory stage of education in the countryside; provision of free textbooks and subsidies for dormitories and living expenses for students of impoverished households; increasing the amount of guaranteed public funds for the primary and middle school levels of rural compulsory education; the upkeep and remaking of school dormitories in primary and middle schools; and a protection mechanism for the salaries of teachers of rural primary and middle schools.

In 2006, this policy was first enacted in some areas of China's western and central regions. In 2007, this policy was extended nationwide, and the government increased standards for basic living subsidies for boarding students and unit price standards for upkeep and remaking of school dormitories; at the same time, officials expanded the scope of free provision of textbooks to all students in the compulsory education stage of rural education. In 2008, the government issued a benchmark amount for public funding of rural primary and middle school students and placed emphasis on resolving heating issues for schools in high-altitude, low-temperature areas of some provinces. This policy had been completely enacted by the end of 2009. Central government outlays for rural compulsory education from 2006 to 2010 totaled 458.8 billion yuan; excluding growth to teacher salaries, the total over this period was still over 370 billion yuan. The proportion of budgetary rural compulsory education funding to total rural compulsory education investments increased from 67% in 1999 to 93% in 2009, marking a historic transition whereby compulsory education was included within the scope of public fiscal protections. Government capital allocations for "two exceptions and one compensation" were the equivalent of reducing expenditures of rural citizens around the nation by over 230 billion yuan, a reduction of 250 yuan in burden per household with primary school students and 390 yuan per household with middle school students. Planning for local government funding of rural compulsory education was handled at the provincial level, and policy provisions were established primarily at the county level. The writing of China's "Compulsory Education Law" of 2006 signified the country's bringing rural compulsory education funding protections within the administrative track of rule by law.

At present, China maintains a net primary school enrollment rate of 99.5, 13% higher than the global average, and a gross middle school enrollment rate of 98.5, 20% higher than the global average, bringing China close to the level of developed nations.

5.3.5.2 New Rural Cooperative Medicine

China's rural cooperative medical system sprouted in the 1940s, went into initial development in the 1950s, hit its first peak in the 1960s and 1970s, and was dissolved in the 1980s. In 2003, the new rural cooperative medical system (NRCM) began rapid promulgation, covering basically all rural citizens by 2008. By the end of 2010, 832 million rural citizens were participating in the program, for an enrollment rate of 96%. The initial per capita standard of the system was 30 yuan, of which the central government and local governments each provided 10 yuan, and citizens provided the last 10. In 2008, that standard was increased to 100 yuan, of which an average of 80 yuan came from different levels of government, and the remaining 20 came from citizens.

By the end of March 2009, fiscal contributions from all levels of government to subsidize the program totaled 133.1 billion yuan, accounting for 71.5% of NRCM's total budget. The standard funding per rural citizen per inpatient hospital stay increased from 690 yuan during the pilot period to 1180 yuan, increasing the amount paid by the system from 25 to 41%, effectively alleviating the economic burden of hospital visits on rural citizens. In 2010 and 2011, the contribution standard paid to NRCM by all levels of government was increased from 120 yuan to 200 yuan, in order to: effectively increase the scale of funding in the program; increase the percentage of inpatient hospital stays covered by the program to 70%; increase the maximum reimbursement standard from 30,000 yuan to 50,000 yuan; and allow for outpatient visits to also be reimbursed to a certain percentage. By the end of 2010, a total of 3.3 billion patient visits were subsidized or reimbursed by the program.

5.3.5.3 Equality in Infrastructure Provision

One, safe drinking water for rural citizens. China has two policy objectives for resolving drinking water issues in the countryside. The first is the safeguarding of the quantity of drinking water for rural citizens: in other words, drinking water year round with no difficulties in water extraction. This policy objective was achieved in 2000. The second is safeguarding the quality of drinking water for rural citizens. In 2000, 379 million people in China's countryside lacked access to safe drinking water, which posed a threat to their health. The safe drinking water issues of 67 million rural citizens were resolved during the "Tenth Five-year Plan" period, and the drinking water issues for 213 million rural citizens were resolved during the "Eleventh Five-year Plan" period. At those rates, by 2013 there should have no longer been any rural drinking water safety issues.

Two, electricity for production and living in the countryside. The policy objective during the first stage was to eradicate all electricity-free counties by the end of the 20th century and eliminate as many electricity-free townships and villages as possible, to bring the rural electrified household rate to above 95%. By 2000, total electricity consumption at the county-level county and below was 520 billion kilowatts, thus achieving the policy objective for the first stage set in 1997. In 1998, the government enacted the policies for rural power grid renovations and for equal grids and equal prices for power consumption in urban and rural areas. The rural power grid structure improved markedly, and power supply became pronouncedly more reliable. At the same time, rural power prices decreased by a large degree, and good conditions were laid for the economic and social development of the countryside. To further close the gap in development of public enterprises between urban and rural areas, during the "Twelfth Five-year Plan" period, the state enacted a new series of rural power grid renovation and upgrading projects per new construction standards and demands. These projects not only thoroughly resolved issues of rural power grids remaining unrenovated, but also brought about upgrading and renovations and increased the output and quality of electricity for parts of the rural power grid that had already been renovated but for which power supply was not reliable because of demand for power outstripping supply. A new rural power grid, more reliable, more environmentally friendly, with advanced technology, and with standardized management, was basically completed. Policy objectives for equal grids and equal prices between urban and rural areas were comprehensively enacted, further reducing the electricity burden of the countryside.

Three, rural roads. Since the outset of Reform and Opening, the Chinese government has placed ever increasing importance on the construction of rural roads, and policy objectives to this end have been raised several times. The goal for the first phase was to increase the rate of road access, in other words making all rural roads accessible to motor vehicles; this objective was basically completed by the end of the 20th century. The goal of the second stage was to increase the width of thoroughfares, up to a standard of 3.5 meters in townships and towns and 3.0 meters in incorporated villages; this objective was basically completed during the "Tenth Five-year Plan" period. The goal of the third stage was to increase the patency rate and unobstructed passenger and cargo movement rate, the standard for patency being a hard road surface on a foundation of connectivity; this goal was basically accomplished during the "Eleventh Five-year Plan" period. The goal for the fourth stage was integration of the urban and rural road networks. By the end of 2010, there was a total of 3.45 million km of rural roads in China. In the eastern and central regions, 94% of roads in incorporated villages were made of asphalt (or concrete), and 98% of incorporated villages in the western region had accessible public roads. Rural passenger transportation was further promoted on a foundation of road connectivity. By the end of 2009, there were 340,000 passenger transportation vehicles, over 140,000 rural passenger stations, nearly 80,000 rural passenger routes, and about 1 million person-trips made from passenger stations daily in the nation. Passenger vehicles reach 35,000 towns and townships, 98% of the national total, and 553,000 incorporated villages, 87.8% of the national total. A rural road network meeting the standard of connectivity between counties and townships, townships and townships, and townships and villages is now basically in place.

In terms of rural provision of infrastructure, the state has put in place rural television, telephone, and Internet facilities, on top of postal and radio services that had been earlier established.

5.3.5.4 Minimum Living Standards Guarantee for Rural Residents

In 1996, China launched a pilot for the minimum living standards guarantee system in a small number of provinces and cities under direct command of the central government; the system was extended to cover all rural areas in China in 2007. The concrete method employed was for the government to put up capital in order to pay subsidies to rural residents living below the minimum living standards line, to ensure their basic living needs were met. The procedure for this program is as follows. A rural citizen fills out an application, and then the local village organization or village assembly appraises the economic situation of the applicant; applications of all people meeting standards are passed onto the township or town government. A civil affairs officer in the town or township government then examines the household assets, income, labor potential, and actual living standards

Table 5.9 Evolution of China's minimum living standards guarantee for rural residents system

	2001	2002	2003	2004	2005	2006	2007	2008	2009	2010
No. of households covered (mn)	1.179	1.567	1.768	2.359	4.061	7.772	16.085	19.822	22.917	25.287
No. of people covered (mn)	3.046	4.078	3.671	4.88	8.25	15.931	35.663	43.055	47.6	52.14
Program funding (bn)							10.91	22.87	36.3	44.5
Program standard (yuan/month)							70.0	82.3	100.8	117.0

Data source Ministry of Civil Affairs

of the applicant, and then passes the results of said examination onto the county level civil affairs bureau for approval. To ensure fairness and transparency in the process, village committees, township and town governments, and county civil affairs bureaus publicize applications and the results of assessments, examinations, and approvals on third party media or on community bulletin boards. Households under this program are assessed annually to ensure they meet program criteria. This is done to both bring households recently fallen into extreme poverty within the scope of the program and also to delist households no longer in poverty as per adjusted subsidy standards from the program. Local governments across the country have also implemented the "incremental reduction of aid-dependency" policy in order to encourage those who are able to work themselves out of poverty to do so. One should note that there is a great degree of differentiation between the standards set by policy for this program and the standards actually implemented, and there are disparities between local government standards for the program and the results of village appraisals of applicants (Table 5.9).

5.3.5.5 Social and Pension Insurance for Rural Residents

From 2006 to 2010, the state again launched the New Rural Resident Social Pension (NRRSP) system, aimed at rural seniors 60 years and older. As of 2010, 143 million rural residents were enrolled in pilot zones of the program, and enrollees 60 years and older were receiving 55 yuan in basic pension subsidies per month from the program. This symbolized transitions from rural senior care dependent on younger generations and on land resources to dependency on economic surpluses, from senior care provided by the family to senior care provided by society, and from social pension institutions being available in only urban areas to China to their availability across the countryside.

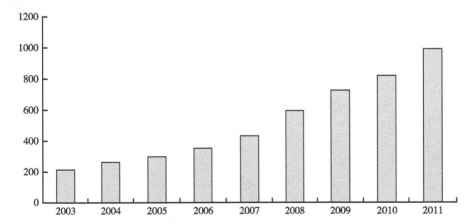

Fig. 5.7 Total central government expenditures for the "Three Rurals" (billion yuan)

As indicated in Fig. 5.7, since 2003, as policy strength for promotion of agriculture and rural development has picked up, central government expenditures on "three rurals" issues have grown ever greater. During the "Eleventh Five-year Plan" period, central government expenditures on "three rurals" issues increased from 339.7 billion yuan to 818.3 billion yuan, meaning the share of central government expenditures on such issues increased from 14.5 to 17.5%.

Chapter 6
Grain Production and Food Security in China

6.1 Grain Production

6.1.1 Changes to Grain Yields and Per Capita Grain Shares

6.1.1.1 Grain Yields in China

China's grain production grew more or less continuously, despite fluctuations, over the period 1949 to 2014 (see Fig. 6.1). If we take 50 million tonnes (1 trillion *jin*) as a step, then China has taken 10 steps upward over this 65-year period. China's total grain yield in 1949 was 113 million tonnes, up to 150 million tonnes (one step) by 1952, 200 million tonnes (two steps) by 1958, 250 million tonnes (three steps) by 1971, 300 million tonnes (four steps) by 1978, 350 million tonnes (five steps) by 1982, 400 million tonnes (six steps) by 1989, 450 million tonnes (seven steps) by 1995, 500 million tonnes (eight steps) by 1996, 550 million tonnes (nine steps) by 2011, and 600 million tonnes (10 steps) by 2013.

Over the 30-year period from 1952 to 1982 (grain production had been restored to its pre-war level by 1952), grain production grew 190 million tonnes from 160 million to 350 million. Over the 30-year period from 1982 to 2012, grain production grew 240 million tonnes from 350 million to 590 million, 50 million more in growth than over the former period.

Minor fluctuations in Chinese grain yields can be explained as being the result of climatic disturbances, whereas policy interventions were responsible for the three consecutive years of reductions from 1959 to 1961, the four consecutive years of reductions from 2000 to 2003, the nine consecutive years of growth from 1949 to 1958, and the 11 years of consecutive growth from 2004 to 2014.

In terms of safeguarding food security, the most valuable lesson for us to consider is that of sending grain up the steps. We needed eight years, 1958 to 1966, to

© Social Sciences Academic Press and Springer Nature Singapore Pte Ltd. 2017   141
Z. Li, *Reform and Development of Agriculture in China*,
Research Series on the Chinese Dream and China's Development Path,
DOI 10.1007/978-981-10-3462-6_6

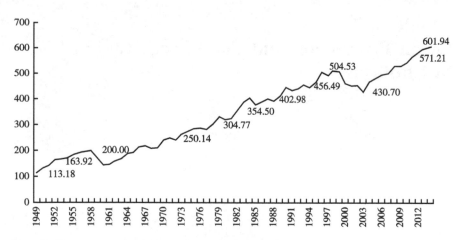

Fig. 6.1 Changes to grain yields in China, 1949–2014 (million tonnes)

step up 200 million tonnes from a base of 200 million tonnes. There is a certain degree of correlation between the nine consecutive years of increased grain yields in the 1950s, and the enthusiasm thus created, with the three years of consecutive decreases in yields thereafter. Grain yields ascended four steps over the 18 years from 1978 to 1996. Notably, there is also a certain degree of correlation between the enthusiasm caused by four years of grain yields holding steady at 500 million tonnes, from 1996 to 1999, and the four consecutive years of decreases that followed (from 508.39 million in 1999 to 430.70 million in 2003). This was followed by 11 consecutive years of increased yields, from 2003 to 2014. Given such circumstances, an important question is how to prevent reduced grain yields in coming years (Table 6.1).

Table 6.1 Grain yields in China, 1949–2014, Unit: mn tonnes

Year	Yield	Year	Yield	Year	Yield	Year	Yield	Year	Yield	Year	Yield
1949	113.18	1960	143.50	1971	250.14	1982	354.50	1993	456.49	2004	469.47
1950	132.13	1961	147.50	1972	240.48	1983	387.28	1994	445.10	2005	484.02
1951	143.69	1962	160.00	1973	264.94	1984	407.31	1995	466.62	2006	498.04
1952	163.92	1963	170.00	1974	275.27	1985	379.11	1996	504.53	2007	501.60
1953	166.83	1964	187.50	1975	284.52	1986	391.51	1997	494.17	2008	528.71
1954	169.52	1965	194.53	1976	286.31	1987	402.98	1998	512.30	2009	530.82
1955	183.94	1966	214.00	1977	282.73	1988	394.08	1999	508.39	2010	546.41
1956	192.75	1967	217.82	1978	304.77	1989	407.55	2000	462.17	2011	571.21
1957	195.05	1968	209.06	1979	332.12	1990	446.24	2001	452.64	2012	589.57
1958	200.00	1969	210.97	1980	320.56	1991	435.29	2002	457.06	2013	601.94
1959	170.00	1970	239.96	1981	325.02	1992	442.66	2003	430.70	2014	607.10

Data source National Bureau of Statistics, every edition of *China Statistical Yearbook*

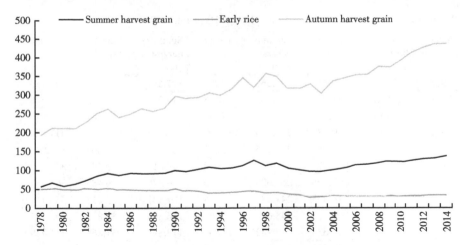

Fig. 6.2   Changes to China's seasonal grain yields, 1978–2011 (million tones)

6.1.1.2   Changes to Seasonal Grain Yields

Changes to China's seasonal grain production (see Fig. 6.2) have been as follows. There has been growth to yields of both summer harvest and autumn harvest grains, with the total yield of summer harvest grains increasing from 59.27 million tonnes in 1978 to 136.60 million tonnes in 2014, and yields of autumn harvest grains growing from 194.56 million tonnes in 1978 to 436.49 million tonnes in 2014, respective increases of 130.1 and 124.3%. The yield of early rice decreased from 50.81 million tonnes in 1978 to 34.01 million tonnes in 2011, a drop of 33.1%. From 1978 to 2014, summer harvest grain yields increased 241.925 million tonnes, autumn harvest grain yields increased 77.225 million tonnes, and early rice yields decreased 16.80 million tonnes; their respective contributions to overall increases in grain yields were 80.0, 25.5, and −5.5% (Table 6.2).

6.1.1.3   Changes to Yields of Major Grain Crops

Yields of the three major grain crops of rice, wheat, and corn have all trended upward (see Fig. 6.3), but their contributions to grain yield increases are all different, and this has caused changes to the share each occupies in the overall grain structure. Rice occupied the largest share for a very long time, but its share of the grain structure has fallen from 67.1% in 1953 (65.0% in 1949) to 37.4% in 2013 (slightly up to 37.7% in 2014), a drop of nearly 30% points, because rice yields are growing the most slowly. Corn originally occupied the smallest share of grain production, but its yields have grown the fastest, making it China's number two grain crop over the years 1998 to 2011, and China's number one grain crop since 2012. Corn's share of the grain production structure grew from 16.6% in 1949

Table 6.2 Seasonal grain yields in China, 1978–2011, Unit: mn tonnes

Year	Summer harvest grain	Early rice	Autumn harvest grain	Year	Summer harvest grain	Early rice	Autumn harvest grain
1978	59.375	50.81	194.565	1997	127.682	45.776	320.713
1979	67.865	51.975	212.26	1998	113.224	40.523	358.548
1980	59.285	49.14	212.13	1999	118.503	40.967	348.917
1981	63.99	49.535	211.495	2000	106.793	37.519	317.864
1982	73.335	53.06	228.105	2001	101.734	34.003	316.90
1983	84.44	50.77	252.07	2002	98.613	30.29	328.155
1984	91.985	53.305	262.02	2003	96.376	29.483	304.837
1985	88.735	48.805	241.57	2004	101.141	32.217	336.112
1986	93.29	49.62	248.60	2005	106.399	31.873	345.751
1987	91.062	47.633	264.282	2006	113.892	31.868	351.719
1988	90.988	47.014	256.079	2007	115.34	31.96	354.20
1989	92.69	47.33	267.53	2008	120.749	31.595	376.365
1990	100.129	50.575	295.539	2009	123.485	33.355	373.981
1991	98.405	46.249	290.639	2010	123.10	31.32	391.99
1992	103.276	46.487	292.895	2011	126.27	32.76	412.18
1993	108.419	41.339	306.731	2012	129.95	33.29	426.33
1994	104.303	40.862	299.937	2013	131.89	34.07	435.97
1995	106.927	42.22	317.47	2104	136.60	34.01	436.49
1996	114.274	43.813	346.449				

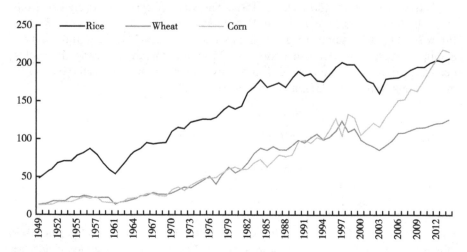

Fig. 6.3 Changes to yields of China's three major grain crops, 1978–2014 (million tonnes)

(15.1% in 1951) to 40.2% in 2013 (slightly down to 39.4% in 2014), an overall increase of 23.6% points. Growth of wheat yields is slower than that of corn and faster than that of rice. On the one hand, wheat has fallen from second to third place

Table 6.3 Yields of China's three major grain crops, 1978–2014, Unit: mn tonnes

Year	Rice	Wheat	Corn	Year	Rice	Wheat	Corn	Year	Rice	Wheat	Corn
1949	48.6	13.8	12.4	1971	115.2	32.6	35.9	1993	177.5	106.4	102.7
1950	55.1	14.5	13.9	1972	113.4	36	32.1	1994	175.9	99.3	99.3
1951	60.6	17.2	13.8	1973	121.7	35.2	38.6	1995	185.2	102.2	112
1952	68.4	18.1	16.9	1974	123.9	40.9	42.9	1996	195.1	110.6	127.5
1953	71.3	18.3	16.7	1975	125.6	45.3	47.2	1997	200.7	123.3	104.3
1954	70.9	23.3	17.1	1976	125.8	50.4	48.2	1998	198.7	109.7	133
1955	78	23	20.3	1977	128.6	41.1	49.4	1999	198.5	113.9	128.1
1956	82.5	24.8	23.1	1978	136.9	53.8	55.9	2000	187.9	99.6	106
1957	86.8	23.6	21.4	1979	143.8	62.7	60	2001	177.6	93.9	114.1
1958	80.9	22.6	23.1	1980	139.9	55.2	62.6	2002	174.5	90.3	121.3
1959	69.4	22.2	16.6	1981	144	59.6	59.2	2003	160.7	86.5	115.8
1960	59.7	22.2	16	1982	161.6	68.5	60.6	2004	179.1	92	130.3
1961	53.6	14.3	15.5	1983	168.9	81.4	68.2	2005	180.6	97.4	139.4
1962	63	16.7	16.3	1984	178.3	87.8	73.4	2006	181.7	108.5	151.6
1963	73.8	18.5	20.6	1985	168.6	85.8	63.8	2007	186	109.3	152.3
1964	83	20.8	22.7	1986	172.2	90	70.9	2008	191.9	112.5	165.9
1965	87.7	25.2	23.7	1987	174.3	85.9	79.2	2009	195.1	115.1	164
1966	95.4	25.3	28.4	1988	169.1	85.4	77.4	2010	195.8	115.2	177.2
1967	93.7	28.5	27.4	1989	180.1	90.8	78.9	2011	201	117.4	192.8
1968	94.5	27.5	25	1990	189.3	98.2	96.8	2012	204.2	121	205.6
1969	95.1	27.3	24.9	1991	183.8	96	98.8	2013	203.6	121.9	218.5
1970	110	29.2	33	1992	186.2	101.6	95.4	2014	206.4	126	215.7

in the grain structure, but on the other hand, its share of that structure has grown from 18.4% in 1949 to 23.0% in 2014, a growth of 4.6% points (Table 6.3).

6.1.1.4 Changes to Regional Grain Production

Research performed into the grain planting intensiveness of the 13 major grain producing regions of China—Hebei, Inner Mongolia, Liaoning, Jilin, Heilongjiang, Jiangsu, Anhui, Jiangxi, Shandong, Henan, Hubei, Hunan, and Sichuan (see Table 6.4)—indicate the following two characteristics of these regions: first, highly intensive grain production, and second, a rising trend for said intensiveness. The general trends are as follows. (1) The heart of Chinese grain production has gradually transitioned toward the northeast, moving a total of 148 km. (2) There has been an increase to the degree of spatial clustering between provinces producing grain, with the cluster effect growing increasingly apparent. (3) Grain production has become concentrated in the 13 major grain production regions (Zhang Jun et al. 2011).

As demonstrated in Table 6.5, the primary grain producing regions accounted for about 70% of nationwide grain yields for along time, but in recent years their share of grain yields have slowly risen, up to 76% in 2011. It is noteworthy that

Table 6.4 Changes to the grain intensiveness index for all of provinces, autonomous regions, and cities under direct command of the central government

Province	49–59	60–69	70–79	80–89	90–99	00–09	14-Oct
Beijing	0.39	0.52	0.56	0.56	0.55	0.21	0.18
Tianjin	0.29	0.41	0.41	0.37	0.42	0.29	0.29
Hebei	4.79	4.92	5.21	4.91	5.4	5.5	5.53
Shanxi	2.24	2.32	2.31	2.11	1.95	1.99	2.12
Inner Mong.	1.99	2.09	1.7	1.52	2.57	3.33	4.32
Liaoning	3.48	3.26	3.76	3.25	3.28	3.35	3.37
Jilin	3.21	3.01	3.12	3.47	4.41	4.94	5.64
Heilongjiang	4.51	4.25	4.53	4.1	5.72	5.99	9.8
Shanghai	0.6	0.87	0.85	0.58	0.47	0.26	0.2
Jiangsu	6.57	6.95	7.15	8.02	7.01	6.21	5.77
Zhejiang	4.08	4.74	4.46	4.23	3.17	1.87	1.31
Anhui	5.05	4.67	5.35	5.56	5.25	5.67	5.56
Fujian	2.27	2.19	2.29	2.21	1.98	1.53	1.14
Jiangxi	3.41	4.03	3.81	3.87	3.49	3.62	3.55
Shandong	7.21	6.5	6.9	7.66	8.44	8.04	7.68
Henan	6.61	5.82	6.42	7.02	7.54	9.55	9.64
Hubei	5.21	5.63	5.47	5.54	5.18	4.51	4.19
Hunan	5.85	5.94	6.3	6.59	5.7	5.62	5.05
Guangdong	5.99	6.65	5.74	4.89	4.27	3.4	2.64
Guangxi	3.1	3.16	3.47	3.22	3.1	3.07	2.53
Sichuan	11.32	10.21	9.26	10.12	9.32	8.82	7.65
Guizhou	2.4	2.33	2.02	1.74	1.97	2.36	1.8
Yunnan	2.94	3.17	2.69	2.49	2.51	3.14	2.96
Tibet	0.1	0.15	0.14	0.13	0.15	0.2	0.16
Shaanxi	2.7	2.64	2.64	2.48	2.3	2.2	2.06
Gansu	2.11	1.63	1.66	1.41	1.57	1.7	1.84
Qinghai	0.27	0.29	0.29	0.26	0.25	0.2	0.18
Ningxia	0.32	0.37	0.34	0.38	0.48	0.63	0.63
Xinjiang	1.02	1.3	1.15	1.32	1.56	1.82	2.22

Heilongjiang's grain yield was 55.71 million tonnes, and Henan's 55.43 million tonnes, meaning that both have broken the 55 million tonne benchmark. The combined yields of these two provinces alone is equivalent to China's total nationwide yield in 1949.

Data collected on grain production in the 13 major production regions since 1949 (see Fig. 6.4) indicate that prior to 1972, the share of total area planted of area planted with grain in the primary production regions has consistently been larger than the share of grain produced. That is to say that the primary contribution to nationwide grain yields of these regions comes not from higher grain yields per unit of area, but rather from a larger area of land planted with grain. There was, however,

Table 6.5 China's primary grain producing regions, 1978–2014

	Area planted with grain (kha)		Grain yield (mn tonnes)		Percentage of nationwide grain area planted in primary production regions	Percentage of nationwide grain yield attributable to primary production regions
	Nationwide	Primary production regions	Nationwide	Primary production regions		
1978	120,587	79,196	304.77	212.86	65.7	69.8
1979	119,263	78,917	332.12	224.88	66.2	67.7
1980	117,234	76,905	320.56	213.68	65.6	66.7
1981	114,958	76,262	325.02	221.02	66.3	68
1982	113,463	75,159	354.5	236.76	66.2	66.8
1983	114,047	75,873	387.28	267.51	66.5	69.1
1984	112,884	75,232	407.31	282.21	66.6	69.3
1985	108,845	73,184	379.11	264.59	67.2	69.8
1986	110,933	75,233	391.51	277.01	67.8	70.8
1987	111,268	75,085	402.98	286.36	67.5	71.1
1988	110,123	74,177	394.08	282.08	67.4	71.6
1989	112,205	75,344	407.55	285.54	67.1	70.1
1990	113,466	75,988	446.24	318.57	67	71.4
1991	112,314	75,075	435.29	304.54	66.8	70
1992	110,560	73,854	442.66	314.12	66.8	71
1993	110,509	74,722	456.49	327.4	67.6	71.7
1994	109,544	73,776	445.1	321.59	67.3	72.3
1995	110,060	74,148	466.62	336.72	67.4	72.2
1996	112,548	75,888	504.54	363.62	67.4	72.1
1997	112,912	76,510	494.17	352.63	67.8	71.4
1998	113,787	76,759	512.3	363.16	67.5	70.9
1999	113,161	76,402	508.39	365.18	67.5	71.8
2000	108,463	73,143	462.18	326.07	67.4	70.6
2001	106,080	72,406	452.64	323.79	68.3	71.5
2002	103,891	71,234	457.06	329.13	68.6	72
2003	99,410	68,549	430.7	305.79	69	71
2004	101,606	70,388	469.47	341.15	69.3	72.7
2005	104,278	72,568	484.02	354.43	69.6	73.2
2006	104,958	73,739	498.04	368.24	70.3	73.9
2007	105,638	76,156	501.6	376.4	72.1	75
2008	106,793	76,717	528.71	399.18	71.8	75.5
2009	108,986	78,010	530.82	397.1	71.6	74.8
2010	109,874	78,550	546.41	411.85	71.5	75.4
2011	110,572	79,104	571.21	434.22	71.5	76

(continued)

Table 6.5 (continued)

	Area planted with grain (kha)		Grain yield (mn tonnes)		Percentage of nationwide grain area planted in primary production regions	Percentage of nationwide grain yield attributable to primary production regions
	Nationwide	Primary production regions	Nationwide	Primary production regions		
2012	111,266.8	79,417	589.57	460.21	71.4	75.7
2013	111,951	80,232	601.94	457.64	71.7	76
2014	112,738	81,080	607.1	446.1	71.9	75.8

Data source Materials published by the National Bureau of Statistics

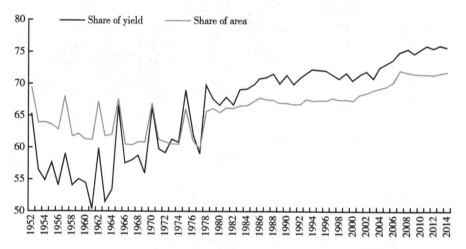

Fig. 6.4 Changes to the shares of nationwide area planted with grain and nationwide grain yields of primary grain production regions

a trend whereby the share of grain area and the share of grain yields have gradually come closer together. Since 1973, the share of grain yields in primary production regions has nearly consistently been higher than the share of area planted with grain (the share of area planted of area planted with grain in 1977 was greater than the grain yield share by 0.7% points, but I ignore this). In this period, the contribution of these regions to nationwide grain yields has come from higher yields per unit of land planted and not from greater area planted, and the trend now is for the share of grain yield to grow greater than the share of area planted with grain.

6.1.1.5   Field Area and Grain Field Productivity

There was for a long time a disparity between the actual amount of LuC in China and the reported amount (see Chap. 2). So to assess grain production in China's agricultural regions, one must first make adjustments to the data, and cannot directly use reported figures for LuC area planted since 1949 to determine the truth behind grain production.

Analysis indicates that the following are the factors we should consider: (1) LuC area used for grain production. The reason I use this indicator instead of "area of land planted with grain" is that there is a relatively large difference in the intensiveness with which land in China is planted as compared to other countries. Agricultural land intensiveness in China is high, and in many areas double cropping in the same year on the same plot of land is common. Land usage intensiveness is much lower in many other countries, with many areas abroad producing a single crop only every other year on a single plot of land. If I were to calculate average grain yields per unit of area planted with grain, I would greatly underestimate the productivity of china's agricultural land. (2) Prior to Reform and Opening, all primary agricultural products were subject to the state monopoly, and all rural citizens had to work in agriculture. During this period, the proportion of total land planted with grain remained mostly stable, and the quantity of grain yields was determined mostly by production per unit of land. Thus, the central government established grain production per unit of land as the most important indicator of performance. Agricultural collective economic organizations often employed two methods to receive praise from superiors. The first was to increase multiple cropping. The results of investigations that proved that "two times five to get ten is better than three times three to get nine" (meaning it was better two plant two crops per year at 500 *jin* yields per harvest to arrive at 1000 *jin* than to plant three crops at 300 *jin* for a total of only 900 *jin*), as well as the fact that many areas which planted three crops a year quickly reverted to two crops a year after Reform and Opening, demonstrate that the positive effect of increasing multiple cropping on increasing yields is extremely limited. The second was to underreport newly cultivated virgin land. Grain yield increases during this period were primarily the result of newly cultivated virgin land, and so rural citizens called such land "helping fields." (3) After the advent of Reform and Opening, with industrialization and urbanization rapidly picking up, there was ever greater room for rural citizens to engage in non-agricultural industries, and there was ever greater motivation for rural citizens to pursue comparative advantages in agriculture. At this time, grain production suffered a double blow of shifting agricultural labor and adjustments to the agricultural production structure. The central government then established area of land planted with grain as the most important indicator for assessing performance in order to further safeguard the nation's food security. To avoid censure from superiors, officials from some township and county governments began overreporting area planted with grain in their jurisdictions. This is an important reason that led average grain yields calculated per reported area planted to be lower than actual yields. All this goes to show that one must jiggle the data a little to make an objective assessment of changes to China's agricultural productivity.

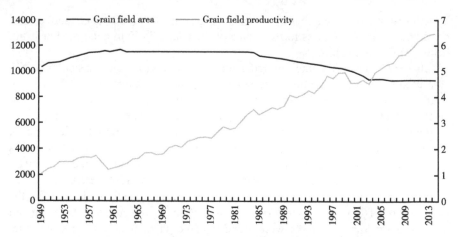

Fig. 6.5 Area planted with grain and average unit grain yields, 1949–2014 (Kha)

Analysis further indicates that the following are the conditions for adjusted data to be usable: (1) Reconstructed LuC area data. (2) The share of area planted with grain of total area planted with crops. (3) Total grain yields. It is much easier to make observations of total grain yields than total area planted with grain, and so the disparity between actual grain yields and reported grain yields is much smaller than the disparity between actual area planted and reported area planted.

As indicated in Fig. 6.5, the total area of land planted with grain in China gradually increased from 104 million hectares in 1949 to 117 million hectares in 1962. Over the 20-plus years from 1963 to 1984, this area held steady between 115 million and 116 million hectares. After 1985, the area of land planted with grain steady fell, down below 100 million hectares in 2001, owing to adjustments to the planting structure and the increasing amount of non-agricultural uses of farmland. Thereafter, the government began to ramp up administration over grain fields, and so total area planted with grain held steady between 93 million and 94 million hectares from 2006 to 2014. Over these 65 years, grain field productivity has gradually trended upward. In 1984, the average grain yield per hectare planted was 1.09 tonnes, up to two tonnes in 1971, then three tonnes in 1982, then four tonnes in 1990, then five tonnes in 2005, then six tonnes in 2011, and finally to 6.51 tonnes in 2014 (Table 6.6).

6.1.2 Per Capita Grain Yields in China

From 1949 to 2014, per capita grain yields in China mostly increased, despite some fluctuations (see Fig. 6.6). Here I take 50 kg as one step, and so over this 65-year period, per capita grain yields in China increased by four steps. The per capita grain

Table 6.6 Grain field area and grain field productivity in China, 1949–2014, Units: kilo hectares and tonnes/hectare

Year	Area	Average yield	Year	Area	Average yield	Year	Area	Average yield
1949	104,279	1.09	1971	115,793	2.16	1993	106,883	4.27
1950	106,213	1.24	1972	115,780	2.08	1994	106,100	4.20
1951	107,551	1.34	1973	115,765	2.29	1995	105,302	4.43
1952	108,014	1.52	1974	115,746	2.38	1996	104,486	4.83
1953	109,467	1.52	1975	115,723	2.46	1997	103,822	4.76
1954	110,867	1.53	1976	115,697	2.47	1998	103,161	4.97
1955	112,264	1.64	1977	115,668	2.44	1999	102,371	4.97
1956	113,657	1.70	1978	115,635	2.64	2000	100,881	4.58
1957	115,048	1.70	1979	115,599	2.87	2001	98,855	4.58
1958	115,607	1.73	1980	115,559	2.77	2002	97,210	4.70
1959	115,991	1.47	1981	115,517	2.81	2003	94,491	4.56
1960	116,140	1.24	1982	115,471	3.07	2004	94,320	4.98
1961	116,515	1.27	1983	115,422	3.36	2005	94,270	5.13
1962	116,886	1.37	1984	115,370	3.53	2006	93,900	5.30
1963	115,757	1.47	1985	112,902	3.36	2007	93,587	5.36
1964	115,774	1.62	1986	112,157	3.49	2008	93,549	5.65
1965	115,788	1.68	1987	111,413	3.62	2009	93,534	5.68
1966	115,798	1.85	1988	110,669	3.56	2010	93,458	5.85
1967	115,805	1.88	1989	109,922	3.71	2011	93,442	6.11
1968	115,807	1.81	1990	109,172	4.09	2012	93,392	6.31
1969	115,806	1.82	1991	108,417	4.01	2013	93,341	6.45
1970	115,801	2.07	1992	107,655	4.11	2014	93,290	6.51

Note Calculated based on reconstructed LuC data, the share of area planted with grain to total planted area, and total grain yields

yield in 1949 was 209 kg, up a step to 250 kg in 1951, up another step to 300 kg in 1956, up another step to 350 kg in 1983, and up the last step to 400 kg in 1996.

Of the 18 years after 1996, per capita grain yields exceeded 400 kg in only seven: 1998, 1999, and then again from 2010 to 2014.

In terms of maintaining food security, the lesson learned most worthy of attention is that of per capita grain yields going up and down the steps. The per capita grain yield in 1956 hit 300 kg for the first time, but it took another 16 years before the per capita grain yield returned to this step, in 1974. The per capita grain yield first hit the 400 kg step in 1999, but it took another 11 years for it to return to that step, in 2010. Maintaining food security does not mean ceaseless increases to grain production, but rather the stable maintenance of an appropriate per capita grain yield. The closer actual grain yields come to a suitable per capita figure, there is not only less risk to food security, but there are fewer costs and losses required for maintaining grain reserves (Table 6.7).

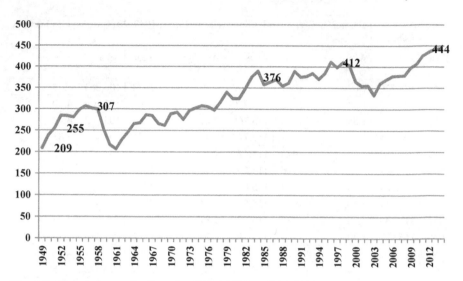

Fig. 6.6   Changes to per Capita grain yields in China, 1949–2014 (Kg)

Table 6.7   Per Capita grain yields in China, 1949–2014, Unit: kilograms

Year	Yield	Year	Yield	Year	Yield	Year	Yield	Year	Yield	Year	Yield
1949	209	1960	217	1971	293	1982	349	1993	385	2004	361
1950	239	1961	207	1972	276	1983	376	1994	371	2005	370
1951	255	1962	229	1973	297	1984	390	1995	385	2006	378
1952	285	1963	246	1974	303	1985	358	1996	412	2007	379
1953	284	1964	266	1975	308	1986	364	1997	399	2008	380
1954	281	1965	268	1976	306	1987	370	1998	411	2009	398
1955	299	1966	287	1977	298	1988	355	1999	404	2010	407
1956	307	1967	285	1978	317	1989	362	2000	365	2011	426
1957	302	1968	266	1979	340	1990	390	2001	355	2012	435
1958	300	1969	262	1980	325	1991	376	2002	356	2013	442
1959	252	1970	289	1981	325	1992	378	2003	333	2014	444

Data source National Bureau of Statistics, every edition of *China Statistical Yearbook*

6.2   Analysis of Factors Affecting Grain Production

6.2.1   Technological Advances

One can use the production function method to assess the impact of technological advances. We can also employ the stochastic frontier production function method to further break down the effects of technological advances. There are two methods for making assessments with the stochastic frontier model. The first is the two-step

Table 6.8 Breakdown of grain production TFP growth (regional averages)

Year	TFP growth	Technological advances	Growth of technological efficiency	Changes to scale efficiency
1979	0.0108	0.0022	0.0093	−0.0008
1980	0.0100	−0.0001	0.0114	−0.0012
1981	0.0120	0.0001	0.0109	0.0010
1982	0.0090	−0.0016	0.0116	−0.0010
1983	0.0105	−0.0020	0.0119	0.0006
1984	0.0075	−0.0020	0.0116	−0.0021
1985	0.0111	−0.0011	0.0113	0.0009
1986	0.0084	−0.0010	0.0112	−0.0018
1987	0.0088	−0.0004	0.0107	−0.0015
1988	0.0089	−0.0014	0.0109	−0.0006
1989	0.0076	−0.0018	0.0120	−0.0026
1990	0.0080	−0.0021	0.0128	−0.0027
1991	0.0105	−0.0024	0.0140	−0.0011
1992	0.0112	−0.0021	0.0140	−0.0007
1993	0.0104	−0.0018	0.0142	−0.0019
1994	0.0125	−0.0018	0.0155	−0.0012
1995	0.0109	−0.0017	0.0153	−0.0026
1996	0.0110	−0.0013	0.0153	−0.0030
1997	0.0144	−0.0007	0.0155	−0.0004
1998	0.0151	−0.0002	0.0153	−0.0001
1999	0.0177	0.0006	0.0161	0.0010
2000	0.0212	0.0001	0.0176	0.0037
2001	0.0175	0.0006	0.0187	0.0007
2002	0.0178	0.0006	0.0185	0.0002
2003	0.0192	0.0015	0.0191	0.0016
2004	0.0110	0.0006	0.0162	0.0045
2005	0.0111	0.0013	0.0131	0.0033
2006	0.0114	0.0025	0.0110	0.0021
2007	0.0085	0.0025	0.0110	0.0050
2008	0.0082	0.0042	0.0093	0.0053

method. First one estimates the technological structure equation and then estimates technological efficiency (TE) using a fitting residual. Then one estimates the TE equation, and finally analyzes the impact on TE. The second is the one-step method. Here one employs the maximum likelihood method to simultaneously estimate the technological structure equation and the TE equation. The results of using the second method demonstrate that since 1979, total factor production of grain in China has grown at a rate of about 1% per year. The effects thereupon of TE growth are also striking, and there are also changes to scale efficiency (Table 6.8).

6.2.2 Impact of Climate Change

First, let's demarcate meteorological yields. Then we can break down the temporal sequence of grain yields per unit of area per the nature and duration of the impact, as based on the ultimate impact on crops of natural and non-natural factors:

$$Y = Yt + Yw + \varepsilon \qquad (6.1)$$

where: Y represents actual grain yields; Yt represents the grain yield trend; Yw represents meteorological yields; and ε is the stochastic yield. The share of the stochastic yield is very small and is often omitted from calculations. Thus, this formula can be simplified as follows:

$$Y = Yt + Yw \qquad (6.2)$$

Here we use a linear moving average simulation to determine Yt. Once we've determined Yt, we can determine Yw as follows:

$$Yw = Y - Yt \qquad (6.3)$$

The above methods yield the following results: First, climate change is now an important factor influencing water usage and grain yields in Chinese agriculture. Palmer Drought Severity Index (PDSI) data indicate that climate change is causing average increases to the amount of water used to irrigate crops in China in excess of 100 billion cubic meters annually, and reductions in grain yields in excess of 1000 kg per hectare planted. Second, human activities, such as technological advances, policy protections, and increased inputs, can mitigate the negative impact on Chinese water usage and grain yields of climate change. Before the 1980s and 1990s, climate change exerted a pronounced impact on both agricultural water usage and grain production in China, whereas the impact of human activities was relatively small. After the 1980s and 1990s, however, the impact of human activities on climate change grew gradually greater. In particular, as droughts worsened, the amount of water used for irrigation per unit of land area planted steadily decreased, while grain yields per unit of area planted steadily increased. The contribution of human factors to per unit of area grain yield increases is 40% or higher.

6.2.3 Agricultural Policies

Table 6.9 indicates a few things. First, there is a positive correlation between area of land planted with grain, labor inputs, quantity of chemical fertilizers used, total horsepower of agricultural machinery, and the amount of fiscal support for agriculture, with the food price index and total grain yields. Second, farmland

Table 6.9 Ridge regression (RR) estimates of the impact of agricultural policies (K = 0.2)

	Estimated value	Normalization factor		Estimated value	Normalization factor
C	3.420*	–	Ln, arable land protection policies	0.023**	0.177
	(2.737)			(3.073)	
Ln, area planted with grain	0.216*	0.416	Ln, policies to support and benefit agriculture	0.163**	0.182
	(2.662)			(2.794)	
Ln, planting labor	0.259*	0.172	Ln, grain prices	0.021***	0.223
	(3.231)			(6.168)	
Ln, quantity of chemical fertilizer used	0.128***	0.207			
	(8.446)				
Ln, total horsepower of agricultural machinery	0.051***	0.203	Adjusted R^2	0.948	
	(7.477)		F statistic	24.002	

protection policies, policies for supporting and benefiting agriculture, and grain price protection policies all play a positive effect in increasing grain yields. The elasticity coefficients of those three are, respectively, 0.023, 0.163, and 0.021. Of those, the intensity of farmland protection policies increases by 1% annually, and overall grain yields increase by 0.023% annually. From 1982 to 2008, the intensity of China's farmland protection policies increased from five to 51 (see Table 6.10). Over the same period, grain yields increased 49.14%. The contribution of farmland protection policies to grain yield increases is 21.16%, and the contribution rate thereof is 43.06%. To better compare the relative importance of these different factors to grain yield increases, I have listed out normalization factor values within the results of my analysis.

Table 6.10 Quantization of the intensity of China's arable land protection policies

	Awakening stage	Initial policy establishment stage		Policy system formation stage		Consummation stage	
	1982–1986	1987–1992	1993–1996	1997–1999	2000–2003	2004–2005	2006–2008
Results of policy endowment accumulation	5	10	14	27	33	42	50
Results of consulting and revisions of experts	5	11	13	29	32	41	51

Ridge regression analysis is a biased estimate regression method used to analyze collinear data. It is essentially an improved version of the "least squares" method. In this method, one eliminates the unbiased nature of the least squares method and discards some data, sacrificing precision to end up with a regression method with regression coefficients closer to reality. This method makes poor data much more usable than does the least squares method.

6.2.4   Reductions of Farmland

Since the 1980s, the rate at which industrialization has occupied farmland has outstripped the rate of addition of new farmland, and so it was inevitable that China endure gradual losses to overall area of farmland. Over the 23-year span from 1980 to 2003, China lost a net total of 5.229 million square hectometers of farmland, an average annual reduction of 227,400, or 8.77%. The loss over this 23-year period is equivalent to 3.8% of the 1980 total area. The three major production regions lost a net total of 2.791 million square hectometers, an average annual reduction of 121,400, or 3.99%. The loss in these regions over the 23-year period is equivalent to 4% of the total farmland area in 1980. We should make special note of the fact that proportionally more farmland was lost over this period in the primary grain producing regions than in the country on the whole. Urbanization, industrialization, and economic development have proceeded rapidly in the mid to lower reaches of the Yangtze River Basin, and so it is here that losses to the area of farmland have occurred most rapidly. Over the period 1980 to 2003, a total of 1.5693 million square hectometers of farmland was lost in this region, an average annual loss of 68,200, or 6.4%. The total loss of farmland over this period in the Huang-Huai-Hai Region was 1.2135 million square hectometers, for an average annual loss of 52,700, or 5.1%, putting this region second only to the Yangtze River Basin. Changes to the total area of farmland were the least pronounced in the three provinces of the Northeast, which lost a net total of only 8890 square hectometers over this period, for an annual loss of 390, or only 0.04%.

There are four reasons for reductions to farmland: one, use for construction; two, returning farmland to nature; three, occupation of farmland for agricultural restructuring; and four, ruin by natural disaster.

6.3   Changes and Trends to Grain Production Distribution

6.3.1   North Outstrips South in Grain Production

Grain production in the North completely outstripped that of the South in 2008, with area planted with grain in the north accounting for 54.79% of the national total, and the North accounting for 53.34% of nationwide grain yields. Those two figures for the South were, respectively, 45.21 and 45.66%.

6.3.2   Grain Production Concentrating in Central Region

Only four of the 12 provinces (or autonomous regions or cities under direct command of the central government) of the East are primary grain production regions, but the share of nationwide grain production of this region is on the decrease, and will continue to decrease if the present trend holds. Eight of the nine provinces (or autonomous regions or cities under direct command of the central government) of the Center, Shanxi alone excluded, are primary grain producing regions, but the share of nationwide grain production of this region is on the increase, and will continue to increase if the present trend holds. Only one of the ten provinces (or autonomous regions or cities under direct command of the central government) of the West, Sichuan, is a major grain producing region. The absolute value of grain production there has not changed much, but Sichuan's share of nationwide grain production will fall steadily if the trend holds.

6.3.3   Expansion of Northeastern Superior Round-Grain Rice, Stable Advantages of Southern Rice

From 2004 to 2008, the North's share of nationwide area planted with rice increased 3.34%, and the North's share of nationwide rice production increased 3.01%. These two figures for the South have fallen, but the South's comparative advantage in rice production remains stable. The four major northern rice production provinces are the three northeastern provinces of Liaoning, Jilin, and Heilongjiang, plus Henan. Of these, Heilongjiang accounts for nearly half of all rice production and area planted with rice in the North. Droughts will be a limiting factor on future expansion of rice production in the North.

6.3.4   Wheat Production Concentrating in Huang and Huai River Basins

The North accounts for over two thirds of nationwide area planted and production of wheat, leaving the South to account for less than one third. Wheat production is expanding in the East and Center but declining in the West. In 2008, the Center and East accounted for 77.6% of nationwide area planted with wheat and 83.9% of wheat production, growth of over 1 and 2%, respectively, over 2004. There was steady growth to the nationwide share of wheat yield and area planted in the five provinces of Shandong, Henan, Jiangsu, Anhui, and Hubei, benefitting from the comparative advantages in planting and processing technology of the Huang-Huai-Hai Region. Wheat yields and area planted also increased in Hebei and Inner Mongolia, where there is a rising trend. Wheat production in the West has fallen steadily, as other crops are supplanting it, owing to such factors as natural conditions and product quality.

6.3.5   Corn Production Concentrating in Northeastern and Central Regions

Corn production has grown to a relatively large scale in China. The North's comparative advantage in domestic corn production has been further solidified. From 2004 to 2008, the North's share of nationwide area planted with corn increased from 76.47 to 78.60%, and the region's corn yield share increased from 79.51 to 82.15%, both growths of over two percent. Over the same period, the Center's nationwide corn area planted share increased from 45. 64 to 46.27%, a growth of 0.63%, and the region's corn yield share increased from 46. 13 to 49. 72%, a growth of 3.59%. The two combined provinces of Heilongjiang and Inner Mongolia collectively accounted for 4.27% of nationwide corn planting area and 4.99% of corn yield.

6.3.6   Overall Shrinking of Soybean Production

Soybean production has been overall down in recent years, with decreases to both area planted and yields. The North accounts for over 70% of nationwide soybean planting area and soybean yields, leaving the South to account for less than 30%. Area planted and yields are down in the East, which has lost between 2 and 3% of the nationwide share of both. In the Center, area planted has increased, but yields are slightly down, but in both the region accounts for over 70% of the nationwide share. There has been a slight reduction to the area planted in the West, but a slight growth in yields. The region has consistently accounted for slightly over 10% of nationwide soybean production.

6.4   China's Food Security Strategy

6.4.1   Enactment of the Prime Farmland Protection Policy

1.1 The Red Line of 1.8 Billion *Mu* of Farmland.
1.2 The Red Line of Water Resource Management.

6.4.2   Strengthening Construction of Prime Farmland Infrastructure

Agricultural infrastructure in China has already reached a certain size, but there remain several weak links in the chain; there are still many floods and droughts every year. If we calculate assuming an annual area of 340.16 million *mu* affected by disaster and 30% reduction in yields, that comes to 24.95 million tonnes of lost production, approximately six percent of total annual production. The construction or rebuilding of a great amount of irrigation and drainage works and augmentation of capacity to resist disasters is of special significance to increasing comprehensive grain capacity. First, we should accelerate the remaking of corollary infrastructure and water-conserving equipment in irrigation areas, increase the service functions of irrigation works in farming areas, and restore and expand the area of effective irrigation. Second, in regions of relatively abundant water resources and strong capacity for increased grain production, we should launch agricultural and irrigation water resource projects and increase the area of irrigation. Third, we should establish dedicated subsidy funds for the construction of small irrigation works, adopt many different methods, such as replacing subsidies with rewards, and encourage rural citizens to invest time and labor into the construction of small irrigation works. Fourth, we should subsidize water-conserving irrigation equipment and facilities and exert great efforts to develop water-conserving irrigation. Fifth, we should establish a system for government subsidization of water used for agriculture. These water subsidies should be paid directly to rural households per verified area of effective irrigation.

6.4.3   Optimizing the Distribution of Grain Production

We should develop the Yangtze River Region into an advantageous production zone for grain crops, and develop improved varieties of wheat to an appropriate scale. We should hold the area planted with wheat stable in the Huang-Huai-Hai Region, but increase the amount of improved, specialized wheat planted. We should strive to promote the planting of corn specialized for processing with a high content of oil, protein, and starch. In the Northeast, we should expand the area planted with corn for processing and feed use, increase the area planted with high-oil soybeans, and reasonably control the area planted with rice.

6.4.4   Promoting International Trade of Agricultural Products

6.4.4.1   Establishment of the Prime Farmland Protection System

We should comprehensively implement the "Prime Farmland Protection Region Regulations" and establish a permanent prime farmland protection area of stable area, focused on grain production. This should be our unshaking foundation for maintaining food security.

6.4.4.2   Strengthening Remaking of Mid and Low Yield Fields

There are 120 million hectares of arable land in China, of which two thirds, or 80 million hectares, consists of mid and low yield fields. So calculating based on two thirds of nationwide arable land and assuming that 1500 kg of additional annual grain production could result from remaking mid and low yield fields, then total untapped potential grain production per year is 40 billion kilograms.

6.4.4.3   Driving Technological Advances in Agriculture

By compiling data from the Ministry of Agriculture's nationwide agricultural technology promulgation station and other relevant research bodies, I conclude that technological means can bring about grain yield increases of between 50 and 75 billion kilograms. Primary technological measures are as follows: (1) Promulgate improved varieties. A one-time nationwide replacement of varieties planted could increase grain yields by 10 billion kilograms. (2) Improved cultivation management technology. By promoting standardized high yield cultivation techniques for crops like rice, wheat, and corn, and promoting the use of plastic sheeting cultivation for corn and other crops in high, cold, mountainous, and dry regions, we could increase grain yields by between 10 and 15 billion kilograms. (3) Fertilization by formula and deep fertilization techniques. If promoted to an additional 700 to 800 million *mu*, we could increase annual grain yields by 10 billion kilograms. The promulgation of the method of fertilizing based on soil testing has increased fertilizer usage efficiency and has kept the quantities of phosphorous and potassium fertilizers steady while reducing the amount of nitrogen fertilizers used. We have now more or less ended the period of depending on increasing amounts of fertilizer to increase grain yields. (4) Water-conserving irrigation techniques. By increasing the area of land on which water-conserving irrigation is practiced by 10% or more and

Table 6.11 Economic efficiency of grain production in China

Region	Technological efficiency	Scale efficiency	Region	Technological efficiency	Scale efficiency	Region	Technological efficiency	Scale efficiency
Beijing	0.766	0.999	Anhui	0.786	0.878	Sichuan	0.861	0.81
Tianjin	0.745	0.98	Fujian	0.795	0.94	Guizhou	0.708	0.94
Hebei	0.748	0.907	Jiangxi	0.834	0.995	Yunnan	0.574	0.998
Shanxi	0.57	0.984	Shandong	1	0.905	Tibet	1	1
Inner Mong.	0.719	0.951	Henan	1	0.831	Shaanxi	0.524	0.985
Liaoning	0.868	0.993	Hubei	0.864	0.954	Gansu	0.536	0.974
Jilin	1	1	Hunan	0.908	0.971	Qinghai	0.623	0.96
Heilongjiang	1	1	Guangdong	0.796	0.951	Ningxia	0.625	0.997
Shanghai	1	1	Guangxi	0.698	0.966	Xinjiang	0.954	0.957
Jiangsu	0.989	0.938	Hainan	0.648	0.961			
Zhejiang	0.917	0.969	Chongqing	0.596	0.98	Nationwide	0.795	0.957

Yang and Lu (2009)

adopting such dry land farming techniques as soil moisture preservation, returning stalks to the fields, increasing fertilizer usage, and the planting of stress-resistant varieties in northern regions dependent upon rainwater with annual precipitation of between 300 and 500 mm, we could increase grain yields by between 10 and 20 billion kilograms. (5) Reduce losses of grain crops during the harvest, transportation, and storage. By reducing losses by between 3 and 5%, we could reduce total annual grain losses by 10 to 20 billion kilograms.

As demonstrated in Table 6.11, China's grain production technological efficiency is 0.795, which means that we have a lot of room for improvement. Our scale efficiency is 0.957, meaning little room for improvement. The research of Xu Qing et al. demonstrates that the overall scale return coefficient for wheat, rice, and corn is 1.049, meaning that there is nearly no pronounced scale efficiency. Thus policies that consider land operation scales from the perspective of only increased grain yields are not enough. Increasing the scale of land operations has a pronounced effect on decreasing overall costs per unit of production. In concrete terms, for every additional *mu* one adds to operations, one achieves an overall cost reduction of between 2 and 10%. Thus increases to the scale of agricultural operations is advantageous to increasing the income of rural citizens (Xu Qing et al. 2011). This further proves that the acceleration of technological advances is highly important to maintaining food security.

6.4.4.4 Promoting Consumption of Scientific, Healthy Products

In China's present food consumption structure, we are near the levels of developed nations and regions in daily consumption of calories, protein, and fat. We lag behind nations such as the US and Japan in such consumption areas as beef and dairy. We must guide the people toward scientific food intake and healthy consumption, drive the formation of a scientific and reasonable food structure, and increase the standards of living and level of nutrition of the people.

6.5 The Implications of Food Security

One can analyze food security from the perspectives of products, resources, and the environment. Comparatively speaking, observations and adjustments are easiest at the product level of food security; the time and space of impact at this level are both relatively minor. Observations and adjustments are difficult at the environmental level, where the time and space of impact are relatively greater. The resource level falls in between the other two. So when discussing food security, one must begin at the product level and then move on to the resource level and finally the environmental level.

6.5.1 Food Security at the Product Level

In the past 10 years, China has experienced 10 consecutive years of grain yield increases. China's total grain yield in 2013 was 601.935 million tonnes, propelling us past the 600 million benchmark. At the same time, net grain imports have steadily increased as our ability to make international payments has increased. Supply and demand of grain on domestic markets has remained stable, as driven by these two factors; there have been no worrisome aberrations. This is a fact beyond all doubt and is also an observable phenomenon.

Over the long term, there are several factors that influence food security at the product level. The first is acceleration of replacement of improved varieties. Grain crops in China long ago achieved a wide coverage rate of improved varieties. In recent years, as there have been more sources of improved varieties, the replacement rate has accelerated, laying an important foundation for preserving stable increases to grain yields. The second is increases to the area of effective irrigation. The area of effective irrigation in China increased from 45.00 million hectares in 1978 to 53.82 million hectares in 2000 to 63.40 million hectares in 2012. The increase over the first 22-year period was 8.82 million hectares, but 9.58 million hectares over the latter 12 period, over which annual growth was markedly faster than the former. The state will place increased emphasis on the construction of irrigation works and will increase investments in this area over the coming seven years. Focus investment projects will become more prominent, and conditions for irrigation in primary grain production regions will be further improved. The third is increases to the area covered by plastic agricultural sheeting. Plastic sheeting is an important measure for maintaining stable grain production in dry regions. The area of plastic sheeting coverage in China increased from less than six million hectares in 1993 to 23.33 million hectares in 2012, nearly quadrupling. Advances to plastic sheeting technology and expansion of coverage area will effectively restrict fluctuations to grain yields caused by climate change and will make a contribution to ensuring food security. The fourth is increases to the comprehensive mechanization rate. China's comprehensive agricultural mechanization rate increased from 18.8% in 1978 to 56% in 2012, nearly tripling. The rate grew 10.2% over the 22-year period from 1978 to 2000 and then a further 27% over the 12-year period from 2000 to 2012, meaning that growth to the rate of mechanization is clearly accelerating. Increases to the comprehensive mechanization rate of grain production help to improve matching of hydrothermal conditions and help to satisfy seasonal demand for grain crop growth, making a contribution to grain yield increases and grain yield fluctuation decreases. The fifth is increases to the concentration of grain production. An analysis of statistical data indicates that the share of nationwide grain production of the 13 primary grain production regions increased from 69.21% over the years 1949 to 1959 to 77.78% over the years 2010 to 2012, for an increase of 8.57% (despite the fact that the former figure includes Chongqing, but not the latter). The concentration of grain production to planting areas more economically suitable is helpful to targeting the space for improvements of policy interventions, and thereby plays a positive role in increasing grain yields and holding production stable.

Food security at the product level is now facing some challenges. The first is ever increasing costs of labor. Although ever smaller inputs of labor are required per unit of area for grain production, labor costs are rising even faster, and so average labor costs per unit of grain produced are growing ever higher. The second is constant increases to land costs. As the scale of land transfers increases, and as land transfer costs increase as a result of demand outstripping supply, the land costs for grain production will grow ever greater. At present the average annual price for grain fields is up to 600 yuan per *mu*. The third is ever increasing costs of chemical fertilizers, pesticides, plastic sheeting, and other important materials. As these three factors will continue to exist over the long term, how to respond to continued increases to grain production costs will be a challenge we must face.

Food demand in China has already left the era of subsistence and entered an era where the people pursue flavor and health. From here on out, the primary question regarding food security will be quality safety. In order to ensure the quality of food, we must: strengthen management of farmland and logistics; allocate grain production to fertile land to the greatest extent possible; increase the freshness of foods available on the market to the greatest extent possible; and leave the mistaken era of excessive storage and excessive processing, just like leaving the mistaken area of excessive packaging, all per the agronomist's logic of: "once our food is all produced on fertile soil, and once everybody has access to these fresh food sources, humanity will see at least half of its diseases disappear." Then we must establish rigorous standards for food production and eliminate such practices as excessive use of chemical fertilizers and pesticides. Third, we must develop effective oversight, ensure that all foods allowed on the market meet minimum food safety standards, and enable all citizens to eat food without worries. This is a duty the government must fulfill. We can allow market mechanisms to establish higher standards for food.

6.5.2 Food Security at the Resource Level

The traditional pursuit of agriculture in China was maximization of production. This was done primarily through two methods. The first was to cultivate all land capable of producing grain, and the second was to practice cultivation in the seasons during which grain could be grown. Thus, water resources available to agriculture were limited. Cultivating virgin land marginally good for grain production and multiple cropping from the single-minded pursuit of increased grain yields inevitably led to the planting of grain in areas and in seasons with poorly matched hydrothermal conditions. This led to water resource scarcity, and particularly to constant decreases to groundwater levels. The natural fertility of farmland is limited, and so in the single-minded pursuit of maximization of yields, one has no choice but to use a great deal of chemical fertilizers to satisfy the fertility requirements of crops. One also has no choice but to use a great deal of chemicals to enable crops to absorb the nutrients in the soil and grow healthy. This has given rise to pollution of farmland, the reduction of nutrients in the soil, and another slew of issues. If the pollution of the soil and water caused by chemical fertilizers, agricultural chemicals, and plastic sheeting continues to grow worse, then our water and soil resources will eventually be unusable for grain production.

If the cost of product level food security is lowering of groundwater levels, pollution of farmland, and reductions to soil nutrients, then the longer we maintain food security at the product level, the worse food security will become at the resource level. If one observes food security at the resource level, then the greater the amount of land reclamation and the more crops grown per year, the better. So we must discard the traditional concepts of cultivating all land that can be used to produce grain and planting in all seasons in which grain will grow. We must also stop phrasing the fallowing of farmland to restore fertility as "allowing farmland to go to waste."

The most observable phenomenon of fallowing is for rural households to employ only single planting, and not double planting, on single units of land. The benefits of "changing double to single" are as follows: (1) High yields and low disaster risk for single cropping. Single cropping is done in the season in which hydrothermal conditions are best matched. As such planting is suited to the season, yields are higher, and the risk of natural disaster low. (2) Increased incomes for rural citizens. This is actually the economic reflection of increased yields and lower risk of natural disaster. (3) Reductions to water for irrigation, chemical fertilizers, and pesticides used are helpful for resolving such problems as decreasing groundwater levels and pollution of the soil and water. (4) Single cropping (or allowing soil to lie fallow for a season) is beneficial for the maintenance of soil fertility. The disadvantage of "changing double to single" is a decrease in overall yield per unit of area planted, but the amount of decrease to overall yields is markedly lower than the decrease to area planted. If one considers that more seeds must be purchased to plant an extra crop in a year, then the amount of grain yield lost to life consumption is also slightly lower. Shortly after the advent of Reform and Opening, some people were triple cropping in areas where double cropping is now prevalent. As "two times five for ten is better than three times three for nine," they changed to only double cropping. We must now make sober observations to see whether the case is indeed that "one times ten for ten is better than two times five for ten."

In the long run, the stability of grain production capacity is more important than the stability of grain yields, and so grain yield stability at the product level must be established on a foundation of stability of grain production capacity at the resource level. When there is a conflict between the two, the only time it is acceptable to employ exhaustive modes of resource usage in grain production will be when there is not enough food to eat. Once there is again enough food, the focus of food security must be transferred to preservation of grain production capacity. We must not sacrifice long term goals for short term goals, or overall goals for partial goals. We must not exert great pressure on our resources for grain yields alone.

We can remedy short term grain supply shortages through imports. When we import grains, what we are really doing is importing usufruct to the water and soil resources of other nations. As most grain exporting nations in the world are nations with rich endowments of water and soil resources (and not nations that force agriculture to make contributions to their economic takeoff), this is a win-win scenario.

6.5.3 Food Security at the Environmental Level

There are limitations to both ecological carrying capacity and to the environment's ability to self-purify. The principle of the conservation of mass dictates that pollution will accumulate in any environment the self-purification ability of which is exceeded, and this will exert an ever greater negative impact on certain ecological systems. If soil and water pollution caused by chemical fertilizers, pesticides, and plastic sheeting is allowed to accumulate in the soil, then the ecological systems upon which we currently rely may one day prove unable to support human life. If the share of total ecological systems of those systems suitable for supporting human life continues to decline, then the external environment for the survival and development of the human race will become increasingly worse. This will be the result regardless of the quality of our observations. Sustainable food security is food security that protects resources and the environment. So it is not enough for us to pay attention to food security only at the product level while ignoring food security at the environmental level. Per my understanding, when the central government emphasizes "holding the rice bowl firmly in one's hands," they are referring primarily to food security at the resource and environmental levels.

Relatively speaking, food security problems at the product level can be resolved with some help from the two markets, and food security problems at the resource level can be solved with help from the two kinds of resources. Food security problems at the environmental level, however, must be solved by reliance upon ourselves. So we must elevate food security problems at the environmental level to a more important status. If we want to be responsible to our descendants and to the future, then we should firmly recall the lessons taught to us by those human civilizations that have completely or partially disappeared (such as the Maya civilization). We should completely eradicate all behaviors of extending payment while reaping early rewards for the pursuit of maximization of profits and minimization of costs over the short term. This is an even more important duty for governments at every level to fulfil.

6.5.4 Food Security at the Consumption Level

6.5.4.1 Losses in Grain Consumption

Food security is related not only to production and imports, but also to consumption. Problems in Chinese food consumption at present can be divided into the following four categories.

One, food losses in transportation and storage. Technology for food circulation and storage is backward in China. We lose as much as 25.0 billion kilograms of food per year to spoilage, spillage, and pests, and annual farmer losses of stored grain run as high as 17.5 billion kilograms. If we could hold food loss rates below three percent, the level of developed nations, we would reduce annual food losses by 25.0 billion kilograms.

Two, food losses in daily life. In 2012, China's per capita grain yield was 435 kg, the per capita meat yield 54.6 kg, and the per capita fisheries product yield 43.6 kg, all of which below global averages. The same is the case in per capita yields of vegetables and fruits, the only exception to the rule being dairy products. China has now by and large resolved its problem of insufficient nutrition for its people. Data issued by the Ministry of Health indicate that 200 million people in China are overweight, and of those 90% are overweight because of eating too much. In recent years, it has been extremely common for restaurants, schools, government organs, and private companies to throw away their leftover food; the same is the case for private households. If we conservatively estimate that leftover food thrown away accounts for 10% of all food consumption, then we throw away about 50 billion kilograms of food every year in China. Even if you cut that figure in half, we still throw away 25 billion kilograms of food. We also waste grain through excessive consumption of *baijiu*. In 2011, China produced 102.56250 billion kilograms of *baijiu* (calculated at the commercial alcohol content of 65%), which exceeded the target production quota for 2020. At least 20% of that consumption comes from excessive alcohol consumption, detrimental to health. If we could cut back this amount of *baijiu* consumption, we could save 10 billion kilograms of grain per year.

Three, grain losses incurred due to excessive processing. In 2011 the total nationwide rice yield was 200.78 million tonnes. If we assume 85% was grade-two rice and 15% grade-one rice, that means that 139.65 million tonnes of that rice could be processed. Excessive refining requirements in processing led to an actual yield of 120.15 million tonnes of processed rice, a reduction of 19.5 billion kilograms. In 2011, total flour production in China was 117 million tonnes, of which special flour accounted for 25%. If we converted 10% of that production into standard flour production, and if we assume a production rate of 75% for standard flour and 60% for special flour, we could save a total of 4.0 billion kilograms of wheat used for processing per year.

Four, food wastes caused by excessive processing. The amount of corn subject to deep processing in China has held steady around 77.50 million tonnes per year. The deep processing industry now accounts for 47% of domestic corn demand. Deep processing of corn not only causes it to no longer be a grain, but also causes some of the nutrition in corn to become pollutants. This has led to a high degree of organic wastewater pollution, and has become an important duty for environmental cleaning.

In summary, if all the above measures were enacted, we could reduce grain losses by 83.5 billion kilograms annually. If we added rigorous controls on processing that changes the nature of food, we could effect a total decrease of

120.0 billion kilograms of grain consumption. This would ensure more effective protection of China's food security.

6.5.4.2 Properly Executing Grain Consumption Management

One, grasp grain consumption. We should rectify the wastes in grain consumption via strengthening management of grain consumption. We should restore the positive tradition of conserving grain. This tradition of grain conservation should be extended to every school, government organ, company, and household. We should improve the infrastructure for grain circulation. We should accelerate the universalization of technology for circulation, transport, packaging, discharging, and storage of bulk grain. We should gradually promulgate such technologies as low-temperature grain storage and grain storage under gas. We should bring the grain loss rate of both circulation and storage below three percent as quickly as possible. We should adjust marketing policies, including, for example, the common sales strategy of buy one, get one free. Such a practice is very likely to lead to waste. Some foreign supermarkets have changed such practices requiring purchasing two objects at once and allowed for the second object to be purchased later, allowing the consumer to first buy the product desired and then claim the second object later on the strength of a certificate. Such methods ought to be encouraged.

Two, reduce grain waste. The government should bear the burden of promulgating knowledge about food and health. The government should make the people understand that overly refined rice, overly white flour, and overly light oil are bad not only for the bodily health of the people, but also bad for food security, as they add to waste and pollution. Russia has experienced many changes in the past several centuries, but they have never stopped consuming whole grain bread as a staple. Their bread is made from all of the grain, with very little loss of nutrition, and this strengthens both the bodies and souls of the Russian people. This is an experience worthy of being summarized. The government should establish processing standards and lead companies to engage in processing of a reasonable degree, to preserve as much nutrition as possible from rice, wheat, and oil. We should no longer encourage the sacrifice of nutrition to excessive processing.

Three, limit grain denaturation. Value can be added to any resource via processing. We must broaden the field of vision of entrepreneurs as regards adding value through processing, and no longer limit them to adding value by the processing of grains. Such policies should be put in place as quickly as possible. To preserve food security, the state has already issued policies prohibiting the deep processing of corn, to prevent such from overrunning grain resources. However, there is still a great deal of space left open by existing policies, making them difficult to thoroughly implement. Entrepreneurs currently engaged in deep processing of corn will very likely resort to opportunism as a response. Deep processing of corn is to a certain extent a distortion of resource allocations attributable to government subsidies and tax exemption policies. It is the government's responsibility to eliminate the threat of deep processing to food security as quickly as possible.

References

Xu Qing, Yin Rong, and Liang Zhanghui, "Scale Economies, Scale Returns, and Appropriately Scaled Agricultural Operations – Empirical Research of Grain Production in China," *Jingjiyanjiu* (2011) 3.

Yang Tianrong and Lu Qian, "Analysis of the Efficiency of Specialized Production in China's Grain Regions," *Southwest Agricultural University Journal (Social Sciences Edition)*, (2009) 6.

Zhang Jun et al, "Research of Changes to Development and Spatial Distribution of Grain Production in China," *Zhongguonongxuetongbao*, (2011) 24.

Chapter 7
Challenges Facing Agricultural Development

In the preceding chapters, I gave a brief analysis and summary of the development of agriculture in China over the past 60 years. In this chapter, I will discuss the problems and challenges facing the development of agriculture in China.

In China, with a population of 1.3 billion, agriculture has long been viewed as the strategic industry for keeping the peace under the heavens and bringing stability to the people's hearts. Questions that researchers and policymakers must answer are how to maintain stable growth and sustainable development of agriculture, and how to respond to the challenges and problems currently facing agricultural development.

7.1 Challenges Facing Agricultural Production

7.1.1 The Challenge of Non-agricultural Usage of Farmland

Since the mid-1990s, the occupation of farmland is a problem that has grown rather prominent, owing to the dual drivers of industrialization and urbanization. The Chinese people have been cultivating virgin land for thousands of years, and so now there is little land available for virgin cultivation. In the era of rapid industrialization and urbanization, losses of farmland have outstripped new additions, and so, only reasonably, overall farmland area has decreased. We do not, however, think that the occupation of farmland is the necessary outcome of market allocations of resources. Without a doubt, the investments attracted, as well as employment opportunities and GDP growth caused by the occupation of a unit area of land by industrial and service sectors are often greater than would have been the case for agriculture. We should not, however, on the basis of that fact come to the conclusion that such occupation of farmland for non-agricultural purposes necessarily

© Social Sciences Academic Press and Springer Nature Singapore Pte Ltd. 2017   171
Z. Li, *Reform and Development of Agriculture in China*,
Research Series on the Chinese Dream and China's Development Path,
DOI 10.1007/978-981-10-3462-6_7

conforms to economic reason. Nor should we come to the conclusion that the occupation of farmland for non-agricultural purposes is beyond reproach, or that the government has done nothing improper in the management of such land. The following are the reasons for my doubts.

One, it is not appropriate for China to discuss the non-agriculturalization of farmland from a purely economic standpoint at this point. Non-agriculturalization of farmland is now determined by local governments at all levels in China. The goal of local governments for so doing is sometimes to maximize income from land sales,[1] and sometimes to maximize investments attracted. So the true determiner of this phenomenon is not demand on the part of companies for land use, but is rather expectations of local governments for income from land sales or for investment attraction. The primary determining factor for companies to buy land is not their actual need for such land, but rather their expectation that the value of such land will appreciate. The faster land values appreciate, the greater the demand for land reserves becomes. An even thornier problem is that in the present political environment of ever deepening reforms, local governments do not necessarily believe they will perpetually have monopolistic rights to tier-one land markets, and so many local government officials are fond of selling as much land as possible as early as possible (or selling early and giving it away early). Likewise, companies do not necessarily believe they will always have opportunities to buy land at low prices, and so they are fond of stockpiling as much land as possible as soon as possible. Under the combined pressure of these two factors, the amount of farmland used for non-agricultural purposes will necessarily be much greater than the amount for which there is real demand. It is evidently impossible to optimize the amount of farmland going to non-agricultural purposes in such a macro-environment. So one will necessarily come to specious conclusions if one discusses China's problem of non-agriculturalization of farmland entirely from the perspective of the theory of perfect competition.

Two, there is much greater room for increases to land usage efficiency for non-agricultural use land than for agricultural land in China. China produces 20% of the world's agricultural products on about nine percent of the world's arable land. This means that China's agricultural land usage efficiency is much higher than the world average, even higher than the average of developed nations.[2] China's land

---

[1] One way to visualize this is: A local government buys land rights from a rural citizen collective with a fixed term, using non-market methods. That government then sells those land rights, for the entire duration of the established term, at market prices (or extremely low prices) and using market methods (or non-market methods). The government earns enormous profits (or promises of investment) from such transactions.

[2] In 2005, 10.1% of all arable land in the world was in China, but China accounted for 21.8% of global grain production. India has slightly more arable land than China, but that country produces only half of the grain that China does. The US has 12.3% of the world's arable land and 16.4% of global grain production. Among all the primary grain producing nations in the world, only France and Germany have higher land productivity rates than China.

usage efficiency for non-agricultural land is quite low,[3] producing only a fraction of the GDP output per square kilometer on non-agricultural land of developed nations.[4] Although China's low land usage efficiency problem is mostly confined to non-agricultural land, local governments at every level and companies are putting most of their energies into increasing the usage efficiency of non-agricultural land. It is not, therefore, appropriate to simply convert agricultural land into non-agricultural land. The reason that there is more room for improvement to land usage efficiency on non-agricultural land than on agricultural land is that it is difficult for farm owners to allocate crops to different spaces on the same plot of land (different crops can't be planted one on top of the other), but it is very easy for factory owners to allocate different factory functions to different floors of the same building.

Three, farmland is not the only source of land that can be used to meet the demands of industrialization and urbanization. There is not only a great deal of farmland in China's countryside, but also a great deal of construction use land and other agricultural use land, the usage efficiency of both of which is very low. Such land could just as easily be used to meet the land demands of industrialization and urbanization. In simple terms, when rural land is needed to meet the demands of urbanization and industrialization, it should be allocated in this order: rural construction use land, non-farmland, poor farmland, mid-grade farmland, and finally superior farmland. The reasons for this order are as follows: (1) The fertility requirements of farmland are high. The quality of food is to a large extent determined by the quality of the land on which it is grown. There more elements contained in farmland, the more nutrition it has, and thus the better the quality of the food that can be produced on it. Land for construction use, however, has zero fertility requirements, and so it is a waste of soil fertility to convert highly fertile farmland into construction use land. (2) Farmland requires a very smooth surface. The smoother and flatter the surface of farmland, the higher its productivity and irrigation efficiency. There is a strong positive correlation between these two factors. Land for construction use also needs to be flat, but its requirements are much less stringent than those of farmland. Again, it is a waste to convert very flat farmland into construction use land. (3) China's high-speed rail network and

---

[3]In China, both within development zones and elsewhere, the rate of land occupation for industrial uses is low. Particularly in "development zones" in which local governments invest their own funds, most factories occupy only a few *mu* of land, and the whole zone might require the enclosing of only several dozen *mu*. The primary reason for this is that local governments offer such land to companies at very low prices, sometimes for free. Owners clearly place importance on operational efficiency of their factories, but also on the potential for value appreciation of their land reserves.

[4]China's current per capita constructed urban area is 126 m^2, higher than the figures for developed nations, 82 m^2, and developing nations, 87 m^2. China's investment per unit of area constructed is one third that of the US, one seventh that of Germany, and one tenth that of Japan and the UK. In 2011, the average investment per square kilometer of urban constructed area in China was USD $140 million. In 2007, that same figure was $772 million for New York, $798 million for Hong Kong, and $1.479 billion for Tokyo.

freeway network are growing better all the time; these have brought development of industry and urban areas in areas of small mountains and hills. If we make full use of these conditions, we will increase the balance between industrial and urban distribution and create more economic growth poles, and will also effectively protect fertile farmland.

Four, the stage of Chinese development in which large amounts of farmland are occupied for industrialization and urbanization is basically over. China's current total area of 190 million μ of construction use land accommodates 700 million people. If we use this standard to calculate, then the addition of another 100 million μ of land should suffice to meet the land requirements of industrialization and urbanization. China already experienced a period of development of over 20 years during which urbanization of land occurred more quickly than urbanization of population. The major problem during this period was the fervor for securing land rights, not the uncovering of potential uses for non-agricultural use land. The most pressing burden at present is to convert from our current extensive method of land usage to a finer method of land usage, and unleash the potential efficiency of non-agricultural use land currently sitting idle. If we can do this, much less new land will be required to meet the demands of urbanization and industrialization.

Five, the red line for farmland protection must be strictly enforced. Some academics think that market mechanisms should be relied upon to balance supply and demand for agricultural products, and that it is not appropriate to protect farmland by establishing a red line. They firmly believe that so long as agricultural product prices are high, there will necessarily be balance in supply and demand for agricultural products, and so there is no need to protect farmland. This viewpoint is clearly biased. Most countries in the world, including all forerunner developed nations, achieve their goals of farmland protection through land use planning, and have established rigorous procedures for the non-agricultural use of farmland. Farmland in most forerunner developed nations is almost entirely privately owned, but the rights to develop farmland belong to the state. It is not the case that land owners can do whatever they please with their land.[5] Two things are protected under such systems. The first is prime farmland of high fertility and nutrition

---

[5]The UK government had basically no protections in place for farmland prior to the Second World War. Most domestic demand for agricultural products at the time was met by imports. This policy led to rapid decreases of farmland. To reverse this trend, the UK government passed the "Town and Country Planning Act" in 1947. The law stipulates that land development rights belonged to the government, and that any person wishing to develop land had to apply and receive a permit before proceeding. Any land owner or developer wishing to change the use of a plot of land had to receive permission from a planning body, even if their designs did not conflict with existing development plans. The US also established a comprehensive system for farmland protection. The "Farmland Protection Policy Act," passed in 1981, divided all farmland in the country into four categories and imposed rigorous controls on the usage of said land. The "Agricultural Risk Protection Act" of 2000 safeguards the production capacity of farmland by limiting non-agricultural uses of prime farmland and special farmland. The "Urban Planning Act" of China stipulates that farmland not be willfully occupied or transferred. China's "Farmland and Countryside Protection Act" stipulates that planning permits are necessary for all development endeavors.

content in agricultural, forestry, and husbandry production areas. The second is farmland that produces characteristic agricultural products.

7.1.2 The Challenge of Uses of Farmland Other Than Grain Production

The crux of agricultural reforms is empowering rural households to make decisions for agricultural production and operations. Once given autonomy in operations and production, rural households can convert some grain fields to planting vegetables, fruits, flowers, and other high value agricultural products, and can build pens for raising livestock and fowl or ponds for raising fish, as driven by comparative profitability and improvements to the domestic food structure. Adjustments to the planting structure and agricultural production structure have increased the profitability of agriculture and rural citizen incomes, but have nevertheless exerted a negative impact on food security.

Although cash crop cultivation requires a relatively limited amount of farmland, adjustments to China's agricultural and planting structures are already basically completed, and so it is not appropriate to exaggerate the severity and danger of the use of farmland for purposes other than grain cultivation. However, China, a nation of insufficient farmland resource endowment, has opted for a strategy to respond to the use of farmland for purposes other than grain planting. First, we should establish oversight mechanisms for the conversion of farmland to purposes other than planting grain. Investigations demonstrate that most such conversions happen on land that has been transferred from original contractors to a third party. The rate of non-grain-planting on transferred agricultural land in the four major grain producing provinces of Henan, Shandong, Hebei, and Anhui is 61.1%. The more land transferred, the stronger the non-grain-planting trend. Therefore, we must establish oversight mechanisms for the non-grain-planting usage of transferred agricultural land, supported by a rural land transfer service platform that covers the county, town, and village levels. Second, we should demarcate prime farmland in primary grain production areas. The foundation of this will be the establishment of high-standard prime farmland as the basis for safeguarding the nation's food security, thereby increasing the comparative advantage of grain planting for rural citizens. Third, we should develop leading rural households by expanding the scale of agricultural operations. There are three characteristics of leading rural households. The first is that their net household per capita income is not less than that of non-agricultural households. Existing research demonstrates that rural households engaged in multiple industries can be divided into two categories: those who earn most of their income from agriculture, category I, and those who earn most of their income from non-agricultural industries, category II. Actually it is more important to divide specialized households into categories: those whose per capita income is less than that of non-agricultural households are category I, and those whose per capita incomes are higher than non-agricultural households are category II.

Category I specialized households are traditional rural households, and category II specialized households are leading rural households. Their second characteristic is their viability. Their production operations are not reliant upon government subsidies. The third characteristic is that they follow all the rules. In other words, their production operations conform to the demands of relevant laws and regulations, and to the demands of market and social rules of upholding agreements and promises. Only those household farms that meet those three conditions, along with large agricultural households that offer outsourced services and companies that engage in agriculture, can be called leading rural households.

7.1.3 The Challenge of Low Efficiency Usage of Farmland

To prevent rural households from sitting on farmland without planting it, most village and community committees in areas lacking abundant farmland resources have established rules that stipulate all contracted land must be planted, lest it be returned to the collective and re-allocated. Thus, there is a new trend of planting land just for the sake of retaining rights to it. Most households that do so have their primary laborers working elsewhere earning good replacement income. The goal for planting the land of these households is to retain their rights thereto, and so they pay attention to minimization of investment and maximization of yield, rather than maximization of profits. Such behavior on the part of such households affects their household income very little, but affects overall agricultural yields very negatively.

This problem is not unique to China. We can look to the experience of other nations to resolve this problem. For example, to address the same problem, the South Korean government passed a law stipulating that owners and users of agricultural land are obligated to plant the land and to seek to increase its fertility. Local governments are authorized to enforce a "disposition order" on violators of the law. That is to say that except in cases of natural disaster or force majeure, the government may "disposition" anybody from their farmland if they fail to meet harvest benchmarks or cultivation benchmarks set by the Ministry of Agriculture, Food, and Rural Affairs for two consecutive years, and transfer the rights to cultivate that land to a new operator for a term of one to three years for farmland and a term of five to ten years for pastureland or land cultivated with perennials. On land for which two or more disposition orders have been served, the government may accept an application from the new operator of the land and order the owner to sell the land to said operator.

7.1.4 The Challenge of Decreasing Cultivation Intensiveness

Agriculture in China is currently transitioning from traditional agriculture into modern agriculture. The pursuit of traditional agriculture is maximization of yields;

additional investments into marginal production are nil. The pursuit of modern agriculture is maximization of profits; additional investments into marginal production are equal to marginal production. As marginal returns are less than investments in the stage of marginal investments, it is normal after the agricultural transition for cultivation intensiveness to decrease. The most observable aspect of this phenomenon is the adoption of single cropping by farmers who previously practiced double cropping. There are three benefits to "changing from double to single." The first is increased income for rural citizens. In 2006, the net profit per hectare of land used to plant two crops of rice was 3813.7 yuan, but 4504.5 yuan for single cropping of rice. That is to say that it was more profitable to plant one crop than two. The second is decreases to the amount of water used for irrigation, chemical fertilizers, and agricultural chemicals. This is the inevitable consequence of growing one fewer crop per year. The third is maintenance of soil fertility, which is also an inevitable consequence of growing one fewer crop per year. The downside to "changing from double to single" is a decrease in overall yield per unit of area cultivated, but total yields of single cropping are in no way only half of the yields of double cropping. From 1998 to 2006, the area of land planted with rice shrank by 13%, but rice production shrank by only 5.4%. When one considers the rice used to sprout seedlings for a second crop, the loss to total yield is even smaller. As it is difficult to reverse the trends of high cultivation intensiveness and multiple cropping, responding to this change is a challenge that must be faced in Chinese agriculture.

Relevant data indicate that both the area planted with wheat and wheat yields are decreasing rapidly in China. The primary reason for this trend is that the growing season for wheat is too long, over half a year in the North, and the crop is highly susceptible to all manner of disasters and risks. Corn ripens reliably in 80 to 90 days, and is much less susceptible to disasters and risks, and its yields are more stable. A single crop of corn in the north yields 1400 *jin* of grain per μ. Even if one plants both wheat and corn, the wheat will yield 600 *jin* and the corn 1000 *jin*, for a total of 1600 *jin*. Corn prices are currently not lower than wheat prices. Rural households who plant only one crop instead of two can increase their agricultural income (the costs of planting another crop outweigh the losses of not planting a second crop), reduce depletion of soil fertility and water resources, and reduce the negative impacts on the environment of the usage of chemical fertilizers and pesticides. So there are advantages to decreasing cultivation intensiveness and promoting seasonal fallowing of fields.

Soil fertility is limited, and so it is not necessarily better to plant the land as intensely as possible, or to plant as many crops a year as possible. Shortly after the outset of Reform and Opening, three crops were planted in some areas that now plant only two crops, but they changed their ways on the strength of the "two times five for ten is better than three times three for nine" logic. Now we must watch and wait to see if "one times ten for ten is better than two times five for ten." From here onward, we must discard the traditional notion of planting as much as possible and in every season suitable for planting. We must promote abandonment of the term "wasting farmland" for allowing fertility to naturally replenish in fallowed fields.

When grain is in tight supply, the state can begin issuing subsidies to encourage farmers to plant two crops of grain, but when grain is relatively abundant, we should respect the "changing from double to single" method of farmers.

7.1.5 The Challenge of Decreasing Agricultural Competitiveness

In recent years, China's net imports of agricultural products have tended to increase, driven by dual factors of rapid increases of agricultural production costs and the opening of new markets for agricultural products. Chinese imports are increasing for not only land-intensive products like soybeans and corn, but also for labor-intensive agricultural products such as rice and cotton. There are two reasons for decreases to China's agricultural competitiveness. The first is falling prices of agricultural products abroad. The delivered duty paid (DDP) price of imported agricultural products within quotas are lower than prices for domestic agricultural products. For example, the per tonne DDP price of lamb and beef is 26,000 yuan, and 12,000 for pork, both of which half the prices for the same on domestic markets.The second is rapidly increasing domestic prices for agricultural products, owing to increases to agricultural factor prices. The first is ever increasing agricultural labor costs. Wage rates in agriculture and non-agricultural industries are roughly equal, indicating that China's labor markets are now fully developed. The second is constant increases to land costs. Land transfer prices continue to rise, owing to insufficient supply to meet land transfer demand. The current average annual land transfer fee per hectare is between 9000 and 12,000 yuan, equivalent to roughly one third of annual grain production per hectare. The third is constant increases to costs of other factors, such as chemical fertilizers, pesticides, and agricultural plastic sheeting. Prices for these three factors are not likely to drop in the short term, and so responding to a drop in agricultural competitiveness is another challenge that China must face.

Development of agriculture requires support from the government. Government support should be concentrated in the construction of public products, such as agricultural infrastructure, and should not be concentrated in private products, such as on agricultural products. The issuance of agricultural subsidies causes internal losses of resource allocation efficiency and external limitations imposed by the WTO. Per WTO calculations, China's subsidies for grains and soybeans have hit the limit of 8.5%, and cotton subsidies have exceeded the 8.5% limit. The common international practice is to convert subsidies for agricultural products into living subsidies for rural citizens, which brings such practices within the green box and avoids limitations imposed due to yellow box policies. For example, when the US government passed agricultural legislation in 2014, the number of yellow box policies in that country fell to an extreme low. We should also transform our yellow box policies into green box policies. China's agricultural resources are relatively sparse. It is thus necessary that we use foreign agricultural resources and international agricultural product markets to adjust domestic supply of agricultural products and alleviate pressure on domestic agricultural resources, while at the same time avoiding the impacts on domestic employment and income of importing agricultural products.

7.2 Challenges in Other Areas

7.2.1 The Challenge of Promoting Cooperation Among Rural Citizens

There are many advantages to cooperation between rural citizens, but many still lack the desire to cooperate. Analysis indicates that there are three reasons for this. First, there are many "rural elites" in China who use state policies to seek personal profit, but few rural elites are willing to help their fellow rural citizens. This is the primary reason that it is difficult to promote cooperation between rural citizens. Second, the formation of an outsourced service market for agricultural production has satisfied the demand of rural households for mechanized tilling, planting, and harvesting. The replacement of regional cooperation between rural households within a community by outsourced mechanized agricultural services on cross-regional markets has, to a certain extent, weakened demand for cooperative organizations of rural households. Third, the rapid rise of agricultural companies and their operations model of "company + rural households" has also replaced the role of rural cooperatives. Other challenges the Chinese government must face are how to increasecohesiveness and cooperation between rural citizens while at the same time reducing the external forces constricting cooperation.

7.2.2 The Challenge of Rural Citizens Unwilling to Abandon the Land

Prior to 1978, all rural citizens in China were subject to policies substituting land for employment and to the household registration system. Shortly after the dawn of Reform and Opening, rural citizens in developed regions like Shanghai no longer accepted those policies. The basis for this judgment is that for land occupied in the same village, rural citizens actively wanted to go work in state-owned enterprises, but after Reform and Opening, they drew lots to determine who went to work in state-owned enterprises. A survey conducted a few years ago demonstrates that rural citizens living around urban areas in the West no longer accept policies for substituting employment with land and the household registration system. A more recent survey demonstrates that 90% of rural citizens are no longer willing to accept these policies. Analysis indicates that there are more development opportunities in rural parts than in urban parts of developed areas. It is very easy for rural citizens to find development opportunities in such areas without relinquishing rights to contracted land. Most obstacles preventing rural citizens from entering cities in under-developed areas have been removed, and so these citizens likewise do not need to relinquish land rights to gain non-agricultural employment opportunities. A challenge China will have to face in promoting the development of modernized agriculture will be how to encourage rural citizens to relinquish their rural status via increasing employment stability and wage growth for rural citizens employed in cities.

7.2.3 The Challenge of Rural Citizens Retaining Land Rights

The average scale of operations of Chinese households has not only long been small, but has also tended to grow even smaller over time as a result of the system for dividing land equally among all sons. This is one facet of the issue. Another facet is that mechanization, the promulgation and application of chemical fertilizers, pesticides, and agricultural plastic sheeting, ever increasing labor inputs per unit of area cultivated, ever decreasing labor strength, and ever diminishing demands of physical strength from laborers for agricultural production are driving the scale of operations suitable for rural households to grow ever larger.

Per household farmland area is very small in China, meaning that the amount of agricultural income one family can earn is limited. On the basis of that, some academics think that it should not be difficult to convince rural citizens to renounce their land rights. That, however, is not the case. First, land is an even scarcer resource than capital and labor, and land grows more valuable the scarcer the resource is. Rapid increases to land prices in recent years have further heightened rural households' expectations of value appreciation of their land, making land the most valuable resource in their possession. Rural households could not possibly relinquish their most valuable possession so lightly. Second, land rights held by rural households are insufficiently clear, and so there is ultimately a risk for them to relinquish land rights. Before land rights are clearly defined and demarcated, rural households will not lightly turn over their land rights for the long term. Third, the issuance of land rights certificates will greatly drive assumptions that rural households will abandon land rights over the long term; observations are required in this area. Fourth, it is possible to find cases of land transfers made across regions and which are perfectly marketized, but that is not the case for most land transfers. Land transfers are not highly dynamic and marketized like labor and capital flows. It is likely not practical to hope that land transfers will soon be as dynamic as flows of capital and labor.

7.2.4 The Challenge of Agriculture Transitioning to Scale Operations

Transfers of land rights between rural citizens or between citizens and companies, and by extension the promotion of scale operations in agriculture, are the very essence of agricultural transformation. They are also a key measure for increasing the competitiveness of China's agriculture and sharing economies of scale. However, rural citizens place importance not only on scale efficiency, but also on the risks of sharing scale efficiency. They are unwilling to bear the risk of transferring land rights in order to share in the benefits of scale efficiency; this is the primary reason that it has been impossible for a great deal of scale operations to form. In addition, obstacles preventing rural citizens from entering cities and non-agricultural industries have yet to be completely eliminated, and the rural social security system is not yet in place; these are also major factors inhibiting rural land transfers. Challenges facing China in the promotion of scale operations of land are how to ensure that rural citizens have no risk of losing their land rights, how to ensure that rural citizens transferring into non-agricultural industries have steady employment opportunities and sources of income, and how to complete the transition from "land security" to social security. Before these issues are completely resolved, we should avoid overestimating the advantages of scale operations of land while underestimating the true difficulty of bringing about scale operations of land.

As noted above, the greatest advantages of scale operations of land, as far as grain production is concerned, are reductions of costs and increases of income; nevertheless, there are limitations to how much one can increase grain yields. Most land transfers actually competed involve the use of land for non-grain purposes; that is to say that scale operations of land do not necessarily equate with scale operations of grain production. Even more important is that scale operations in agriculture must be made appropriate to the level of economic development and the foundation of agricultural formation.[6] We should not measure ourselves based on the agricultural operations scales in other nations.

There are many other ways to increase agricultural efficiency beside scale operations. First, we can proactively encourage rural households to develop mutual aid and cooperation in such areas as purchasing production factors, sales of agricultural products, land management, construction and maintenance of agricultural infrastructure, and so on. Second, we can adopt advanced agricultural technologies. Third, we can establish and consummate the agricultural mechanized services outsourcing system. Fourth, we can optimize industry distribution and upgrade the industry structure. Such methods are less difficult to operate than land transfer methods and should thus be the priority for government guiding policies.

---

[6]In general, scales of agricultural operations are relatively larger in nations where agriculture is dominated by immigrants, such as the US, Canada, Brazil, and Argentina, as well as the Northeast and Xinjiang in China. Agricultural operations scales tend to be smaller in nations where agriculture is dominated by non-immigrants.

In 2012, China's per capita grain yield was 435 kg, the per capita meat yield 54.6 kg, and the per capita grain fisheries products yield 43.6 kg. All those figures were higher than global averages, 30.7% higher than the 332.7 kg global per capita grain yield average, 29.7% higher than the 42.1 kg global per capita meat yield average, and 97.3% higher than the 22.1 kg global per capita fisheries product yield average. China's per capita vegetable and fruit yields are also higher than global averages; dairy products are an exception. However, unsound management measures have led to a slew of problems of both waste and unreasonable consumption. Another challenge China must face is how to effectively resolve these problems and safeguard sustainable development of agriculture.

Measures we should adopt include the following: improving conditions for grain storage and reducing losses from storage; establishing processing standards and encouraging companies to process agricultural products to reasonable degrees; strengthening policies restricting processing that denatures grain and stopping the opportunistic behavior of deep processing of corn; spreading knowledge about food and health; helping the citizenry understand the limitations of their senses; letting citizens know that excessively refined rice, over-white flour, and excessively lightly colored oil are bad not only for their personal health, but also for food security, and that these things lead to waste, increased production costs, and increased pollution; and changing marketing strategies of commercial enterprises that are disadvantageous to food conservation.

7.2.5 The Challenge of Protecting Rural Citizen Land Rights

Most land occupied for urbanization at the beginning of that process was farmland. After the central government strengthened administration of prime farmland, priority was placed on using old urban areas for new urbanization. Old urban areas were limited, however, and costs for rebuilding them high, and so focus was eventually shifted to use of rural construction use land. From 2000 to 2010, the number of rural residential areas decreased by about 20%, from over 3.30 to 2.70 million. This was objectively inevitable; what we need to discuss is the method employed to drive this process.

Sacrifices must be made when developing urban areas. Losses thus incurred are fast variables felt all at once, while the benefits of development are slow variables felt only much later. An even thornier problem is that the victims of such sacrifices are not the beneficiaries of development. So the key to promoting urbanization does not lie in the audacity of sacrifices made, but rather in the wisdom required to skillfully, effectively handle the relationship between development and sacrifices.

First, arrangements of rural construction use land should be made gradually and orderly, not rashly. An investigation I performed indicates that a small amount of officials in some local governments do not make arrangements for rural construction use land on the basis of urbanization, but rather are anxious to complete arrangements for rural construction use land during their term in office. Second, special arrangements for rural construction use land must be linked to the urbanization of special groups. One must safeguard the endogenous nature of arrangements of rural construction use land, and not coerce rural citizens to give up their construction use land to be urbanized for other people. Third, one should not discuss land in terms of only the land itself. Urbanization is the result of development, not its prerequisite. The government should bring about more stable employment opportunities and sources of income for rural citizens and bring about the replacement of "land security" by social security, by eliminating obstacles for entry into non-agricultural industries and into urban areas and establishing a rural social security system. Fourth, the government should issue policies to endow rural citizens the right to build cities on the construction use land that is granted to them; this will resolve the problem of rural citizens' passively losing their land. A challenge we must face in the promotion of urbanization is how to resolve the above issues.

7.2.6 The Challenge of the Rural Community Administration System

To strengthen rural community administration, we must first increase the organizational level of rural citizens, as well as the public service capacity and coordinated administration level of the government. The primary tasks of rural community administration are as follows: strengthen community cohesiveness and promote development of rural communities; resolve all manner of conflicts and maintain stability in rural communities; open channels for dialogue, allow rural citizen groups to express their interest appeals, and make the government able to hear the will of rural citizens. To promote democratic administration of rural communities, the government must accept oversight from rural citizens groups and must make institutional arrangements for rural citizens to participate in government administration. We should shore up the fiscal reward and subsidization mechanism for village-level public welfare affairs of "one matter, one debate." We should improve methods of rewarding and subsidizing, and increase the scale of both. We should promote healthy development of village-level public welfare enterprises and change the government's method of monopolizing power. A challenge that all levels of government must face is how to bring about change in government administration by giving authorities to rural citizens' collectives.

7.2.7 The Challenge of Rural Differentiation and Stability

There are two processes currently taking place in China's countryside: sharp differentiation in traditional rural communities, and rapid changes to the rural employment structure. Market mechanisms and government support are two important drivers of these processes. The primary effect of market mechanisms is to promote differentiation in traditional rural communities, and the primary effect of government support is to maintain stability in rural communities. Differentiation is advantageous to multiplying development opportunities for rural citizens, while stability is advantageous to reducing the risks of rural citizens. When these two powers are combined reciprocally, they yield double the reward for half the effort, but when they fight to usurp one another, they lead to double the effort and half the reward. Markets spontaneously exert their effects, so it is governments that determine whether these two powers work together or against each other. The challenge the government must face in handling the relationship between rural differentiation and rural stability is how to cause their measures to conform to the choices of rural citizens, rather than trying to change the decisions of rural citizens, and organically merge the needs of the state and rural citizens alike.

Chapter 8
Outlook and Vision for Agriculture in China

8.1 Objectives for Agricultural Development

8.1.1 Objectives of Agricultural Reforms

China's strategic objective for agricultural development is as follows: by around 2030, initially establish modern agriculture, with appropriately scaled operations as its foundation; with high-caliber rural citizens, new high technology, and advanced equipment as motive force; with a socialized services system, agricultural product market system, agriculture-supporting industrial system, and macro adjustment system as its supports; and suitable to the demands of moderate prosperity, international competitiveness, and sustainable development. Deepening reforms is the major measure to be taken to achieve the strategic objective of agricultural development. In simple terms, the objectives of agricultural reforms can be summarized as follows: marketization, non-agriculturalization, and rule by law.

8.1.1.1 Marketization

Marketization reforms for agricultural products in China are basically complete. The next step of reforms is to establish the market as the fundamental determiner of resource allocations, primarily by establishing financial markets, land markets, and labor markets. Of those, rural financial market reforms should be a combination of reforms to existing entities as well as new growth. On the one hand, we should cut the umbilical cord that tethers state-owned commercial financial organizations to the government and push them back onto the market. At the same time, we should convert policy (non-commercial) banks that engage in only "grain" business into comprehensive policy banks that support agricultural development, rural infrastructure construction, adjustments to the agricultural structure, and imports and

© Social Sciences Academic Press and Springer Nature Singapore Pte Ltd. 2017
Z. Li, *Reform and Development of Agriculture in China*,
Research Series on the Chinese Dream and China's Development Path,
DOI 10.1007/978-981-10-3462-6_8

exports of agricultural products. On the other hand, we should grant legal status to the financial operations of private banks, appropriately reduce the threshold for entry into rural financial markets, promote the development of small and medium rural banks, and effectively resolve the problem of the enormous scale of private lending despite such lending being illegal. We should pass laws to endow rural households with the right of occupation, the right of usufruct, the right to profit, and the right to punish for their land, while giving collectives the right to know, the right to participate, and the right to make decisions regarding land use changes. These are necessary conditions for rural land marketization reforms. The core of agricultural land marketization reforms is as follows: the standardization of rural land markets; the safeguarding of equal rights between those whose land is appropriated and the appropriators, and equality of rights between land appropriators; preventing local governments from abusing their authority to appropriate land; and compensations to the rural citizens who contribute to holding the 1.8 billion farmland red line. The core of labor marketization reforms is as follows: elimination of all systemic obstacles preventing population movement; encouraging and supporting the development of intermediary bodies serving labor markets; and acceleration of the development of an urban-rural integrated labor market.

8.1.1.2   Non-agriculturalization

Since the dawn of Reform and Opening, ever greater amounts of rural laborers have left the countryside. This trend has contributed ever greater amounts of urban and rural development and increases to rural citizen incomes. However, this trend of non-agriculturalization of rural citizens has become stunted in the stage of labor outflows; this is disadvantageous to expansion of agricultural scale operations and to urbanization. We must organically combine expansion of non-agricultural employment, reductions of the rural population, and expansion of agricultural scales of operation by deepening reforms, eliminating barriers preventing rural citizens from becoming urban citizens, and completing the transition from rural labor outflows into urban migration as quickly as possible.

8.1.1.3   Rule of Law

Inactivity and abuse of public powers on the part of some village officials are what rural citizens hate the most; this is the primary reason for conflicts between officials and the masses. To reverse this trend, we must adopt effective measures to increases the self-control of rural officials, but even more importantly, we must make institutional arrangements that force government officials to govern per the law. The only way to effectively solve these problems will be to work on both ends at the same time.

8.1.2 Tasks of Rural Development

8.1.2.1 Increasing Agricultural Competitiveness

Promote strategic adjustments to the agricultural structure; continue to optimize the regional distribution of agriculture; promote concentration of superior and characteristic agricultural products into advantageous production zones; form an advantageous agricultural production industry belt; drive scale operations, quality, and standardization in agriculture; continuously increase the level of industrialized operations in agriculture. Continue to increase the capacity of processing conversion of primary agricultural products; augment the added value of agricultural products; continue to accelerate development of the forestry, husbandry, and fisheries industries; and comprehensively increase the efficiency of agricultural resource usage.

8.1.2.2 Increasing Rural Incomes

In the present stage, the government is not capable of maintaining constant rapid increases to rural citizen incomes on the strength of fiscal transfer payments, and nor is there a need for the government to even establish such a goal. Fiscal transfer payments made by the government to increase rural citizen incomes should be targeted at the low income segment of the rural population, in order to bring their per capita daily income, as calculated by purchasing power parity (PPP), above USD $1, and to ensure a gradual shrinking of the gap between the living standards of low income rural citizens and average income rural citizens.

During the stage of transformation of the "dual economic structure," maintaining "institutionalized wages" is advantageous to increasing social reproduction, to increasing employment opportunities, and to accelerating the replacement of the dual economic structure. One cannot look at only the "cruelty" of "institutionalized wages" while ignoring their reasonability. In reality, the difference in wages between urban workers and rural migrant workers, as determined by the market, has not exceeded the range of 30–80%. Disparities in income between urban and rural areas are to a great extent determined by excessively fast income increases of that segment of the population with special powers (monopolistic powers, administrative powers, enterprise powers, and so on). So we should check this trend of increasing incomes on the strength of special powers; this is an important measure in the prevention of growth of the income gap.

8.1.2.3 Increasing the Safety of Foods

For the coming decades, food demand in China will continue to grow. Food security is an important component of national security. To safeguard food security, we must first put in place most rigorous protections for farmland to ensure that the amount of comparable farmland does not decrease.[1] Second, increase the amount of fiscal payments into agricultural insurance and establish mechanisms for agricultural risk prevention, in order to maintain the incentives for rural citizens to engage in agricultural production. Third, reasonably establish the size of national grain reserves. The focus of food security is grain for human consumption. We should adopt more flexible strategies for grain going to produce livestock feed in order to allow international grain markets to play their full role. Fourth, establish food safety goals, strengthen management of food production safety, and comprehensively increase the quality and safety of agricultural products.

8.1.2.4   Increasing the Level of Rural Infrastructure

We must initially form an infrastructure system of reasonable structure covering the countryside and settle prominent disputes regarding the inhibition of rural economic and social development caused by infrastructure. First, expand the focus from water quantity security alone to also include water quality safety, and give more rural citizens the chance to enjoy the same drinking water quality as urban citizens. Second, extend all-weather county and town road networks into village organization road networks, allowing rural citizens to have the same road access as urban citizens. Third, continue promoting agricultural infrastructure construction, major environmental programs, and environmental project construction, including farmland and dry land projects.

For a relatively long time, rural infrastructure construction and maintenance were the duty of local governments within a given jurisdiction. As most county and town governments lived on "hand-to-mouth budgets," in many cases they lacked the capital necessary for rural infrastructure construction. Their only solution was to raise money, apportion local laborers, or encourage local citizens to invest time and labor. This not only was an unreliable, unstable means of augmenting rural infrastructure construction, but also added to the burden of rural citizens. The central government has now established the construction of rural infrastructure as an important means to increasing rural citizen incomes. This has provided an extremely beneficial macro policy environment for accelerating construction of rural infrastructure. Sustained rapid growth of the national economy has laid a solid material foundation for the government to increase investments into rural infrastructure construction. Usage rates of rural infrastructure are relatively low. The amount of construction and maintenance possible using market methods is small compared to the burden the government must bear. That is to say that as the market economy is perpetually improved, the government must continuously increase the

---

[1]"Comparable farmland" is the product of the actual area of farmland and the adjustment factor of farmland quality. On farmland of a certain area, the faster quality is increased, the greater the area of comparable farmland, and vice versa.

amount of investments in rural infrastructure construction at the same time that it removes itself from competitive industries. First, increase the proportion of national debt to total investments in rural infrastructure construction. Infrastructure plays important roles in promoting economic growth and social progress in rural regions, and so naturally should be a focus area for national debt investments. Second, increase the scale of the "disaster relief through work" program. Increasing the supply of rural infrastructure through this program can lay the foundation for economic development in rural regions and can also provide temporary opportunities for employment and income growth of rural citizens.

The government should consolidate investments into resources for the construction of the rural infrastructure system, per the principle of prominent focuses. Increasing the results of fiscal capital used to promote agriculture and increasing the amount of such capital should be given similar importance. In addition to an increases to uncompensated government investments, the government should also use fiscal subsidies to encourage the participation of social capital in agriculture and the construction of rural infrastructure.

8.1.2.5 Increasing the Level of Development of Rural Society

Rural social development is concentrated in the three areas of education, medicine, and senior care. First, augment the supply of non-standard education on a foundation of improvements to rural compulsory education to provide better conditions for the improvement of the quality of rural citizens and their ability to grasp new skills. Second, increase government support of rural medical system construction; expand the scope of coverage of the rural cooperative medical guarantee system; improve the new rural cooperative medical system; enable rural citizens to afford to use the medical system and afford to take medicine; and eliminate the worry of "contracting major illness." Third, further improve the system for caring for and aiding rural "five guarantees households" and persons with major illness or injuries; gradually improve methods of aid; increase standards for care and aid; expand the scope of coverage for care and aid provision; gradually bring about the transition from families and communities caring for the elderly to social security systems caring for the elderly; and effectively resolve issues of providing care to rural seniors, medical treatment to rural sick, and aid to rural populations affected by disasters.

8.1.3 The Course of Agricultural Development

Agriculture is one of the fields in which bio-technology is applied most directly, most extensively, and most dynamically. In the 21st century, development of life sciences, most particularly in genetic research, will drive development of organic sciences while at the same time inciting a new agricultural revolution and driving the formation of a new agricultural industry. Summarily speaking, industrialization of microorganism resource usage will upgrade two-dimensional agriculture composed of plants and animals into three-dimensional agriculture composed of plants, animals, and microorganisms, laying the foundation for the establishment of agriculture primarily friendly to the environment. The industrialization of algae resource usage will upgrade continental agriculture into agriculture that merges land and ocean resources. Creating seeds using plant cell totipotency and sex-less reproduction; using high-protein feed and food products from plants of highly nutritious, highly digestible leaves; using resources of perennial and annual plants, as well as algae, for production—these will all become new industries within agriculture. We should benefit from the new agricultural revolution to: guide and drive; make breakthroughs in development in the areas of key technologies, transformation of the achievements of technology, increasing the quality of rural citizens, innovation in the scientific and technological system, and so on; accelerate the transformation of agriculture from dependence on resources to guidance by technology; cause technological advances to become the fundamental driver of agricultural development; and strive to basically complete the tasks of agricultural modernization by 2030.

In the 21st century, information resources will come to play an ever more important role. Different from hard resources that cannot be collectively used like natural resources and energy, information is a common resource that can be collectively used. Bringing about a high degree of sharing of agricultural information resources through maximum application of modern information technology is advantageous to the following: improving policies for production operations of rural households; driving upgrading of the agricultural industry structure; increasing the levels of science, culture, and quality of rural citizens; optimizing governmental macro-administration policies; and driving comprehensive development of rural society. This is another important symbol for the formation of modern agriculture.

The 21st century will be a century in which organic sciences and life sciences drive global development. Marx's prediction that differences between productivity of industrial and agricultural laborers would shrink as the differences in the levels of scientific development shrank might just come true in the 21st century.[2] Rapid growth of the national economy will provide a better external environment for agricultural development. Diversification of demand for agricultural products will create more opportunities for agricultural development, and the agricultural

---

[2]As far back as 140 years ago, Marx had already come to think that the speeding of industrial development was the inevitable result of arriving in a certain stage. "Once industry develops to a certain point, such imbalances will necessarily start to shrink. That is to say that agricultural productivity will necessarily grow faster than industrial productivity." He adds: "In particular, the true scientific foundation of big industry—mechanics—had already reached a degree of perfection by the 18th century. Those other sciences that more directly became the foundation of specialization in agriculture (as compared with industry)—chemistry, geology, and physics—were developed only in the 19th century, and particularly in the most recent decades of the 19th century." Karl Marx, "Theories of Surplus Value," (1861–1863), *Collected Works of Marx and Engels, Vol. 26* (II), (Beijing: Renminchubanshe, 1973), first edition, 116.

revolution will provide stronger technological support for agricultural development. Against such a background, despite challenges and difficulties, there are abundant opportunities and hope for agriculture in China.

8.1.3.1 Transition from Responding to Quantity Demand Toward Responding to Quality Demand in Agricultural Products

Agriculture in China was for a long time focused on responding to demand for the quantity of agricultural products. As of the late 1990s, however, agriculture in China upgraded to being focused on demands for both quantity and quality of agricultural products.

During the stage of traditional agriculture, increases to productivity of farmland and the cultivation of suitable virgin land were the primary means used to achieve balance between supply and demand of agricultural products. As large amounts of forests, grasslands, and wetlands were developed into farmland, the land being newly included into agricultural production came to be of ever lower quality; at the same time, there were corresponding decreases to the area and quality of forests, grasslands, and wetlands. At the micro level, ecological agriculture was an attribute of traditional agriculture, but at the macro level, this was an agriculture that damaged natural resources and the environment. In recent decades, balance between supply and demand of agricultural products has been entirely established on a foundation of increases to agricultural productivity, with help from chemical fertilizers, pesticides, and agricultural plastic sheeting. There is no longer any need to cultivate appropriate virgin land, but the effects of this are two-fold. The first effect is that shortages of agricultural products no longer limit economic growth, and the other is a series of negative impacts on the environment, such as: the accumulation of a great quantity of chemicals difficult to break down in the soil caused by the use of agricultural plastic sheeting, high contents of dangerous substances in agricultural products, and so on. We have created so many problems over only a few short decades of eradicating traditional agriculture; this is worthy of deep reflection on our parts. The solution, however, is not a simple return to traditional agriculture, but rather to make yet another breakthrough and transition to ecological agriculture.

At the levels of technology and the economy, there are commonalities between ecological agriculture and traditional agriculture. Commonalities at the technological level are: both have a harmonious, give-and-take relationship with nature; resource allocations are complex and cyclical; and products produced are organic and without pollution. Commonalities at the economic level are: they both combine production cycles with ecological cycles; they are both the results of autonomous choices on the part of agricultural producers; and they both can bring about resource allocation methods that achieve anticipated goals of producers. Furthermore, technology chosen for both come from a foundation of science. The differences are: experiential science is the foundation of traditional agriculture, whereas empirical science is the foundation of ecological agriculture. Both seek optimization of labor allocations, but they are different in that: the biggest advantage of traditional agriculture is that marginal production of additional labor is zero, whereas the greatest advantage of ecological agriculture is that marginal production is equivalent to marginal inputs. Traditional agriculture is the product of the natural economy; it is founded on division of labor between family members, and its goal is to maximize household effectiveness. Ecological agriculture is the product of the market economy; it is founded on division of labor in society, and its goal is maximization of profits. The goal of traditional agriculture is to satisfy the food demands of one's own family. From a narrow perspective, production by rural households is diversified and dispersed. From a broader perspective, the micro-allocations of resources of rural households are extremely similar. The goal of ecological agriculture is to satisfy society's demand for agricultural products. From a narrow perspective, production by rural households is specialized. From a broader perspective, micro-allocation of resources by rural households is extremely differentiated. The brands of the products of traditional agriculture usually come from the name of the production region, as inShatian pomelos. The brands of the products of ecological agriculture are commercial trademarks. During the stage of traditional agriculture, the function of the brand was to inform the consumer where the product was produced. In the stage of ecological agriculture, the brand's function is not only to inform the consumer of the quality of the product, but also to inform the consumer of a promise to compensate losses if the product fails to meet quality standards. In the stage of traditional agriculture when place names served as brands, rural households faced the market independently. In the stage of ecological agriculture in which registered trademarks serve as brands, rural households often adopt such methods as group cooperation or agricultural company cooperation.

> Ecological agriculture achieves higher production efficiency and integration with stronger sustainability by replacing non-renewable resources with renewable resources, replacing high-energy resources with low-energy resources, and by allowing products to be returned to the resources cycle after consumption. So after we enter the stage of ecological agricultural development, marginal land that used to enter the system on the basis of average productivity from high to low will begin a reversal of that sequence, from low to high. This will be manifested in the following ways: returning farmland to forests, returning pasturelands to grasslands, and returning fields to lakes; increases to average quality of production on farmland; and a renewal of the practice of fallowing. Fallowing, however, will no longer be practiced to restore fertility, but will rather be used to limit yields of agricultural products, preserve the production potential of the land, and to improve the agricultural environment.

8.1.3.2 Transition from Responding to Demand for Agricultural Products Alone to Responding to Demand for Agricultural Products and Energy

At the level of development trends of agriculture, agriculture in the 21st century will cease to respond to only demand for agricultural products and will being to respond to demand for agricultural products and energy. Worldwide, attention began being paid to bio-energy after the first petroleum crisis in the 1970s. The use of bio-energy in China began with the rural use of methane, but later evolved to include the gasification of grain stalks, the use of bio-fuels to generate electricity, and the production of fuel ethanol.

In China, there are about 100 million hectares of land not suitable for planting crops, but suitable for planting energy plants. If we used 20% of this land, then we could produce 1.0 billion tonnes of biomass a year, which could be used to make a minimum of 50.00 tonnes of fuel ethanol and bio-diesel. There is also an incredibly large amount of algae bio-mass. If we are ever able to successfully develop high-yield oil-algae into an industry, we might achieve several tens of millions of tonnes of bio-diesel production from algae per year. The development of bio-energy will greatly expand the room for development of agriculture. Developing bio-energy will be advantageous for: mitigating shortages in supply of energy and ensuring national energy security; protecting and improving the environment and promoting sustainable development; and improving rural health conditions and the conditions for production and living of rural citizens.[3]

Production of bio-energy in China has now achieved a certain scale. Experts estimate that by 2020, our annual bio-fuel production capacity will hit 19.00 million tonnes, of which 10.00 million will be fuel ethanol, and 9.00 million bio-diesel. The state has already issued laws and regulations setting industry standards for the production of bio-energy, as well as fiscal policies to promote the development of the bio-energy industry. An outlook on the future is that there will be ever greater room for development of the bio-energy industry in China, and applicable technologies will grow ever better. The role these factors play in optimizing China's energy consumption structure, cleaning the environment, and promoting rural economic development, will grow ever more important.

8.1.3.3 Transition from Economic Sustainability to Resource and Environmental Sustainability

At the level of development trends, agriculture in China will transition from economic sustainability into economic and environmental sustainability. Without

---

[3]A study performed by Nobel prize recipient and ozone layer researcher Paul Krutzen and others proved that as compared with the anticipated impact on climate change of fertilizer—two percent—of the Intergovernmental Panel on Climate Change (IPCC), the contributions of NO_2 to the greenhouse effect of planting grains used as biofuels was twice as high (three to five percent). NO_2 emissions of bio-diesel made from rapeseeds make 2–2.7 times the contributions to warming of CO_2 emissions from burning fossil fuels, meaning that the impact on global warming of such fuel is greater than that of fossil fuels. Contributions to warming of corn ethanol are between 1.9 and 2.5 times those of CO_2 emissions from burning fossil fuels, making this a better substitute product. So the Organisation for Economic Cooperation and Development (OECD) issued a report demanding an assessment of the complete life cycle of bio-fuels, to keep the problem from growing worse.

sustainability of the usage of agricultural resources, agricultural growth will eventually prove unsustainable, and rural social development will eventually stagnate.

Stable, healthy, sustainable development of agriculture is determined by: the investment capacity of agricultural capital; the coordinative capacity of agricultural policies; the capacity of agriculture to support the environment; the buffering capacity of the agricultural environment; the protection capacity of agricultural facilities; and in particular, the capacity to innovate of human capital. At the level of innovations by human capital, education is the source, technology the force, and people the foundation. To allow them to play their full role, we must accelerate transmissions and cycling between them. In no way is the natural environment perfect and lacking nothing for agricultural production. There is an objective need to use factor inputs to mitigate the shortcomings of the natural environment. There is in particular a need to bring about sustainability of resource usage, economic growth, and the environment by increasing resource usage efficiency via technological inputs. China's per capita endowment of agricultural resources is insufficient, and so we must establish an intensive sustainable agricultural technology system that conserves resources and reduces pollution, through high efficiency of resource usage. We cannot emphasize intensification of agriculture while overlooking sustainability, and nor can we emphasize sustainability while looking down on intensification. The core of intensive, sustainable agriculture lies in technological intensiveness of high efficiency use of resources. As a developing nation lacking major agricultural corporations, China has to establish the government as one of the major investors in agricultural technology innovations. The government must also effectively resolve insufficiencies in scientific and technological investments, inappropriateness of investment mechanisms, and poor management of scientific research. All of this will make a contribution to increasing the competitiveness of China's agriculture, upgrading the agricultural structure, and increasing rural citizen incomes. Although it will be very difficult to develop intensive, sustainable agriculture, it is possible to integrate the two with help from great support and positive guidance from the government, from technological innovation on the part of the multitudes of scientific researchers, and the capacity to action of China's rural citizens.

8.1.3.4 Transition from Safeguarding Demand Equilibrium for Agricultural Products to Increasing International Competitiveness of Agricultural Products

For a long time, the primary objective of China's agricultural policies was to bring about equilibrium between supply and demand for grain, and thereby to maintain national food security. After Reform and Opening, we achieved the historical transition from shortages of primary agricultural products to overall equilibrium and surplus production every year, on the strength of 20 years of bitter labors. However, prices for domestically produced agricultural products are growing ever higher, and the government is issuing ever greater quantities of agricultural subsidies. It is, furthermore, an incontrovertible fact that China's agriculture has become more competitive. In order to meet the demands of specialized division of labor, scale operations, commercialized competition, and intensive development, rural citizens must continue to transfer from agriculture into non-agricultural industries and continue to move from the countryside to urban areas, while at the same time gradually expanding the scale of agricultural operations via voluntary land transfers. This is a major issue that affects the nation's long-term development, and we must attach sufficient importance to it.

In the early 1980s, the Household Responsibility System, the connotation of which was the separation of land ownership and usage rights, achieved a return to "land for the tillers" while simultaneously eliminating many obstacles preventing rural citizens from organizing for common production. What we must do now is to develop voluntary land transfers to expand the scale of agricultural operations. Voluntary land transfers are an active choice made on the part of rural citizens who have another means to make a living, similar to the depositing of idle capital into banks or other investments on the part of rural citizens.

In reality, as the capital functions of land are growing increasingly stronger than the agricultural production functions of land, the trend whereby rural citizens maintain small production by hiring laborers is stronger than the trend for transferring land rights away. If it is the case that specialized rural households can earn their living from agriculture only by hiring many part-time workers from other households, then it will be difficult for China to increase its international competitiveness in agriculture. In order to promote voluntary land transfers and thereby increase the scale of agricultural operations and China's agricultural competitiveness, the central government must give rural citizens land rights that preserve their ability to participate in land transfers as quickly as possible, particularly in institutional arrangements that increase land rights the more the economy develops or the more land prices rise. We must issue policies that encourage rural populations to migrate and drive agricultural development on the strength of these population migrations.

8.1.3.5 Transition from Increasing Rural Incomes to Protection of Rural Citizen Rights

In recent years, there have been many people who bring up rural income when discussing gains to rural income, but few people who bring up rural income while discussing rural citizen rights. The greatest influence on rural incomes is possibly not taxes, but rather the infringement on rural citizens' rights, or the outright loss thereof. Prior to Reform and Opening, the central government obtained 600.0 billion yuan in agricultural surpluses by worsening conditions for industrial and agricultural trade (price scissors for industrial and agricultural products). Since Reform and Opening, local governments at all levels have earned a total of 15 trillion yuan by appropriating land from rural citizens at low prices and selling it at high prices, while compensating rural citizens less than five percent of that figure.

Giving rural citizens all manner of subsidies for low agricultural productivity is a method approved by the citizenry of China. The logic of reforms, however, is to first give rural citizens the rights to which they are entitled, and give rural citizens equal opportunities for employment, equal citizen treatment, equal opportunities for political participation, and only then consider giving them subsidies. On the one hand, the government has accumulated a great amount of revenue by maintaining inequality in employment, unequal citizen treatment, and unequal opportunities for political participation, and by coercively selling the land of rural citizens. On the other hand, reforms that pay some subsidies to rural citizens are clearly focusing on one aspect while ignoring the other.

8.1.4   Policies for Agricultural Development

Current infirmity in agriculture is one of the major reasons that many people emphasize the necessity of protection of agriculture. At the most, however, agricultural protections can only eliminate the negative impacts of infirmity in agriculture, and not the infirmity itself. International experience demonstrates that developing modern agriculture is the key measure needed to eliminate infirmity in agriculture. As it is possible to eliminate infirmity in agriculture only by developing modern agriculture and making agriculture an industry able to compete equally with all other industries, the only way to treat the root cause of infirmity in agriculture is to develop modern agriculture. So agricultural protection is merely a means to treat the symptoms and negative impacts of agricultural infirmity.

Since 2002, central and local government investments in agricultural subsidies have grown ever greater, but infirmity in agriculture still persists, and agricultural competitiveness has yet to be increased. The satisfaction with agricultural product prices and incentives to engage in agricultural production of rural citizens have also yet to increase. Given such circumstances, we need to make an assessment: in the end, will we continue to dispatch ever-increasing government subsidies to protect agriculture, an industry that has never been competitive with other industries, or will we go to great pains to build an agricultural industry that is competitive with other industries? The answer is clear. As a true modern agriculture cannot be formed in an environment where it is separated from market competition and lacks needed protection against market risks, we must first change agricultural policies in order to build a modern agriculture. In concrete terms, we need to make changes to agricultural policies in the following three areas.

8.1.4.1 Replace Policies for Risk Evasion of Rural Households with Policies that Reward the Pursuit of Efficiency of Rural Households

Shortly after the dawn of Reform and Opening, the Household Responsibility System was enacted. The true nature of that policy was to encourage rural citizens to increase productivity via the endowment of rights. The true nature of measures currently being adopted, such as minimum purchase prices for grain and temporary storage, on the other hand, is to ensure that rural citizen incomes do not decrease via the dissolving of market risks. One should affirm that these policies played a positive effect in ensuring stable agricultural production and protecting the rights of rural citizens, but one must also not overlook the negative effects these policies had on distorting prices and increasing reserves. Price distortions reduce the allocative efficiency of resources in agriculture. Distortions to resource allocations in agriculture put pressure on the production of other agricultural products, and increases to reserves destroy market stability. All of these policies are effective in the short term, but in the long term, they will grow increasingly difficult to sustain as the accumulated losses gradually build up.

Food security is an essential strategic issue for China, the most populous nation in the world; we cannot ever afford to lower our guard. The key measure to safeguarding food security is to eliminate natural risks and market risks to agriculture. The government's duty in terms of eliminating natural and market risks is to establish an agricultural infrastructure system that behaves as a public product. In concrete terms, that includes the following: systems for researching and developing and promulgating agricultural technology; collection and organization of climatic information and information from agricultural products; a system for analysis and dissemination of said information; an agricultural infrastructure system including roads and irrigation works; and enabling all rural households prompt access to needed technologies, information, and services. The duty of rural households or farm owners is to optimize resource allocations and allow their regional comparative advantages and competitive advantages on the market to play their full role. The only way to allow active governments, efficient markets, and driven rural households to be fully effective will be for governments to bear their proper burdens and not those of rural households, and vice versa.

8.1.4.2 Replace Yellow Box Policies with Green Box Policies

Although agricultural production subsidies in China actually serve as subsidies to increase rural citizen incomes, we still call them agricultural production subsidies. The major reason that we emphasize that these are agricultural production subsidies is worry that rural citizens stop planting grain. If there were transfers of agricultural labor but not of agricultural land, and if there were no limitations whatsoever on the usage of agricultural land, there would indeed be many rural families not planting their land. The situation in China, however, is not at all like that. In recent years, there have been gradual reductions to the number of rural households as urbanization and industrialization have proceeded. The micro scale of operations in agriculture, on the other hand, has gradually increased as the number of land transfers increases. The larger the scale of micro operations in agriculture, the more suitable such operations are to the intensive planting of crops. As this process is driven by such an endogenous crop selection mechanism, drops to grain yields will certainly prove to be short-lived and limited. Theoretically speaking, such a short-term drop is a necessary prerequisite for rural product price formation mechanisms.

Government support of agriculture is necessary and reasonable. However, such support should not become an obstacle to the normal operations of market mechanisms. Agricultural production subsidies lead domestically to drops in allocative efficiency of resources and internationally to restrictions from the WTO. So government support of agriculture should be concentrated in the construction of agricultural infrastructure for public good. Subsidies used to increase rural citizen incomes should not be linked to agricultural production. Per WTO calculations, China's subsidies of grain and soybeans have already hit the 8.5% limit, while cotton subsidies have exceeded the 8.5% limit. The common international practice is to convert subsidies for agricultural products into living subsidies for rural citizens, which brings such practices within the green box and avoids limitations imposed due to yellow box policies. For example, when the US government passed agricultural legislation in 2014, the number of yellow box policies in that country fell to an extreme low. We should also transform our yellow box policies into green box policies.

In recent years, the costs of agriculture in China have risen rapidly. At present, the delivered duty paid (DDP) price of imported agricultural products within quotas are lower than prices for domestic agricultural products. For example, the per tonne DDP price of lamb and beef is 26,000 yuan, and 12,000 for pork, both of which half the prices for the same on domestic markets.

Under such circumstances, increasing the prices of domestic agricultural products increases the incomes of rural citizens while also increasing pressure on domestic products from abroad. China is a highly populous nation of relatively sparse per capita agricultural resources and so it is necessary for us to use foreign agricultural resources and international agricultural markets to regulate domestic supply of agricultural products and reduce the pressure of domestic agriculture on both resources and the environment. However, large quantities of imported agricultural products will affect the employment and income of rural citizens in China. This means that that we have little room left to increase rural citizen incomes by increasing the prices of agricultural products.

8.1.4.3   Replace Production Subsidy Policies with Environmental Subsidy Policies

Some academics explain government subsidization of rural citizens as the result of agriculture being a weak industry, while at the same time viewing all government payments to rural citizens as agricultural subsidies. In fact, there are differences between the stage of economic development and the economic implications of income rural citizens earn from the government. The government's initial goal in paying rural citizens was to ensure yields of agricultural products. Thereafter, that goal was expanded to include protection of agricultural product quality and sustainability of agriculture. Environmental subsidies that have emerged in recent years do not fall within the scope of subsidies. In order to conform to this change, theoretical research of rural reforms should be deepened from subsidy reforms to compensation reforms.

Assessing the value of ecological system services[4] is a complicated task. Such assessments involve economic theories and models, at which economists excel, as well as aspects of ecology, geology, and other sciences, in which economists lack expertise. Most methods we use to assess the value of ecological system services in China were introduced via relevant theories from abroad. In our use of assessment methods for foreign development in this initial stage of case studies, we still do not possess the conditions to establish compensation standards for the value of ecological system services. However, this cannot be used as an excuse for us not to convert ecological subsidies into ecological compensations. A relatively feasible method at present is as follows: establish compensation standards and the scope of compensations per the government's ability to pay for transfers, and on the basis of increases to the government's capacity to pay for transfers, gradually increase compensation standards and expand the compensation scope.

8.1.4.4 Replace Policies for Material Property Rights with Policies for Pricing Property Rights

As the number of rural households transferring away land rights increases, the number of methods of land transfer will also increase, the total area of land

---

[4]There are four kinds of ecological system service value: direct usage value, indirect usage value, selective value, and existence value. (1) Direct usage value can be measured by market prices, such as determining the cost of wood directly from its market price. (2) Indirect usage value is the value of ecological system services that cannot be commoditized, such as the value of function of forests in conserving water and soil resources. (3) Selective value is the willingness to pay for the future use of a function of ecological system services; this can be divided into three categories: personal future use, future use of others, and future use of descendants. (4) Existence value is the willingness to pay to ensure the continued existence of ecological system services. There are roughly three ways to assess the value of ecological system services: (1) Direct market assessment. This means assessing the value of ecological system services by market prices, such as the impact of soil changes on crop yields. (2) Hypothetical market assessment. This means assessing the value by finding replacement products for ecological system services that have no market, such as the impact of environmental improvement on the community. One can assess the value of environmental improvement by sussing out historical changes to real estate prices within a community. (3) Simulated assessment. This method is used to assess the value of ecological services for which there is no market and no replacement product, such as conducting a survey using questionnaires or telephone calls to assess the willingness of people to pay (even if compensated) to determine the value of ecological system services.

transferred will increase, and material land rights arrangements will become increasingly suitable to demand. At present it is said that members of rural collective economic organizations have the right to contract and to operate land, and that the only thing they transfer away is the right to operate the land, as they retain the contracting rights to the land. We should discuss this line of thinking. We should not seek explanations to the questions incited by land transfers within the original property rights structure, but should rather further improve the current rural property rights structure. The most appropriate method of so doing would be to materialize implied land rights. The rural collective economy in the 1950s was formed by rural families being forced to sell their land into communes for shares. The current implied, unclear materialization and concretization of shares is considered a matter of course. There are three advantages to the materialization of land shares. First, members of collective economic organizations are advocating for legal protections of their ownership of collective land and for stability of their membership in collective economic organizations. Second is the effective resolution of the problem of rural households losing their relationship with collective land by contracting out the operations rights thereto. Third is the standardization of land transfer entities. That is to say that only members of collective economic organizations with collective land shares have the right to transfer away operations rights to their land. It is not possible to transfer land a second time that has already been transferred a first time. This is done to prevent the same piece of land being flipped over and over again, and especially the emergence of land agencies profiting from just such transactions.

Shares in rural collective land are fixed over long terms, making them highly stable and appropriate for the method of issuing land certificates. Rights to operate rural collective land change frequently, making them extremely flexible, and making them appropriate for the method of contract signing. Members of collective economic organizations possessing certificates of shares in collective land (similar to deeds for real estate) can both use the land the rights to which belong to them or can contract the rights to part or all of their land to a third party. Even when land is contracted out, the collective land share certificate (deed) remains in their hands.

After collective economic organizations issue land share certificates to their members, ownership of all collective land still belongs commonly to all members of the collective economic organization, preserving the inseparable integrity of such land. Collective land is distributed internally to qualified collective members on the principle of fairness. Such allocated land can be sub-divided or merged together, but collective land is all owned collectively on a shareholding basis.

8.1.4.5 Replace Guiding Policies with Laws and Regulations

CCP Central has issued 12 consecutive "Documents Number One" every year since 2004. These documents have played an extremely important role in promoting growth to agriculture, growth to rural citizen incomes, and rural development. In the long term, however, there are more options for deployment of rural work than the issuance of a new document every year. If things continue this way, there may emerge questions about whether government work is in the end conducted per documents or per the law. If we continue issuing a new document every year, rural citizens and rural officials around the country may come to have new expectations every year. Although this method exerts a degree of influence on short-term policymaking, as it is difficult for this method to produce stable long-term expectations, it will exert a degree of negative influence on long-term policymaking. The method of issuing a document per year is in the end unsustainable, and so there is an objective need to replace the document-guided macro policy environment with a law-guided macro policy environment.

The 12 Documents Number One issued in the new millennium have formed a complete policy system for strengthening agriculture, benefiting rural citizens, and enriching rural citizens. The next step will be to convert mature policy measures into laws, to drive rural reforms within the track of rule by law, and enable all rural citizens to enjoy legal protections and judicial services. In order to promptly elevate effective policies to the status of laws and revise or abolish laws that do not conform to the demands of reforms, we must first issue legal powers per legally-established procedures for pilot reforms. This is the true meaning of rule-by-law construction for strengthening the countryside.

Per the demands of the appeals of rural citizens, the bringing about of a governance system, and the modernization of our capacity to govern, we should: comprehensively plan and promote the establishment of laws and regulations related to the countryside, as well as revision work; shore up the legal system for support and protection of the "three rural issues"; protect the property rights of rural collectives and rural citizens; ensure fair access to markets and market competition for all rural production and operation entities; ensure that the market plays the decisive role in the allocation of resources; allow rural democratic deliberations to play a positive role in rural governance; combine rural rule-by-law construction and construction of rules established by villagers; increase the level of rural governance; and encourage rural citizens to maintain their rights through legal channels.

8.2 Outlook for Agricultural Development in China

8.2.1 Full Citizen Treatment for Rural Citizens

Over the short term, we can adopt policies that demand rural citizens to make more contributions for the government, or we can adopt policies that require the government to make more contributions for rural citizens. In the long term, there will be aftereffects to either policy course. What we truly must implement is a policy for undifferentiated treatment of all citizens and the assurance that all rural citizens enjoy full citizen treatment. In such a macro policy environment, increases to rural citizen incomes will be established on a foundation of increased competitiveness of their identities.

8.2.1.1 Giving Rural Citizens a Full Opportunity for Competition

Since the mid-1980s, ever greater quantities of rural laborers have decided to migrate, and so the hidden unemployment problem in agriculture has been greatly mitigated; this has accelerated economic development in places to which rural laborers migrate. However, it remains difficult for rural populations to migrate, even to this day. To bring about equality in opportunities for both urban and rural citizens, we must continue to deepen reforms to the household registration system. The key of reforms to the household registration system is not the allowance of rurally-registered citizens to obtain urban registrations, but rather to eliminate the special privileges bestowed by the system as it currently exists, to use the system merely as a way of identifying where a given citizen lives, and to thereby remove this institutional obstacle to harmonious development between urban and rural areas. As systemic reforms have been deepened and the economy has rapidly grown, the conditions have already been laid for replacing the current household registration system with a new registration system that allows urban and rural citizens to move about the country freely. Cities can no longer use the excuse that "we lack laborers, not citizens" to continue to uphold the current system.

Reductions to the area of farmland and degree of intensiveness of usage of farmland are a serious problem that has emerged in recent years. An even more serious problem is the government's wanton appropriations of rural citizen's land, their arbitrarily determined compensation standards, and the difficulty for rural citizens to uphold their land rights. The primary measure for resolving the former problem would be the stabilization of land contracting policies, to give rural citizens long-term, stable expectations about their land, and thus encouraging them to improve their land. Develop markets for land operation rights, promote voluntary circulation of land operating rights between rural households, bring about appropriate scales of land operations and organic integration with household operations, and increase the usage efficiency of farmland. The primary measure to resolving the latter problem would be to pass laws granting equal deliberations rights to rural citizens and land appropriators. A majority of collective members whose interests are at stake would have to agree for any collective member to transfer land operation rights outside of the collective. This would effectively prevent village officials from coercively renting out collective land and coercively rescinding land contracted by rural citizens. Reform the approvals system for land occupation and institutionally uphold the land rights of rural citizens whose land is appropriated. As the economy develops, it will be difficult to avoid the problem of some farmland being turned to non-agricultural purposes, but we must reduce the amount of farmland so used to the greatest extent possible. To achieve this objective, we must first establish a set of policies to encourage entrepreneurs to increase their land usage efficiency to the greatest extent possible. This is the key to putting in place strict farmland protection institutions. Next, we must strive to increase the quality of prime farmland and ensure that the area of comparable farmland does not decrease. Next, we must perform well the work of compensations for appropriated land and truly protect the legal rights of rural citizens.

In reality, there are many highly profitable production projects available to rural citizens, and they can accept interest rate on loans even higher than those available in commercial banks, but most banks are not interested in issuing such small loans. To meet the financing demands of rural citizens, we must develop local private commercial banks per the ideology of "increased amount" reforms. In this, the government's duty will be to strictly regulate the activities of such financial businesses and to guide these financial businesses to be responsible to society. Given prerequisites of strict oversight and effective prevention of financial risk, we should encourage rural citizens to autonomously establish local financial organizations that serve their own communities, encourage all manner of credit underwriting organizations to actively develop underwriting services that conform to the characteristics of the countryside, and bestow rural citizens with the right to mortgage their land operations rights for access to bank loans.

8.2.1.2   Giving Rural Citizens All Needed Information and Skills

Rural citizens can acquire needed knowledge and skills through the training system. First, use legislation to stipulate that as long as the disparity between industrial and agricultural laborers persists, growth to the rate of government investments into training programs for rural citizens should be greater than to the rate of overall government investments in the countryside; we should at the same time improve the methods of administration of government capital used for training programs. Second, on the basis of the training for production skills that rural citizens need, we should: innovate new training methods; improve training mechanisms; and increase the production skills of rural citizens, as well as their capacity to operate and their knowledge of markets. Third, we should promote higher education in agriculture and forestry, rural vocational education, and rural adult education. Fourth, we should strengthen government oversight over training markets and promote competition among training organizations. Fifth, we should encourage urban teachers, doctors, technicians, and culture workers to provide temporary voluntary service to the countryside and encourage graduates of vocational schools to work in the countryside.

8.2.1.3   Giving Rural Citizens Full Citizen Treatment

The bestowal of rights is an effective means for allowing rural citizens to realize their full wealth creation potential, and is also a basic experience of rural development since Reform and Opening. Shortly after the dawn of Reform and Opening, the rapid growth of agricultural products was the result of giving rural citizens the right to autonomous land operations. The rapid growth of non-agricultural industries in the countryside in the mid-1980s was the result of giving rural citizens the right to choose their own employment opportunities. Improvements to the relationship of citizens and officials in rural communities in the 1990s were the result of giving rural citizens the right to choose their own elected village officials. However, we have not finished the work of bestowing rights to rural citizens; this remains a focus area for the deepening of rural reforms. Giving rural citizens their due rights is advantageous to increasing reciprocity between government objectives and the objectives of rural households, and encouraging rural citizens to lend their support to the achievement of government objectives.

First, we should give rural citizens the right to migrate freely. Migrant rural laborers now comprise the bulk of industrial labor in China, but very few families of rural migrant laborers have become citizens of the cities where such laborers work, as they lack the right to fully integrate into urban communities. To reverse this trend, we must: give rural citizens the right to migrate freely; form mechanisms that integrate reductions to the rural population and the agricultural labor force with gradual expansion of the average scale of operations of agricultural households; and establish growth of rural citizen incomes on a foundation of increases to factor return rates, upgrading of the employment structure, increases to agricultural competitiveness, and so on. Second, we should give rural citizens the right to reduce the costs of transactions and rights to form associations to increase opportunities for receiving loans. In recent years, rural economic cooperative organizations in China have developed to a certain extent. They have made an indirect contribution to increasing rural citizen incomes by increasing the scale of transactions, improving the technological services environment, and in other areas, thereby reducing the costs of making transactions or studying for rural citizens. However, there is still a great discrepancy in the actual degree to which rural citizens are organized and their demand for organization. So we should give rural citizens the right to form associations to increase their incomes and encourage development of rural citizen economic cooperation organizations through all manner of measures and standards.

8.2.2   International Competitiveness in Agriculture

For China, a nation of 1.3 billion people, the establishment of an agriculture that is competitive and directly enables rural citizens to grow rich is an important obligation that cannot be overlooked. To achieve this goal, we must accomplish the following tasks:

8.2.2.1   Increasing Comprehensive Agricultural Productivity

Increase comprehensive agricultural productivity through constant decreases to the rural population and constant increases to the scale of operations of rural households. Concrete measures are as follows. At the policy level: strengthen training programs for rural laborers and increase their ability to enter cities; grant legal rights to rural citizens who enter cities to labor and live; and decrease the opportunity costs of the "threshold" to entry into cities and the difficulty of rural citizens gaining urban registration. With help from the rapid urbanization and industrialization of the nation, ensure annual decreases to the agricultural share of nationwide employment by one percent (over the 20-year span from 1981 to 2001, the share of agricultural laborers to total nationwide laborers fell by an annual average of 1.3%). At the social level: constantly improve the construction of production-oriented infrastructure for paddy and dry fields, and increase the ability of agriculture to resist climaticabnormalities. At the level of rural households: encourage rural citizens to adopt such methods as soil improvements through fertilization and reasonable land use; constantly increase the fertility of the land; promote branded marketing of agricultural products by standardizing production; and increase the added value of agricultural products.

8.2.2.2 Guiding Rural Citizens to Establish Marketing Cooperatives

The power of rural citizens is not determined by their numbers, but rather by their degree of organization. Dispersed operations of rural citizens leads to poor strength, difficulties for them to get their products to market, and difficulties to protecting their interests. In agriculture, we must, on a foundation of persisting in maintaining the household as the basic unit: develop marketing cooperation between rural households or between rural household groups and companies; expand the scale of transactions; effectively reduce the transaction costs of purchasing production factors and selling products, as well as the costs of study and of technology; and thereby effectively combine the advantages of household production with those of cooperative production.

In recent years, specialized cooperative organizations of rural citizens have developed. They have played a role in providing technology, information, capital, material resources, and product sales services to rural citizens, and thereby in increasing the incomes of rural citizens. However, such organizations remain far from ubiquitous; their service functions are weak, and they lack adequate appeal and cohesiveness for rural citizens. To change this situation, we must: deepen reforms; eliminate factors inhibiting the development of the cooperative economy; feasibly protect the legal rights of both rural citizen cooperative economic organizations and their members; and establish a better policy environment for the development of such organizations. Governments at all levels should provide a degree of fiscal subsidies and more convenience for the introduction of new technologies, for member training, and for agricultural product marketing on the part of such organizations. These governments should encourage financial organizations to issue loans for the production and operation activities of such organizations and at the same time act in accordance with the principle of maintaining the rights of rural citizens to operate independently in operational and financial matters, respect the wishes of rural citizens, and respect the principle of "established by the people, operated by the people, and profits to the people."

To give Chinese rural citizen cooperative organizations the ability to effectively exploit the comparative advantages of China's agricultural resources, to effectively exploit the comparative advantages of the agricultural resources of other countries, and the ability to participate in international competition, rural marketing cooperatives should rely on community organizational resources, expand the scope of cooperation, and exceed the limitations of the community.

8.2.2.3   Establishing a Sound System for Agricultural Technology Promulgation and Services

To deepen reforms to the system for promulgation of agricultural technology, we must: change the current method of establishing agricultural research and development systems demarcated by administrative region; concentrate the power of comparative advantages and unite to tackle key problems in agricultural research and development; and strive to make breakthroughs in areas such as applied research, industrialization of new and high technology, research into agricultural foundations, and so on. To improve the systems for innovation in agricultural technology and promulgation of agricultural technology, at the top level we must: form national bases, regional agricultural scientific research centers, and vocational schools; and establish an integrated system for innovation in agricultural technology and an agricultural information network at the state, provincial, city, and county levels. At the bottom level, we must: form a bond between technicians; take model households as the core; unite the various technical propagation networks of rural households; and constantly increase the contribution rate of science and technology to agricultural growth. We must encourage vocational schools, companies, public enterprises, and social organizations to develop agricultural technological services and gradually form an agricultural science and technology promulgation system with the aforementioned bodies chiefly responsible for technological promulgation. We must develop organs that provide commercialized pre-production, production, and post-production services to rural citizens and enable rural citizens to adapt to the demands of development of scaled, standardized, modernized agriculture.

8.2.2.4   Establishing Mechanisms to Link up with Global Agriculture

Some experts and academics call for an agricultural protection strategy that emphasizes self-sufficiency in such major agricultural products as grains at the national level, pointing to the fact that agriculture is a special industry that touches on the livelihood of the nation and its people as their proof. Actually, there is a need to implement policies for the "two kinds of resources" and "two kinds of markets" in agriculture in China as well. In order to accomplish this, we must establish mechanisms for linking domestic agriculture with global agriculture.

Theoretically speaking, the circulation of resources at the global level is advantageous for the further optimization of resource allocations, and thereby is the result of the benefits experienced by all nations of integrating with the global economy. In reality, our integration into the global economy has brought many benefits to consumers of agricultural products in China. It has also given Chinese agricultural producers more opportunities to participate in international division of labor, international trade, and international cooperation. Although our integration into the global economy has brought uncertainty for the rights of agricultural producers, we absolutely could not choose not to integrate simply because of these uncertainties. First, there are more consumers of agricultural products than producers thereof, and this disparity will grow larger as the economy develops. To eliminate the uncertainties of rights of a minority of producers and sacrifice the benefits of a majority of producers would clearly be a one-sided move. Second, agriculture is a freshwater-intensive and land-resource-intensive industry. Imports of agricultural products are, therefore, tantamount to imports of freshwater and land resources from abroad; this has many benefits for the sustainability of agriculture in China. Third, the more sources of supply of agricultural products, the more options we will have for balancing supply and demand, and the lower the costs will be for government adjustments to supply and demand. Fourth, with pressure from international competition, government agricultural controlling departments will make efforts to establish agricultural economic operating mechanisms and administrative mechanisms to respond to international competition. Producers will then strive to seek comparative advantages and advantages for developing competition per signals from international markets, increase the average scale of operations, increase the degree of organization of rural citizens, and thereby form an internationally competitive agricultural production operations system to share the positive effects of internationalization and avoid the negative effects to the greatest degree possible.

8.2.2.5 Improving Policies for Agricultural Support

The weakness of agriculture is a special phenomenon of the dual economy transition period. Once traditional agriculture is replaced by modern agriculture, this phenomenon will cease to exist. That is to say that agricultural support policies will become decreasingly important, or possibly decreasingly necessary, as modern agriculture develops. China has yet to complete the transition away from the dual economic structure, and so there is still an objective need for policies to support agriculture. In simple terms, there are two reasons for policies to support agriculture: the first is to provide incentives for rural citizens to produce, and the second is to increase the country's capacity for agricultural production. At the level of policy effects, the former is a fast variable with one-time results, and the latter is a slow variable with sustained results. In the long term, the former is the focus of improvements to policies supporting agriculture.

In different stages of economic development, the economic implications of government support of agriculture are different. If one holds to a protectionist perspective of agricultural subsidies, one may become lost in bias. The earliest government policies for agricultural support were indeed related to the protection of rural citizen incomes and national food security. But in addition to those two objectives, modern agricultural support policies also help to maintain sustainable development in agriculture and sustainable use of agricultural resources and the environment.[5] We are now in a new stage of agricultural development in China, and so the objectives of agricultural support policies in China should be upgraded correspondingly. That is to say that we should, given the prerequisite of safeguarding comprehensive grain production capacity, establish a system to ensure sustainable development of agriculture and sustainable usage of resources and the environment.

8.2.2.6 Developing County Economies

Since Reform and Opening, the enormous contributions made by China's countryside to national economic and social development have mostly been transferred to cities, and the competitiveness of the countryside has not been clearly increased, which has led to an expansion of the disparity in development between urban and rural areas. To reverse this trend, the primary measure for comprehensive planning of coordinated urban-rural development should be the acceleration of county-level economic development. In concrete terms, that means replacing the system under which cities manage county affairs with a system where provinces directly administer counties, to give more decision-making power and autonomous development authority to counties. We must improve the policy environment for the development of the private economy in order to invigorate economic development at the county level. We should: build small urban areas, with focus on county capitals; develop competitive, characteristic industries; unearth the economic potential of counties; and broaden the channels for rural laborers to find employment and for migration of rural populations. There are two methods we can adopt for developing county-level economies and characteristic industries: the first is to create regional brands by developing mainstay enterprises, and the second is to seek

---

[5]The Agricultural Adjustment Act, passed by the US Congress in 1933, was aimed at protecting agriculture. After years of improvements by different administrations, it eventually formed into a federal agricultural policy system aimed at protecting agriculture. However, enormous amounts of agricultural subsidies led to budget deficits, which brought about a great deal of fiscal pressure and pressure from public opinion. So the US government passed new agricultural legislation in 1985 and 1996 to bring about market-guided agricultural reforms. Agricultural legislation passed in 2002 expanded the policy's objectives to four areas: preventing and controlling agricultural crises caused by surpluses and maintaining healthy development of agriculture; increasing the safety, nutrition, and convenience of agricultural products and increasing the quality of life of the American people; strengthening protections over resources and the environment and ensuring sustainable development of agriculture; and promoting rural social development. At present, the relationship between government subsidies received by rural citizens in China and their contributions to improving the environment is becoming increasingly tight.

external scales of economy through enterprise clustering. Practical experience in China demonstrates that the method of clustering enterprises to create external economies of scale is more feasible than developing large mainstay enterprises to create internal economies of scale. Brands can be commonly created and shared among enterprises that are clustered.

8.2.3 Comprehensive Development of Rural Society

8.2.3.1 Democratic Decision-Making Mechanisms in Rural Communities

Institutional arrangements for direct village elections have led to improvements in the relationship between village committees and village residents. The next step is to expand the scope of direct elections, increase the level at which elections replace official appointments, and ensure that officials fulfill their duty of serving the electorate at the systemic level. We should now place emphasis on work in two areas. The first is to revise the "Village Committee Organization Law," focusing on the new problems and new experiences that have arisen as a result of village autonomous government, in order to resolve problems that arise where the law is not suited to reality. The second is to deepen accompanying reforms to improve the policy environment for the development of rural democratic governance.

8.2.3.2 Public Administration Mechanisms in Rural Communities

It is neither practical nor reasonable for the government to monopolize power in all rural and community public affairs. We can use the "one matter, one discussion" system to deal with the issue of "club goods" (falling somewhere between public and private goods) by relying on collective action of rural citizens in the community. The goal of replacing the systems of "voluntary labor" and "accumulation labor" with the "one matter, one discussion" system is the protection of the rights of rural citizens to make decisions on and to administer club goods. This is essentially a replacement of coercive institutional arrangements with inductive institutional arrangements. In its method, this is a replacement of top-to-bottom with bottom-to-top, and in characteristics, this is a replacement of "demanding that rural citizens do" with "rural citizens should do."

Standardize and guide the development of rural citizen organizations. The development of rural citizen organizations is advantageous to improving the rural governance structure, to optimizing grassroots government functions, and to maintaining social stability. In recent years, there has been a certain degree of development to village autonomous governance organizations, economic cooperation organizations, and social welfare organizations in China. This has played a role in increasing rural citizen incomes, provision of public services, maintaining rural stability, and resolving community conflicts. So we should continue to use a variety of measures to standardize and guide the development of rural citizen organizations.

Standardize the behavior of governments and officials. Ensure that governments and officials uphold their primary duties of protecting legal property rights, maintaining fair competition, and providing public products.

8.2.3.3 Distribution Planning in Rural Communities

We must strengthen planning and administration of rural areas. The land planning and construction in rural communities of residential areas, roads, water supply, drainage, power supply, garbage collection, fowl and livestock raising centers and other agricultural production projects, as well as living services facilities and public enterprise facilities, must all be made in strict accordance with rural planning and related laws, of legal effectiveness. Rural areas should meet the demands of orderliness, cleanliness, environmental friendliness, and efficient use of resources.

8.2.3.4 Modernization of Rural Governance Structures and Governance Capacity

Officials in China's countryside should establish strengthened services and a fair, transparent agricultural administrative management system with standardized behaviors, and complete the transition from "managing rural citizens" to "serving rural citizens," in conformance with the demands and objectives for modernization of governance structures and the capacity to govern as raised by the 18th National CCP Congress.

First, strict adherence to the principle of governance according to the law. Rural citizens comprise China's largest population segment, and rural stability is the foundation for long, peaceful rule of the state. In all administrative and economic means taken by the government that affect rural stability or the management of rural citizens, agriculture, and the countryside, the government should adhere to the established principle of "governing according to the law" and have legal foundations and clear legal authorities, in order to protect the autonomous operations, production rights, and property ownership rights of rural citizens, uphold the democratic rights of rural citizens, and prevent incursions of government authorities on rural citizen rights.

Second, optimize the arrangements of government organs with the objective of maximizing public services. The objective of enterprises is to maximize profits through allocative optimization of available private resources. The objective of governments is to maximize public services through allocative optimization of available public resources. In recent years, the government may have reduced its total salary expenditures, but the positions cut are often those tasked with providing services to rural citizens. In fact, it is only natural for the number of public servants paid with taxpayer funds to grow as the economy and society develop; one should not make an unwarranted fuss about this. The goal of governmental reforms is for a service-oriented government to replace the administration-oriented government, and for increasing amounts of public servants providing services to taxpayers to replace servants tasked with making decisions for taxpayers.

For the government to establish maximization of public services as its reform goal, it must make changes to the official mentality that has persisted in China for thousands of years, including: replacing the feudal mentality with the democratic mentality; replacing the mentality of making decisions for the people with the mentality of serving the people; replacing the mentality of gloating about government achievements with the mentality of fulfilling government duties; replacing the mentality of leading the people with the mentality of the people managing their own affairs; and replacing the mentality of government allocations of public resources per the fancies of government officials with the mentality that oversight is necessary for government allocations of public resources.

There are greater problems of asymmetry between powers and obligations when the government handles affairs than when companies or non-governmental organizations (NGOs) handle affairs. So the government should hand over all matters that the government itself, companies, or NGOs can handle to companies or NGOs. The government will exist forever; what changes will be who carries out the duties of government. It is difficult for companies and NGOs to exist in the long term, as the greater the difficulty in maintaining the organization's existence, the more careful they become. This is an important basis for the government's being willing to hand off all affairs that it, companies, and NGOs can handle to companies and NGOs. In this way, the government can concentrate its efforts on the provision of services that companies and NGOs cannot provide and on assessing and screening the social obligations that are to be performed by companies and NGOs. The more companies and NGOs undertaking public duties, the greater the space for competition, the more public duties they will undertake, and the stronger will be their mentality of obligation to society. So a wise government is one that hands off as many public duties as possible to companies and NGOs, and not one that insists on performing all public duties on its own.

The thinking of some officials in China is just the opposite. They think that the only way to accomplish great deeds is to concentrate a great amount of money; they see this as the superiority of the socialist system. When officials want to "accomplish great deeds," they invariably just want to trump the historical achievements of their predecessors and elevate themselves to a higher historical status. If we let this continue, we will stay locked in this odd cycle of officials trying to one-up those who came before them, and a cycle of rapid GDP growth but low social wealth accumulation. The effects of the top-to-bottom government achievements mechanisms for official performance assessments and promotions are mostly to blame for such thinking. To overturn this mentality, we must enact a bottom-to-top government achievement assessment mechanism, whereby acceptance of officials by ordinary citizens is the standard for assessments, and official promotions are confirmed by popular elections.

8.2.3.5 Oversight and Assessment Systems in Rural Communities

In reality, people's opinions of major rural issues can vary in the extreme. On the surface, the reason for this is a lack of diversity in data sources, but the substantive reason is that the system for rural oversight and assessments is far from perfect. Some major programs initiated by the government are to a certain extent arbitrary, as they lack full, accurate information, for example: fluctuations to the start and scale of the program for returning farmland to forests. A relatively complete system for oversight and assessment of rural development would play a key role in allowing the government to enact proper macro-adjustments for rural development. In recent years, we have made marked progress in rural oversight and assessments. We must grasp this opportunity and existing foundation to establish a complete system for rural oversight and assessments as quickly as possible.

First, improve methods of rural oversight and assessments, including improvements in the following two areas. One, change top-to-bottom oversight and assessments into a synthesis of both top-to-bottom and bottom-to-top oversight and assessments, with both methods confirming the other. Two, convert oversight and assessments that look to only GDP into comprehensive oversight and assessments.

Second, upgrade the system for rural oversight and assessments. We should convert the oversight and assessments system that places focus on only changes to the economy into one that places focus on the economy, society, and the environment. We should expand oversight of only rural incomes to oversight of rural development. We should expand oversight of environmental changes from oversight of changes to surface plant cover alone to an integrated oversight integrating changes to surface plant cover, changes to groundwater levels, and changes to ecological service values.

Third, implement a publication system for public affairs. County and township governments lack transparency in their financial affairs, and this has given rise to the systemic flaw of corruption. To eradicate the corrupt behaviors of a minority of officials, we must start with systemic innovation. The implementation of a publication system and increasing of transparency in public affairs is advantageous to eradicating corruption, to augmenting the ability of rural citizens to participate in administration, and to increasing the level of fairness between members of rural communities.

Fourth, establish rural emergency response mechanisms. The system for rural oversight and assessments is a source of information for the government regarding rural matters and the improvement of rural policies. So when we establish such a system for oversight and assessments, we should naturally also establish rural emergency response mechanisms at the same time.

References

Dang Guoying, *China's Rural Reforms in the New Century: Reflections and Outlook*.

Liu Jiang et al, *China's Agricultural Development Strategy for the Early 21st Century*.

Lu Liangshu, *Development Trends and Outlook for China's Agricultural Science and Technology in the 21st Century*.

Liu Xunhao and GaoWangsheng, *How to Sustain Development in Agriculture in China in the 21st Century*.

CPSIA information can be obtained
at www.ICGtesting.com
Printed in the USA
LVHW021248200720
661084LV00002B/38